BRITISH
COLUMBIA
OFF THE BEATEN PATH™

Help Us Keep This Guide Up to Date

Every effort has been made by the author and editors to make this guide as accurate and useful as possible. However, many things can change after a guide is published—establishments close, phone numbers change, facilities come under new management, etc.

We would love to hear from you concerning your experiences with this guide and how you feel it could be made better and be kept up to date. While we may not be able to respond to all comments and suggestions, we'll take them to heart and we'll make certain to share them with the author. Please send your comments and suggestions to the following address:

The Globe Pequot Press
Reader Response/Editorial Department
P.O. Box 833
Old Saybrook, CT 06475

Or you may e-mail us at:

editorial@globe-pequot.com

Thanks for your input, and happy travels!

BRITISH COLUMBIA

OFF THE BEATEN PATH™

TRICIA TIMMERMANS

A Voyager Book

The Globe Pequot Press

Old Saybrook, Connecticut

Cover map © DeLorme Mapping
Text illustrations by Julie Lynch

Library of Congress Cataloging-in-Publication Data
Timmermans, Tricia.
     British Columbia : off the beaten path / Tricia Timmermans. — 1st ed.
        p. cm. — (Off the beaten path series)
     Includes index.
     ISBN 0-7627-0122-6
     1. British Columbia—Guidebooks.   I. Title.   II. Series
     F1087.7.T56   1997   97-36763
     917.1104'4—dc21   CIP

11.95 ßß

Manufactured in the United States of America
First Edition/Second Printing

*Dedicated to the
memory of my Aussie parents,
Ed and Molly Gallagher*

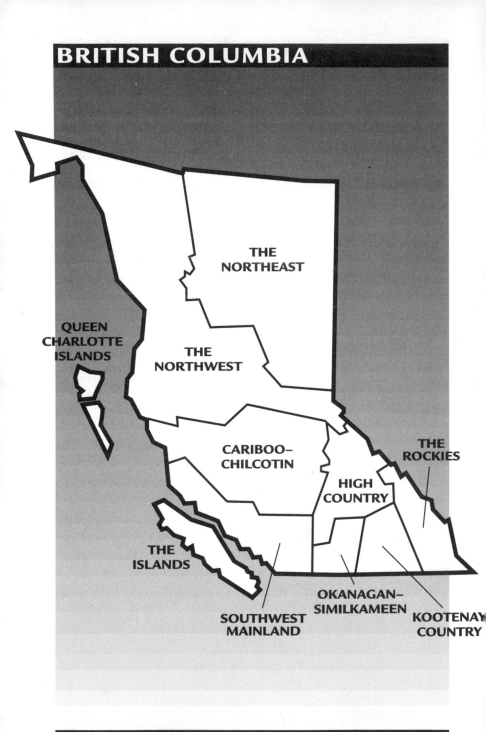

BRITISH COLUMBIA

QUEEN CHARLOTTE ISLANDS

THE NORTHEAST

THE NORTHWEST

CARIBOO–CHILCOTIN

THE ROCKIES

HIGH COUNTRY

THE ISLANDS

SOUTHWEST MAINLAND

OKANAGAN–SIMILKAMEEN

KOOTENAY COUNTRY

CONTENTS

ACKNOWLEDGMENTS

Sometimes that strong seducer, opportunity, knocks loudly enough that the door must be opened. Shortly after I graduated from Victoria's Western Academy of Photography, travel writer and teacher, Isabel Nanton, handed me that opportunity, and to her I am deeply grateful. My daughter Mary-Louise with her daily E-mailed encouragement, was heaven-sent. Thanks, Weez. Friends Jan Gravlev and Ginny Storey were always there for one of my procrastination chats on the phone. And fellow photojournalist and friend, Sandy Carter, unselfishly read chapters, added valuable ideas, and dragged me away when she knew it was time. Thanks too to BC Tourism's Stephen Puddister and the regional contacts. And finally, thanks to the many decent, hospitable British Columbians who invited me into their homes and enthused about their neck of the woods. They, and their stories, convinced me that I was indeed living in a beautiful part of the world.

I shall be telling this with a sigh
Somewhere ages and ages hence:
Two roads diverged in a wood, and I—
I took the one less traveled by,
And that has made all the difference.

—**Robert Frost** (1874–1963), *The Road Not Taken*

The prices and rates listed in this guidebook are quoted in Canadian dollars and were confirmed at press time. We recommend, however, that you call establishments before traveling to obtain current information.

INTRODUCTION

British Columbia (or BC, as we locals say) is alive with unexplored, tucked-away treasures. Many are remote and inaccessible, but most are easily unearthed. This book is intended to guide you to some of the best of them. Your fun will be in tripping over a few more on the way.

I feel enriched and enlightened after many months of researching, digging around in back alleys, and adding at least 6,000 miles (almost 10,000 kilometers) to my 4-Runner's odometer. My problem now is that I am addicted to it and am not sure if there is a practical cure. So many places I would have loved to linger—to hear that other story, to hike that other trail.

Often I was overwhelmed by the immensity of the snow-covered mountains and clear blue lakes, the friendliness and courage of people who had dared to venture, and the exciting history of the land and its people. Always, I was overwhelmed by British Columbia's extraordinary beauty.

I will not burden you with metric conversions and money exchanges, liquor and gun laws, and government taxes. There are countless information offices for that. Instead, I invite you to hop right in and start exploring BC's nooks and crannies, her high roads and byroads, her oceans and lakes, mountains and valleys, 366,275 square miles (948,596 sq kms) of sheer excitement. Take this book, a good road map, and get going. Before you know it, you will have picked up my addiction, and will soon be writing your own Off the Beaten Path™ guide. Happy Trails.

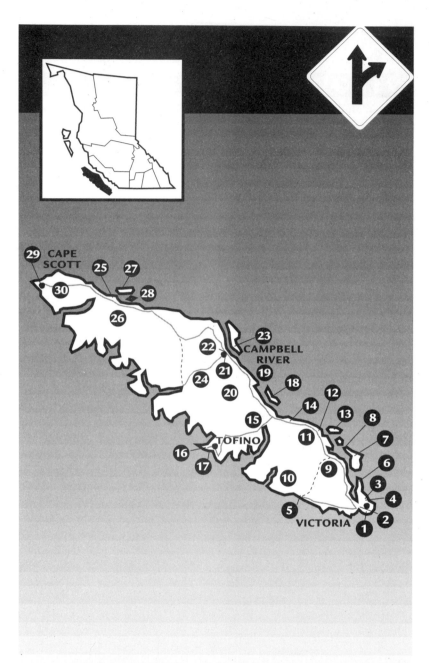

CAPE SCOTT

29 30

25 27 28

26

22 23 CAMPBELL RIVER

21 19

24 20 18

14 12

15 11 13 8

TOFINO 7

16 9 6

17 10 3

5 2 4

VICTORIA 1

THE ISLANDS

1. Sam's Deli
2. Market Square
3. Oak Bay Marina
4. Windsor House Tea Room and Restaurant
5. Botanical Beach
6. Sidney Harbor Cruise
7. Naikai Gallery
8. Anne's Oceanfront Hideaway
9. Native Heritage Centre, Duncan
10. Carmanah Walbran Provincial Park
11. Bungy Zone Adrenalin Center
12. Dinghy Dock Pub
13. Gabriola Island petroglyphs
14. Horne Lake Caves Provincial Park
15. MV *Lady Rose*
16. Jamie's Whaling Station
17. Wickaninnish Inn
18. Denman and Hornby Islands
19. Outback Emuzing Ranch
20. Mt. Washington Resort
21. Sea Tangles on the Beach Bed and Breakfast
22. Campbell River Optical Maritime Museum
23. Kwagiulth Museum and Cultural Centre
24. Strathcona Park Lodge
25. Mothership Adventures
26. Henschel Fine Arts Gallery and Studio
27. Sointula
28. U'mista Cultural Centre
29. Cape Scott Provincial Park
30. Bernt Ronning Garden

THE ISLANDS

Whether it's the warm Pacific air or the billions of blossoms counted each February in Victoria's Flower Count, Canadians are moving west to the islands in droves. I had lived in three provinces and two territories before I discovered that this 282-mile-long (453-km) island, with its Gulf Island neighbors, are the pièce de résistance of this country I now call home.

Separated from mainland British Columbia (BC) by Queen Charlotte, Johnstone, and Georgia straits, and from Washington's Olympic Peninsula by the 100-mile-long (160-km) Juan de Fuca Strait, Vancouver Island, with more than 2,100 miles (3,400 km) of coastline, is North America's largest island.

Starting in Victoria's Inner Harbor and suburbs, we'll head out to explore colorful tide pools, meet the artists of Salt Spring Island, camp among the giant, old-growth trees at Carmanah Pacific Park, and go whale watching from aboard a converted mission boat. In an island off the far north, we'll visit the past in a unique aboriginal cultural center. This is but the tip of the overflowing cornucopia of exciting adventures in store.

VICTORIA

Rated by *Condé Nast Traveler* as Canada's number-two tourist choice (after Vancouver) and number eight in the world, the local joke is that Victoria is the land of the newly wed and the nearly dead. Perhaps this is but a reflection that younger people, like their grandparents, are now seeing the light and choosing to settle in Canada's *Garden of Eden*.

On any warm spring or summer day, the downtown core of Victoria hums with activity as both locals and tourists alike head to the **Inner Harbor,** where dozens of mime artists, balloon twisters, didgeridoo players, face painters, bagpipers, fiddlers, and Japanese calligraphers all vie for a spot along the waterfront promenade. Above them, beside baskets of brilliantly colored blooms hanging from nineteenth-century-style street lamps, frightfully English, red, double-decker buses, horse-drawn carriages, and kabuki cab pedalers carry tourists from one end of town to the other, giving the city a festive feel.

If you prefer to explore Victoria from sea level, try a three-hour kayak lesson and harbor tour from **Ocean River Sports** (1437 Store Street, Market Square, V8W 3J6; 250-381-4233). Rates start from $49, or if you're more experienced and prefer a half-day rental, a single kayak costs

$24, and a double kayak, $34. For those wishing to learn more about the Islands' marine life, its old-growth rainforest ecology, or its Native peoples' plant use, **Coastal Connections Guided Nature Adventures** (1027 Roslyn Road, V8S 4R4; Victoria, 250-480-9560 or 1-800-840-4453; E-mail: coastcon@islandnet.com), using experienced naturalist guides, runs fascinating trips ranging from three-hour walks ($42) to ten-hour instructional, sail-kayak-hike Gulf Islands explorations that include gourmet picnic lunches ($199).

With the sea so close, try a tasty seafood lunch. One of my favorites is right downtown across from the **Victoria InfoCentre** (812 Wharf Street, V8W 1T3; 1-800-663-3883). ♦ **Sam's Deli** (805 Government Street, 250-382-8424) piles the shrimp high to produce delicious shrimp and avocado sandwiches. Their date squares are made fresh daily from owner Barb Housser's grandma's recipe. Thick clam chowder, freshly squeezed orange juice, and tasty spinach salad is what keeps clients returning. It's open from 7:30 A.M. till 11:00 P.M. in summer (shorter hours in winter) and is a great spot to sit outside and watch the passing crowds.

Shoppers looking for the offbeat will enjoy ♦ **Market Square,** on the waterfront between Johnson and Pandora streets. Bordering Canada's oldest **Chinatown,** you'll find forty-five stores with curious names such as **Seeing Is Believing, Fat Phege's Fudge Factory, Royal Holographic Art Gallery,** where $19.95 will buy a pair of holographic sunglasses; **Molly's,** with medieval and Victorian specialties made by local artists; and the **Rubber Rainbow Condom Company,** where you might be surprised what $3.49 will buy. They glow in the dark!

And after dark, enjoy a meal at **John's Place** (723 Pandora, 250-389-0711), where my favorite is the Thai Chicken. Laced with crunchy cashews, it's awfully addictive, and there's an endless supply of hot, herby bread. But spare some room for a big piece of apple pie. Breakfasts are huge, too. A Wurlitzer and great photos give it a fifties feel.

Over in Oak Bay (head east along Fort or Johnson Street), you'll be taken back further than the fifties. Just ten minutes from the city, million dollar Tudor-looking waterfront homes with perfectly manicured gardens reinforce the more-English-than-England-itself reputation Victoria has acquired. But this suburb, with the added color of billowing spinnakers, has its own peculiar charm.

And none more charming than *Chocolate,* a nine-year-old harbor seal who spent his first year at Sealand after his mother abandoned him. When Sealand closed in 1990, Chocolate hung around. If you want to

Chinatown, Victoria

feed him (and his mates), the Marine Store at the top of the ramp at
◆ **Oak Bay Marina** sells a tray of herring for $2.00. You'll find them
salivating at the bottom of the ramp. If they're not around, run the tap
in the fish-cleaning sink.

For more scuttlebutt on Chocolate and his pals, phone **Oak Bay
Marina Boat Rentals** (250-598-3369) and talk to Steve. Not only is he
the local marine life expert, but he'll also rent you a 16-foot Double
Eagle boat for a day of cruising or fishing. Two hours will cost you $50.
But if you'd rather someone else bait the hook and clean your catch, try
the marina's 61-foot *Discovery Princess*. Four hours of painless fishing is
$24 (kids $15). All you have to do is land something, and the crew can
help with the rest, even package your catch. The cruises run from June
15, at 8:30 A.M. and 1:30 P.M. daily till September.

While at the marina, there's fine dining at the **Marina Restaurant**
(250-598-8555). Ask about their early-bird specials. More downscale,

the **Café Deli** is right below. Sit out on the sunny deck and watch yachts gently rock, while a great blue heron fishes nearby.

Up in the village of **Oak Bay,** there's a kaleidoscope of shops, tea-houses, and galleries. The easiest way to explore the whole area is to hop on the green double-decker, the *Oak Bay Explorer* (250-598-4556). From late May to September, it transports tourists from the Empress Hotel and the downtown ferry terminals to Oak Bay and back. A cheerful English Bobby welcomes you aboard the ninety-minute tour that costs but a dollar. Runs start at 11:00 A.M., stopping at nine points in Oak Bay.

Down the road from the village, at the corner of Newport and Windsor, is the ◆ **Windsor House Tea Room and Restaurant** (2450 Windsor Road, 250-595-3135). It sounds British, and if that's what you want, you won't be disappointed! Pick up a London *Express* or *Telegraph* at **Windsor Park Place** (250-592-5315) next door and settle into your hot, buttered crumpets, classic cream scones, butter tarts, finger sandwiches,

Chocolate, a harbor seal at the Oak Bay Marina

BRITISH COLUMBIA TRIVIA

The worst streetcar disaster in North American history occurred on May 26, 1896 in the capital of British Columbia, Victoria, when fifty-five partygoers died after a span of the Point Ellice Bridge collapsed as a result of overloading. The streetcar (Car 16), together with passengers, weighed approximately twenty-one tons, whereas the bridge load capacity was estimated to be about ten tons.

and a pot of steaming English tea. The more down-to-earth ginger carrot soup is delicious too. It's open Tuesday to Saturday from 11:00 A.M. to 6:00 P.M. Friday nights it's open till 9:00 P.M. If you're lucky, you'll catch a game of cricket being played on the pitch across the road in Windsor Park. Only in Victoria!

The theme continues at the **Oak Bay Guest House** (1052 Newport Avenue, Victoria, V8S 5E3, 1-800-575-3812 or 250-598-3812), a 1912-built bed and breakfast inn with claw-foot bathtubs, period furniture, and lots of charm. You may even be greeted by a fully dressed butler. Breakfast is a four-course, genteel feast. Rates are from $55 for a single room in off-season to $165 for a double studio suite in high-season.

It's not all Old World charm in this municipality, though. Kids will love the tropical decor at the **Oak Bay Recreation Center** (near Fort and Foul Bay at 1975 Bee Street, 250-595-7946). With an ozone-purified pool, sauna, hot whirlpool, and waterslide, you'll leave imagining you've had a trip to Hawaii.

To return to the city, take Beach Drive past the gloriously posh Victoria Golf Course to Clover Point, where huge ships, paragliders, and high-flying kites are often part of the scenery. From Victoria, turn south off the Trans-Canada onto Highway 14 to the village of Sooke, a haven for fabulous bed and breakfasts. Find one listed on a comprehensive photoboard at the **Sooke Region Museum** (Box 774, Sooke, V0S 1N0; 250-642-6351). Next door, take a peek in tiny **Moss Cottage,** Sooke's oldest building. And don't leave Sooke without trying the area's best halibut burgers at **Mom's Café** (2036 Shields Road, 250-642-3314).

Continue west past driftwood-strewn beaches through Jordan River and Port Renfrew to the colorful tide pools at ❧ **Botanical Beach.** In all, it's about a two-hour journey from Victoria, but don't miss a low-tide visit to this virtual aquarium, with its brilliant red gumboot chitons, giant green sea anemones, purple sea urchins, and blood stars.

SIDNEY

Highway 17 (locals call it the *Pat Bay*) runs the length of the pastoral Saanich Peninsula, linking Victoria with Sidney and Swartz Bay, where BC Ferries connect to the mainland and the Gulf Islands. **Sidney by the Sea** is to many merely a town you pass to and from the ferry, but there's lots happening.

To see the area from a nautical perspective, try a ◆ **Sidney Harbor Cruise** with **Barbara and the Starships** (250-655-5211). A ninety-minute cruise in a glass-enclosed boat is in effect a mini-wildlife tour. There's an optional lunch stop at Canoe Cove's **Stonehouse Pub** (250-656-3498), or Shoal Harbor's **Blue Peter Pub** (250-656-4551), after which you can hop on the next ferry back past Sidney's waterfront homes. Tickets run $14.00 for adults, $12.50 for seniors, and $7.00 for children.

While in Sidney, don't miss the **Sidney Museum** (9801 Seaport Place, 250-656-2140). It has an echolocation chamber, demonstrating how marine mammals orient themselves, and the skeleton of Scar, a 23-foot (7 m) killer whale. Drive to the end of Beacon Avenue and turn left into Seaport Place. In summer, it's open daily from 10:00 A.M. to 5:00 P.M.; admission is by donation.

Nearby, a foot ferry (250-727-7700) runs to **Sidney Spit Marine Park, 3** miles (5 km) across on Sidney Island. From wooded trails you'll see lots of deer and even a few exotic birds. The ferry leaves on the hour from the pier at the foot of Beacon Avenue from May 15 till Thanksgiving, 9:00 A.M. to 5:00 P.M.

> **BRITISH COLUMBIA FACT**
>
> BC occupies 9.5 percent of Canada's surface and is its third largest province.

and 10:00 A.M. to 7:00 P.M. weekends, and costs $7.00 (adults), $6.00 (seniors), and $5.00 (children) round-trip. Then, return to the Beacon Avenue beat and discover some of the interesting little shops for which Sidney is renowned.

SALT SPRING ISLAND

North of Sidney, island-hop by BC Ferry to **Salt Spring Island,** home to many of Canada's best-known artists and writers. From the ferry terminal at Fulford Harbor, Beaver Point Road leads off the Fulford-Ganges Road for 6 miles (9.5 km) to **Ruckle Provincial Park,** with walk-in (not far!) beachfront campsites. The area is still a working sheep farm, with the original 1870 Ruckle homestead at the park entrance.

The Fulford-Ganges road runs north for 9 miles (14.5 km) to **Ganges,** through what was once BC's largest fruit-growing area. **Mount Maxwell Provincial Park** (day use only), 5.5 miles (9 km) up a steep, rough road, has spectacular views. Take Cranberry Road, about a mile south of Ganges, and follow the signs. The scenery over Fulford Harbor to the Gulf Islands and west to Sansum Narrows and Maple Bay is worth the wear on your vehicle (or boot soles)!

On Saturdays, the ferries and highways are full of folks heading to the **Saltspring Saturday Public Market** (250-537-1102), running from May to October on the grounds of the **Harbor House Hotel** on Upper Ganges Road overlooking Ganges Harbor. Locals sell flowers, jewelry, and pottery—anything from a slice of watermelon to a sequined frog.

If you've missed the Saturday market, the ❦ **Naikai Gallery** (3102 Grace Point Square, 115 Fulford-Ganges Road, SSI, V8K 2T9, 250-537-4400) has a great variety of locals' works. It's open from 10:00 A.M. to 5:00 P.M. seven days a week, from Easter to Thanksgiving. One local artist of note is Carol Haigh. Her acrylic originals and silk-screened marine scenes grace the Naikai's walls.

Grace Point Square has more than lovely galleries. The **Bouzouki Greek Cafe** (250-537-4181) looks down Ganges Harbor to the Sisters Islands. Its hosts, Steve and Georgia Asproloupos, serve traditional Greek fare from recipes Georgia learned from her mother in Ithaca. The Bouzouki is open daily for lunch and dinner from 10:00 A.M. to 9:00 P.M. (closed Sundays in the off-season).

From Ganges, Lower and Upper Ganges roads lead northwest to Vesuvius Bay Road and the twenty-minute ferry to Crofton on Vancouver Island. Sunset Drive, running to the northwest tip of Salt Spring, is a pleasant drive hiding a couple of high-end bed and breakfasts, including the **Beach House on Sunset** (930 Sunset, SSI, V8K 1E6; 250-537-2879) and ❦ **Anne's Oceanfront Hideaway** (168 Simson Road, SSI, V8K 1E2; 250-537-0851), where you wake up to coffee on the deck looking across Stuart Channel, followed by a four-course breakfast. Spend a day mountain biking, then soak in the hydromassage hot tub before bed. Prices range from $135 to $175 off-season and $165 to $200 high-season.

SOUTH CENTRAL VANCOUVER ISLAND

From Crofton, a 6-mile (10-km) drive north along the coast road leads to **Chemainus** (*the Little Town That Did*). It's a mandatory tourist stop. Murals have turned the town into the world's largest outdoor art gallery. The InfoCentre (250-246-3944) has mural maps to help you find them all.

While still in the area, visit Duncan, famous for its totems, more than forty of which (many on Government Street) decorate the city. Visit the ⬥ **Native Heritage Centre** (200 Cowichan Way, Duncan, V9L 4T8; 250-746-8119) to see them being carved. Duncan is 39 miles (62 km) north of Victoria on the Trans-Canada over the Malahat Range. From the Nanaimo Ferry terminal it's 32 miles (52 km) south.

About 3 miles (5 km) north of Duncan, Highway 18 starts its cut across southern Vancouver Island to **Bamfield** on the west coast, a town where the main street is the sea and half the community is accessible only by water taxi. If you have the right vehicle, and better-than-good gear, then hiking along the reservations-only **West Coast Trail** (Box 280, Ucluelet, V0R 3A0; 1-800-663-6000 or 250-726-7721), or camping beside the world's largest spruce trees in ⬥ **Carmanah Walbran Provincial Park** (250-387-4550), or windsurfing on **Nitinat Lake**, may be on your list of things to do.

A Carmanah camping–hiking holiday with my kids, despite rain and rough roads, is one of my camping memory treasures. For public safety and environmental protection, the trail to the tallest tree in Canada (the tallest Sitka spruce in the world), the 312-foot (95-m) **Carmanah Giant**, is out of bounds. From the parking lot, the 2.3-mile (3.8-km) trail upstream along Carmanah Creek to the **Three Sisters** and the 2.9-mile (4.6-km) downstream trail to the **Fallen Giant** are both awesome.

To get to Carmanah from Duncan, take Highway 18 west through Lake Cowichan Village. The InfoCentre (summer only) may have maps. Wind past Cowichan Lake to the Nitinat Main junction. Twelve miles (19 km) on, turn left onto South Main for 3.5 miles (5.6 km) to the **Nitinat General Store** (250-745-3449), where you can have a cafe meal, fuel up, use the Laundromat, and find a bed next door, in the **Nitinat Lake Motel** (250-745-3844). Cross the Caycuse River Bridge, and turn right onto Rosander Main. Carmanah is a further 18 miles (29 km) south, with some interesting switchbacks and great views.

The Trans-Canada heads north from Duncan through Nanaimo, home of the ⬥ **Bungy Zone Adrenalin Center** (1-888-668-7874). It's the only legal bungy bridge in North America, and the drop over the Nanaimo River Canyon is 138 feet (42 m). The local numbers are 716-RUSH and 753-JUMP, and if you do all four jumps (the Flying Fox, the Ultimate Swing, Rap Jumping, and just a plain old Bungy Jump), you get to become an Awesome Foursome Rush Club member! If you're game, a bungy jump costs $95.

The food at the ♥ **Dinghy Dock Pub** (250-753-2373) will also give you a rush. Take a ten minute ($4.50) **Protection Connection** ferry from the dock on Front Street in Nanaimo to Protection Island and try

BRITISH COLUMBIA FACT

6,500 islands and islets lie off BC's coast.

Sex in a Dinghy! Relax, it's but a heavenly dessert. For an entree, try the Louisiana Blackened Halibut Burger. The burger plus dreamy dessert will set you back a whole $13. It's open 11:30 A.M. to 11:00 P.M. (12:00 P.M. on weekends) May 1 to Thanksgiving.

Ferries from Nanaimo take twenty minutes to **Gabriola Island.** While there, take a look at the ♥ **petroglyphs** (prehistoric rock carvings) found along a trail behind the United Church, about 6 miles (10 km) along South Road from the ferry terminal. The whole drive around the island runs barely more than a marathon race, but despite its size, quite a few welcoming artists have studios here. It also has a good sprinkling of moderately priced bed and breakfasts. If you're looking for one right on the ocean, try **Gaviota House Oceanfront** (1364 Sea Lovers Lane, 250-247-9100) on the northwest coast, which has three rooms, from $45 to $65.

PARKSVILLE/QUALICUM AND WEST

Parksville and Qualicum are renowned for having some of the best beaches in Canada, all easily accessible. Entering Parksville on Highway 19A from the south, turn right after the railway tracks and stop off at the excellent **InfoCentre** (250-248-3322) to find out about accommodations, attractions, and restaurants, then visit **Craig Heritage Park and Museum** (250-248-6966) next door to find out about the area's beginnings.

Just north of Parksville, the village of Qualicum Beach is often bypassed, but its interesting stores warrant a stop. Turn off Highway 19A, head up Memorial, and turn right onto West Second Avenue. **Carriage Lane** at 177 West Second houses an eclectic group of stores, ranging from the island's only fly-fishing store, **The Village Angler** (250-752-0704; E-mail: angler@qb.island.net), to **Melrose Place Coffee Cafe and Gift Shop** (250-752-5005), with its extra-good coffee and delicious "melt" sandwiches, to the **Kingfisher Gallery** (250-752-9832) at the entrance, with quality island-made pottery, blown glass, and other gifts.

Back on the highway, about 5 miles (8 km) north, you could be surprised again at the quality inside **Bahari** (5101 Island Highway West, Qualicum Beach, V9K 1Z1; 250-752-9278; E-mail: lhooper@macn.bc.ca). The views are outstanding, especially from the hot tub, sitting at eagle-height above basking seals in Georgia Strait. It's a bed and breakfast you won't forget in a hurry. Rates including gourmet breakfast range from $75 to $100. Or if you prefer total solitude, there's a self-contained apartment with two bedrooms for $120.

From Bahari it's only a few miles north to the turnoff to the ◆ **Horne Lake Caves Provincial Park.** Look for the **Horne Lake Store and Cafe,** and follow the signs for about 12 miles (20 km). Contact **Rathtrevor Beach Provincial Park** District Office (250-248-3931) in Parksville, or the caves info-line (250-757-8687) to obtain information on these caves, some of the most accessible of the thousand known caves on Vancouver Island. Alternatively, tours can be arranged at the **Horne Lake Family Campground** (250-248-7829) at the end of the lake.

To unearth more treasures along this bottom third of Vancouver Island, take Highway 4 to Tofino, 107 miles (173 km) west of Parksville. You'll find colorful parrots in **Emerald Forest Bird Gardens** (250-248-7282), meet **Bill Gruff,** the grazing goat on the sod roof at the **Coombs Old Country Market,** walk along jungle paths at **Butterfly World** (250-248-7026), camp at **Little Qualicum Falls Provincial Park,** and stand in awe in **Cathedral Grove** (MacMillan Provincial Park), where some of the largest Douglas fir trees left on Vancouver Island still stand. Despite the 800-year-old trees misted in moss and sword ferns, you'll quickly realize you're in the heart of logging country as you approach **Port Alberni.**

Underneath an industrialized facade, there are some healthy activities in Port Alberni. Kayakers and hikers are heading south to Bamfield, Ucluelet, or the West Coast Trail on the ◆ **MV** *Lady Rose* or **MV** *Frances Barkley.* If you join them, expect to see sea lions, whales, eagles, and spectacular scenery. Return trips cost $40 to $44, and if you want to stay a while, you can rent kayaks or stay in the **Sechart Whaling Station** lodge accommodation (twenty-five rooms from $30 per person) near the **Broken Group Islands,** one of the three physically separated units that make up the **Pacific Rim National Park Reserve** in Barkley Sound. (The other two are **Long Beach** and the **West Coast Trail.**) Contact **Alberni Marine Transportation** at Alberni Harbor Quay (250-723-8313 or 1-800-663-7192 April–September) for information on the

BRITISH COLUMBIA TRIVIA

The Nuu-chah-nulth *(all along the mountains)* tribe on Vancouver Island's west coast used to whale in open seas in cedar canoes—not a very safe-sounding occupation. As part of their intensive training program, sexual abstinence, fasting, bathing, and learning how to capture the huge mammals, the whalers also visited sacred shrines made up of skulls and images of whales and deceased whalers. As a further aid, the whaler's wife would lie completely still while her husband was on the kill, to ensure that the whale, too, would be docile. Captain Cook, when he came to the coast in 1778, was seen to be drifting too close to a reef. The Nuu-chah-nulth called out to him "Nootka, nootka," meaning "Circle round." His misunderstanding resulted in these people being mis-named as the Nootka.

Alberni Inlet trip as well as for kayak rentals and lodge information. While there, try **The Little Bavaria,** 3035 Fourth Avenue (250–724–2208, or 1–800–704–2744) for a substanial, three-course meal.

Tofino to the north and **Ucluelet,** 26 miles (42 km) to the south, lie at the end of Highway 4, with glorious **Long Beach** between them. The Pacific Rim National Park Reserve headquarters (250–726–4212, or 726–7721 off-season), a mile north of the Ucluelet–Tofino junction on Highway 4, is open daily from March 15 to October 15. Short films and exhibits of marine biology of the Pacific West Coast and the culture of the Nuu-chah-nulth make the **Wickaninnish Interpretive Center** (Box 280, Ucluelet, V0R 3A0; 250–726–4701), 6 miles (10 km) north of Ucluelet, worth a stop. While there, have a meal or a bowl of clam-thick chowder at the **Wickaninnish Restaurant** (open mid-March to mid-October 11:00 A.M. to 9:30 P.M., 250–726–7706) and maybe catch a glimpse of Ukee, Ucluelet's gray whale mascot, somewhere in the pounding waves outside.

Not to be outdone, Tofino's mascot is Orkie, a killer whale. ◆**Jamie's Whaling Station** (250–725–3919 or 1–800–667–9913) guarantees his customers a whale sighting and offers a raincheck "forever" if they don't see any. Three-hour trips on a large, comfortable boat range from $48 to $70, and two-hour trips in a Zodiac range from $35 to $50.

Nearby **Meares Island** is famous for its ancient cedar and hemlock stands, and it was once the site of an extremely bitter antilogging lobby by the Tla-o-qui-aht First Nations people and other environmentalists. Take a water-taxi across and hike on the boardwalks. The **Tofino InfoCentre** (250-725-3414) can help you with this, as well as tours to Vancouver Island's only known **hot springs** in Maquinna Provincial Park, 23 miles (37 km) northwest.

If it's blowing a gale, head to the brand new $8.5-million ❦ **Wickaninnish Inn** (P.O. Box 250, Tofino, V0R 2Z0; 250-725-3100, or 1-800-333-4604) with its **Pointe Restaurant, On-the-Rocks Bar** and wraparound windows to let you see the Pacific in all its fury. Soak in hot tubs in the $100-$260 double rooms or soak up the 180-degree wild Pacific view dotted with wet-suited board surfers and enjoy haute gastronomy. Look for signs on Highway 4 at Chesterman Beach about five minutes south of Tofino.

DENMAN AND HORNBY ISLANDS

From Buckley Bay on the Island Highway (19) a car ferry (250-335-0323) leaves hourly for ❦ **Denman Island** and yet another for ❦ **Hornby Island,** just east of Denman. These islands are steps back in time, so enjoy them leisurely. Cycling on the mostly paved roads is an ideal way to get around, and **JR's Cycledeli** (250-335-1797) can usually oblige with a rental. It's in Denman Village near the junction of Denman and N.W. Roads, up the hill from the ferry dock. Cycle trails through old-growth Douglas fir in **Boyle Point** and **Fillongley Provincial Parks,** both pleasant with drift-wood-littered, sandy beaches. Take the ferry to Hornby Island, where **Tribune Bay Provincial Park** has fine white sandy

BRITISH COLUMBIA FACT

BC's population is approximately 3.5 million

beaches, and **Helliwell Provincial Park** has a 3-mile (5-km) circular track with spectacular bluffs. When the herring are running in March, watch for sea lions on nearby Flora Island.

For campers, Fillongley on Denman has ten beach sites, and **Tribune Bay Campsite** (250-335-2359) on Hornby has hot showers, bike rentals, and nearby cafes. As on many of these small islands, artisans and bed and breakfasts flourish. Drop into the **Denman Island General Store** (250-335-2293) at the top of the hill after you come off the ferry, and ask about anything you need to know! Or write the Hornby/ Denman Tourist Association, at Sea Breeze Lodge, Hornby Island, V0R 1Z0 (250-335-2321).

THE COMOX VALLEY

Courtenay is the city, **Comox** the town, and **Cumberland** the village, three of the communities comprising the Comox Valley, where some of Canada's tallest fishing tales originate. (Federal fisheries records do back the claim that saltwater fishing, in particular, is some of the most productive in the Strait of Georgia.) But as well as on the sea, there's plenty to do on land in the Comox Valley. One attraction 3 miles (5 km) north of Courtenay tweaked my interest. ◆ **Outback Emuzing Ranch** (2301 Clark Road, Courtenay, V9N 5M9 (250-338-8227); E-mail: emuzing @mars.ark.com) is a small emu farm offering tours to the public. Here, just off the Island Highway, Russ and Karen Davis raise these gentle, flightless Australian birds for their meat and hides as well as their valuable healing oil.

High above the emu ranch, 19 miles (31 km) west of Courtenay, looms a mountain rated third in British Columbia (after Whistler and Blackcombe) for the number of skiers it attracts each year. ◆ **Mt. Washington Resort** (Box 3069, Courtenay, V9N 5N3; 250-338-1386) is number one to more than 300,000 skiers per year. It had been a while since I had last clipped into downhill skis, so I chose the **Discover Skiing Again** package. A day-pass, a two-hour lesson, and gear rental, including the latest parabolic skis, were less than $60, and the spectacular views of the Strait of Georgia and the Coast Mountains were free. In summer, the cross-country ski trails of Paradise Meadows become wildflower-thick hiking trails, winding through a corner of Strathcona Provincial Park. Phone 1-800-699-6499 (250-386-9008 in Victoria) for condo or chalet accommodation, or 1-800-715-5534 to inquire about the new luxury hotel opened at **Mt. Washington Village Centre** in 1997.

CAMPBELL RIVER AND SURROUNDS

You've seen the view from the top. It's time to return to sea level and head north to the other Salmon Capital of the World (and you were told it was Port Alberni!), **Campbell River**. At ◆ **Sea Tangles on the Beach Bed and Breakfast** (583 Island Highway, Campbell River, V9W 2B9; 250-286-6886) you can almost cast a line from your bedroom window. You're guaranteed eagles, herons, and cruise ship sightings. Rates at Sea Tangles (meaning *kelp*) are very reasonable ($40–$65), breakfasts are tasty, and there's the use of a private kitchen.

Within walking distance is the downtown **Discovery Fishing Pier.** For a dollar a day, you can fish from the fully lit, 600-foot (183-m) dock,

BRITISH COLUMBIA TRIVIA

The Potlatch is a traditional feast or ceremony common among the Indians of the Pacific Northwest, especially the Kwakiutl. The word is Chinook jargon derived from the Nootka word *patschmati* meaning *"gift."* Its traditional purpose was to validate the status of the chief or clan, although individuals also used it to try to enhance their social ranking. Gifts were exchanged, and property was destroyed in a competitive display of affluence. It was prohibited by the government in 1884, but the practice continued in secret. The ban was lifted in 1951.

which sports built-in rod holders, bait stands, fish-cleaning areas, and picnic tables. Some very large salmon have been caught off this very pier. The concession stand (250–286–6199) will sell you all the necessary gear and bait, licenses, and ice cream. Just across from the pier you'll find something just as tasty but more substantial. **Vincenti's Restaurant,** 702 Island Highway (250–287–2772) brings recipes straight from Italy and serves delicious cappuccinos.

Just north of the pier you can visit the **Otter Gallery** (104–909 Island Highway, Campbell River, V9W 2C2; 250–286–9686) in the green-roofed Georgia Quay building on the waterfront. The quality of the work here, all by BC artists, is outstanding. Look for folksy, wooden CD cabinets, handblown glass, raku, etched brass, and outstanding photography.

There are two interesting museums in Campbell River. For those interested in nautical memorabilia, the ⚐ **Campbell River Optical Maritime Museum** (102–250 Dogwood Street, 250–287–3741) has a collection of maritime artifacts scattered throughout waiting and examining rooms, put together by auxiliary Coast Guard volunteer, Dr. Robert Somerville, who often gives personal tours between seeing clients. It's open during regular business hours, and admission is free.

On a more grandiose scale, the **Campbell River Museum and Archives** (470 Island Highway, V9W 4Z9; 250–287–3103), is on the highway at the corner of Fifth Avenue in a new building overlooking Discovery Passage. Look for historical logging items and a 200-year-old Sun Welcome Mask. It's open daily but closed Mondays in winter.

For more aboriginal history, take a twelve-minute ferry ride to **Quadra Island,** and follow the signs to the ⚐ **Kwagiulth Museum and Cultural Centre** (Box 8, Quathiaski Cove, Quadra Island, V0P 1N0;

250-285-3733), shaped like a giant sea snail to reflect the evolution of Kwagiulth culture. It's in the Cape Mudge Indian Village and houses part of a returned potlatch collection confiscated by the government in 1922. Admission is $1.50 for kids and $3.00 for adults.

While on Quadra, plan to hike on some of the often-deserted trails. The **Morte Lake** trail is an easy, pleasant hike, and the **Chinese Mountain** trail provides a panoramic view of the island. Tour the **Cape Mudge Lighthouse** (250-285-3351), where Captain George Vancouver went ashore in his exploration of Discovery Passage, or visit **Drahanchuk Studios** (250-285-3160), a gallery set in picturesque gardens with views across Sutil Channel to the Coast Mountains.

Before leaving the Campbell River area, head 30 miles (48 km) west on Highway 28 to **Strathcona Park.** It's BC's first Provincial Park, a hiker's wilderness paradise. At 520,000 acres (210,000 ha), not only is it the largest park on the island, but it also has the island's highest peak, **Mt. Golden Hinde,** at 7,218 feet (2,200 m), and Canada's highest waterfall, **Della Falls,** which at 1,443 feet (440 m) is ten times higher than Niagara Falls. The paved road that hugs the eastern shore of Buttle Lake down to Myra Creek is spectacular, with several creeks and waterfalls en route. Stay at the ◆ **Strathcona Park Lodge and Outdoor Education Centre** (Box 2160, Campbell River, V9W 5C9; 250-286-8206), where wilderness skills are taught and healthful meals are standard fare.

Gold River is 6 miles (9 km) west of the park border. It's a town with a logging base but great tourism potential. Good fishing in the Gold River and Nootka Sound (a 65-pound [30-kg] salmon was taken in 1993), and more than fifty caves within a 30-mile (50-km) radius supplement the beautiful views. A short hike along the **Peppercorn Trail** close to town is a great unwinder. The trailhead is near the Secondary School. Steps have been made, and at one point there's a rope to assist you down a slope, with the trail ending at Peppercorn Park parking lot beside a swimming hole and diving cliffs. Call **Gold River InfoCentre** (Box 610, V0P 1G0; 250-283-2418/2202; E-mail: goldriv@goldrivr.island.net) for information.

A lonely logging road runs between Gold River and **Tahsis.** Every June the Tahsis Lions Club hosts the **Great Walk,** indisputably North America's toughest walk. Contact the Tahsis Lions Club (Box 430, Tahsis, V0P 1X0; 250-934-6570) for information. Afterwards, soak your toes at the **Harbourview Bed and Breakfast,** on the oceanfront at 700 South Maquinna Road, Tahsis, V0P 1X0. Rates are $65-$110.

From Gold River, another logging road leads 39 miles (63 km) north through the Nimpkish Valley to Woss, just west of Highway 19. It's rough, but if you're in Gold River and heading north, it will cut off 92 miles (148 km). If you don't mind a few corrugations (maybe a lot!) and have good emergency supplies and the appropriate forestry maps, there's lots more to be explored in this wild, northern part of the island, including **Zeballos, Fair Harbor, Little Hustan Cave Regional Park,** and **Port Alice.**

From Woss, 80 miles (129 km) north of Campbell River on Highway 19, the road skirts the Nimpkish River and **Nimpkish Lake** (noted for its world-class windsurfing) for 40 miles (64 km) to Port McNeill, the ferry terminal for the intriguing island communities of Sointula and Alert Bay.

THE NORTH ISLANDS

Six miles (9 km) before Port McNeill, just before the Nimpkish River Bridge, a 9-mile (14-km) road leads to Telegraph Cove and the **Robson Bight (Michael Bigg) Ecological Reserve,** the most predictable location in the world to see killer whales. ◆ **Mothership Adventures** (Box 130, Victoria, V8W 2M6; 250–384–8422; E-mail: momship@islandnet.com) will take you to them, as well as elephant seals, otters, and black bear, and show you a live-aboard, sea kayaking adventure you won't forget—ever. Captain Bill McKechnie has beautifully refitted the 68-foot (21-m) *Columbia,* an historic mission boat, to take adventurers to Kingcome Inlet, Desolation Sound, and the remote Kitlope. Costs run about $150–$200 U.S. per day, including kayaks, all meals and wine, and comfortable staterooms. Visit the Web site at http://www.islandnet.com/~momship for itineraries.

BRITISH COLUMBIA FACT

Fresh water covers almost 2 percent of BC's land mass.

Just after the Nimpkish River bridge, on Highway 19, look for an ARTISAN sign to ◆ **Henschel Fine Arts Gallery and Studio** (801 Nimpkish Heights Road, Port McNeill, V0N 2R0; 1–888–663–2787 or 250–956–3539), where delicate northern scenes grace modern gallery walls—a little treasure of a place off the beaten path.

Just before the gallery, **Roseberry Manor Bed & Breakfast** (810 Nimpkish Heights Road, Port McNeill, V0N 2R0; 250–956–4788) has antique, knickknacky decor straight out of a Victorian dining room. Candlelit gourmet breakfasts plus afternoon tea and evening cappuccinos are all included in the $65–$75 price.

If you make the 8:40 A.M. ferry in Port McNeill, it's possible to see both ◆ **Sointula** and **Alert Bay** in one day. But you might miss some of the treasures both Malcolm and Cormorant Islands have hidden away.

Sointula, Finnish for *place of harmony,* is aptly named. As soon as you drive off the *Quadra Queen II* thirty-car ferry, you sense the easygoing atmosphere. It wasn't always so though. The old school building off First Street houses the **Finnish Museum** (250-973-6353), where you can learn about the community's colorful history. It started as a Finnish cooperative community in 1901, but after some dissension and debt, and a fire destroyed the meeting hall, the cooperativeness disappeared. Many Finns remained, though, and in some of Sointula's back lanes you'll still hear a smattering of the old tongue.

The **Rogues House Retreat** (Box 276, Sointula, V0N 3E0; 250-973-6222), a fully licensed restaurant and pub, is a good place to chat with locals. A house with lots of character, it has a weirdly curved chimney in the basement, lots of stained glass and bric-a-brac, and froggy ornaments everywhere. The suite downstairs ($156 per night) sleeps from seven to ten persons, plus there's a hot tub on the waterfront deck.

At **Choyces** (250-973-6433), you can buy coffees, local arts and crafts, or rent bikes to pedal around the island to see quaint Finnish farms and beachfront homes. It's by the dock as you come off the ferry and is open Monday–Saturday 10:00 A.M. to 5:00 P.M.

The **Alert Bay Travel InfoCentre and Art Gallery** (118 Fir Street, Box 28, Alert Bay, V0N 1A0; 250-974-5213) is to the right after the ferry along the waterfront. Here, there's quite a collection of photocopied literature about the island's history and attractions.

After the ferry, take a left on Front Street past the pretty Anglican **Christ Church** built in 1892 to the ◆ **U'mista Cultural Centre** (Box 253, Alert Bay, V0N 1A0; 250-947-5403). Here, learn about the Potlatch (perhaps read their informative brochure first), then see the famous **Potlatch Collection** of coppers and masks, originally confiscated by the government in 1921. Hours are Monday–Friday, 9:00 A.M. to 5:00 P.M. year-round, plus noon to 5:00 P.M. weekends and holidays in the summer.

High up on a hill behind the U'mista Cultural Centre, the **World's Tallest Totem Pole** reaches for the sky.

Other attractions on Cormorant Island include the **'Namgis Burial Ground** on the waterfront, and the **Gator Gardens Ecological Park,** where stark, eagle-topped dead trees make for interesting photography.

And don't leave without doing some whale watching. **Seasmoke & Sea Orca Expeditions** (Box 483, Alert Bay, V0N 1A0; 1-800-668-6722, BC only, or 250-974-5225) run $60 per person tours from late May to mid-October.

WINDOW ON A SMALL TOWN

The walls were as thin as brothel sheets, the pillow slips thick with bleach. Buses idled below, their sickly fumes filtering into the rain-battered hotel. My dreams were of gas masks. I was beginning to have doubts about Port McNeill.

The next morning, I stumbled sleepily to the town's one mall. An adorable teapot in The Window, a little hole-in-the-wall studio, tweaked my interest. IT'S MY BIRTHDAY, GONE FOR LUNCH was the greeting on the open door. Of course it wasn't painter and potter Heather Brown's birthday. She invited me in to to see her superb paintings of island gardens and spawning salmon, and her whimsical pottery.

I was captivated. We chatted about the Ronning Gardens (the subject of many of her paintings) near Cape Scott, and of the vicissitudes of living in Port McNeill. I left The Window breathing in deeply the sweet smell of a rain-cleansed earth as speckles of blue broke the grey sky.

And if you never want to leave, **Janet's Guest House Bed and Breakfast** (Box 229, Alert Bay, V0N 1A0; 250-974-5947) on the waterfront at 667 Fir Street is a cozy spot to stay. Rates range from $55 single to $70 double, or $160 for the whole house, handy for groups.

From Port McNeill, Highway 19 runs 20 miles (33 km) north past the twenty-ton **World's Largest Burl** to Port Hardy, the jumping-off point for BC Ferries' fifteen-hour sail through the spectacular Inland Passage to Prince Rupert, 305 miles (491 km) north.

In **Port Hardy,** the curator of the small museum at 7110 Market Street (Box 2126, Port Hardy, V0N 2P0; 250-949-8143) is a wealth of knowledge on the logging, mining, and fishing history of the area. Mr. William Reeve is "the entire permanent staff," and hours vary "according to available funds"! His book/gift store is extensive, considering the tiny area. And, of course, he knows where to eat.

Snuggles (250-949-7575) at the Pioneer Inn has possibly Port Hardy's finest dining. If you prefer a pub-style meal, **I.V.'s Quarterdeck Pub** (6555 Hardy Bay Road, 250-949-6922) has just the right mix of local and marine atmosphere. It's a pleasant walk from town. Go up Market Street past the Green Apple Restaurant, and veer left past the elementary school.

If you've come this far north, spare time for ❖ **Cape Scott Provincial Park** at the far northwest end of the island. Head out of Port Hardy along Highway 19, and take a right onto Holberg Road. The park entrance is 40 unpaved miles (64 km) west of Port Hardy. On the way, you'll pass through Holberg, from which you can drive 12 miles (20 km) south to the tiny fishing hamlet of **Winter Harbor,** where in September the tuna-fishing fleet livens this sleepy port, or west to the park entrance.

En route to the park, stop in at the ◆ **Bernt Ronning Garden** (Box 105, Holberg, V0N 1Z0; 250-288-3724), a heritage site presently being restored by Julia and Ron Moe. It's blooming with a collection of plants from all over the world. Look for the pair of Monkey Puzzle trees at the entrance to the old house site, as well as brilliant rhododendrons, daffodils, and countless squirrels. Bring peanuts!

The entrance to Cape Scott Provincial Park is 10 miles (16 km) from Holberg. Sea caves, giant Sitka spruce, old World War II building ruins, native middens, and the Cape Scott Lighthouse are but some of the points of interest in this sometimes extremely muddy, difficult to traverse, but spectacular area. Stand on the Cape Scott Sand Neck and view both sides of Vancouver Island as the early Danish settlers must have done. A short 1.5-mile (2.5-km) hike along the **San Josef Bay Trail** has some spectacular Pacific views. For information (and don't hike in this area without it) contact BC Parks District Manager (Box 1479, Parksville, V9P 2H4; 250-248-3931).

WHERE TO STAY:

1. **Oak Bay Guest House,** 1052 Newport Avenue, Victoria, V8S 5E3, 800-575-3812 or 250-598-3812.
2. **Anne's Oceanfront Hideaway,** 168 Simson Road, Salt Spring Island, V8K 1E2, 250-537-0851.
3. **Bahari Bed and Breakfast,** 5101 Island Highway West, Qualicum Beach, V9K 1Z1, 250-752-9278.
4. **Sea Tangles on the Beach Bed and Breakfast,** 583 Island Highway, Campbell River, V9W 2B9, 250-286-6886.
5. **Roseberry Manor Bed & Breakfast,** 810 Nimpkish Heights Road, Port McNeill, V0N 2R0, 250-956-4788.
6. **Rogues House Retreat,** Box 276 Sointula, V0N 3E0, 250-973-6222.
7. **Janet's Guest House Bed and Breakfast,** Box 229, Alert Bay, V0N 1A0, 250-974-5947.

WHERE TO EAT:

1. **Sam's Deli** (250-382-8424), 805 Government Street, Victoria.
2. **Windsor House Tea Room and Restaurant** (250-595-3135), 2450 Windsor Road, Oak Bay. Tuesday–Saturday 11:00 A.M. to 6:00 P.M. Open Friday nights for dinner till 9:00 P.M.
3. **John's Place** (250-389-0711), 723 Pandora Street, Victoria.
4. **The Blue Peter Pub** (250-656-4551), 2240 Harbor Road, Sidney.
5. **Bouzouki Greek Cafe** (250-537-4181), Grace Point Square, 115 Fulford-Ganges Road, Salt Spring Island.
6. **Dinghy Dock Pub** (250-753-2373), Protection Island, Nanaimo.
7. **I.V.'s Quarterdeck Pub** (250-949-6922), 6555 Hardy Bay Road, Port Hardy.

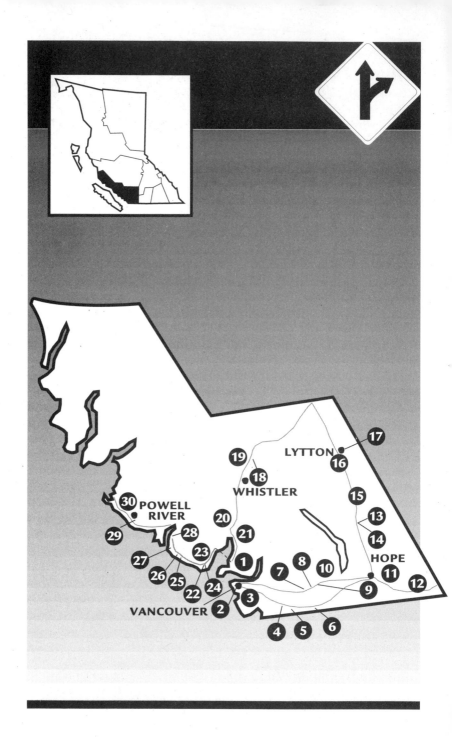

LYTTON

WHISTLER

POWELL
RIVER

HOPE

VANCOUVER

THE SOUTHWEST MAINLAND

1. The Grouse Grind
2. Harry's Take Out
3. Raku Kushiyaki
4. Herder's Haven
5. Domaine de Chaberton Estates
6. Abbotsford International Airshow
7. Westminster Abbey
8. Hatzic Rock Site
9. Kilby General Store Museum
10. Harrison Heritage House and Kottage Bed and Breakfast
11. Othello-Quintette Tunnels
12. Manning Provincial Park
13. Spirit Caves Trail
14. Yale Museum
15. Hell's Gate Airtram
16. Siska Art Gallery
17. Kumsheen Raft Adventures
18. The Spirit Circle, Art, Craft and Tea Company
19. Rainbow Valley Inn Bed and Breakfast
20. Brackendale Art Gallery Theatre and Teahouse
21. Stawamus Chief
22. Molly's Reach
23. Ruphi Fabrics and Ceramics
24. Aladdins Cafe
25. The Blue Heron
26. Beachcomber Bed and Breakfast
27. Pender Harbor
28. Skookumchuck Narrows
29. Willingdon Beach Campsite
30. Desolation Resort

THE SOUTHWEST MAINLAND

Whether you want to be part of the madding crowd, or lose yourself in silent wilderness, this region of British Columbia has it all. Starting out in vibrant Vancouver we'll travel east along the Fraser River to picturesque Hope, then north through amazingly engineered tunnels, to the mercifully untouched Stein River Valley. Then it's south through the Coast Mountain peaks to North Vancouver. From here, ferries cross Howe Sound to the warm Sunshine Coast, where from Gibsons Landing, immortalized in the CBC production *The Beachcombers,* we pass through laid-back villages and holiday homes to Lund, the last vestige of civilization before the yachting paradise of Desolation Sound.

VANCOUVER

Vancouver is at the center of a very beaten path. With its eclectic mix of residents, there's little challenge in finding elegant eateries, a variety of accommodations, and a range of activities, from sailing, to skiing, to golfing, often possible all on one day, in any season. The problem is knowing where to start.

From just about any area of Vancouver, a look up reveals **Grouse Mountain,** at night a sleeping beauty of twinkling lights giving the city a fairy-tale feel. To get there head north through Stanley Park to the Lions Gate Bridge, then east on Marine Drive, north on Capilano Road, and up Nancy Greene Way to the end. For over three hundred stalwarts, (five thousand on weekends!) the 2-mile (3.5-km) daily climb, ❖ **The Grouse Grind,** to the top of this 3,609-foot (1,100-m) pinnacle keeps them in peak form.

But if you're into taking the easy way up, an aerial tramway, **Skyride** (604–984–0661), is an alternative. At the top, view a thirty-five-minute

---

BRITISH COLUMBIA TRIVIA

Greenpeace was originally called the "don't make a wave" committee. It was founded in Vancouver in the early seventies and first drew attention when members hired a fishing boat to go to Amchitka Island in Alaska to protest against a hydrogen bomb test. In the mid-eighties it became the focus of world attention when its ship, the *Rainbow Warrior,* was blown up in New Zealand by French agents.

movie in the multimillion dollar "Theater in the Sky" and eat at the **Grouse Nest Restaurant.**

Stop off on the way down at the **Capilano Suspension Bridge** (604-985-7474) swaying 230 feet (70 m) above the Capilano River, or watch native carvers chiseling colorful totem poles at the Carving Center in **Capilano Park.**

Back at ground level, and smack in the center of the city, you'll find a refueling spot at a little hole in the wall called ◆ **Harry's Take Out** (1087 Robson Street, 604-331-0046). Beside Billie Holiday and Louis Armstrong photos enjoy Harry's excellent pizzas and listen to lively jazz music. For a *loaded* sandwich try **Uptown Market** (538 West Pender, 604-488-1450). It's next door to **The Umbrella Shop** (604-669-9444), a fifty-year-old establishment that perhaps tells a tale about Vancouver's weather! ◆ **Raku Kushiyaki** (4422 West Tenth Avenue, 604-222-8188), a small restaurant out near the university, is run by a couple of adventurous Canadians whose ingredients are equally so. Dishes range from orange-spiced lamb shanks to salmon with Chinese pesto. Raku is open Tuesday through Sunday 5:00–11:00 P.M. and if you're not into nibbling your way to sumo wrestler status, prices are reasonable.

While in the university area visit the **Museum of Anthropology** (6393 Northwest Marine Drive; 604-822-3825), magnificently situated overlooking the Strait of Georgia and English Bay. The museum houses a fabulous collection of Northwest Coast First Nations artwork, as well as artifacts from around the world. It's open daily from 11:00 A.M. to 5:00 P.M. and admission is $6.00 for adults and $3.50 for seniors and students. The family rate is $15. It's also open Tuesday nights from 5:00–9:00 P.M., when admission is free.

There's more free entertainment to be found in one of North America's busiest and most aromatic **Chinatown**s. The area, from Carrall Street to Gore Avenue, and Union to Powell Streets, is second only in size to San Francisco's Chinatown. Don't miss the **Sam Kee Building** at 8 West Pender Street, listed in the *Guinness Book of World Records* as the world's thinnest office building. It's all of 6 feet (1.8 m) deep.

Sample teas at **Ten Ren Tea and Ginseng,** 550 Main Street (at the corner of Keefer) and take your camera along to capture some of the details on the traditional gate framing the entrance to the **Chinese Cultural Center.** It's in front of the **Dr. Sun Yat-Sen Garden** (578 Carrall Street, 604-662-3207), an authentic Ming Dynasty garden, and the first of its kind to be built either inside or outside China since 1492. Admission to the garden is $4.50.

BRITISH COLUMBIA TRIVIA

In bilingual Canada, the second most spoken language in British Columbia is not French but Chinese. Indeed, French is British Columbia's fifth most spoken language, trailing behind German and Punjabi.

EAST TO ABBOTSFORD

From dim sum to dogs. If you'd like to see border collies being trained, John Carter at ◆ **Herder's Haven** (19022 Sixteenth Avenue, RR 3, Surrey, V4P 1M6; 604-541-8739; E-mail: jpcarter@helix.net) will welcome you. To get there, cross the Port Mann Bridge (Trans-Canada Highway), or the Patullo Bridge (Fraser Highway 1A), turn south onto Highway 15 (176th Street) and east onto Sixteenth Avenue. The HERDER'S HAVEN small sign is about 2 miles (3 km) on. John Carter trains border collies to herd sheep and teaches his skill to handlers who pay $12 for a group lesson or $25 for a private lesson. Demonstrations are free to the public.

If you hadn't expected to see sheep dogs, you may be just as surprised to find a winery. ◆ **Domaine de Chaberton Estates** (1064 216th Street, Langley, V2Z 1R3; 604-530-1736, 1-888-DDC-WINE) is the only estate winery in the Fraser Valley. It's about 3 miles (5 km) farther east along Sixteenth Avenue, and south on 216th Street. Tours are held on weekends April through August, at 2:00 and 4:00 P.M., and by appointment in winter. The vintner, Claude Violet, came from the south of France in 1981 and chose the area both for its closeness to the Vancouver market and its dry microclimate (it gets 56 percent less rainfall than downtown Vancouver).

After tasting Mr. Violet's award-winning wines, continue east along Sixteenth Avenue to Highway 13 (264th Street) and north to Aldergrove. From here Highway 1A travels east to Abbotsford, Canada's raspberry capital, and the place to be the second weekend of August when awe-inspiring aerobatics such as the Wall of Fire and incredible wing-walking are performed at the world-famous ◆ **Abbotsford International Airshow** (604-328-JETS).

THE FRASER RIVER VALLEY

Cross the Fraser River to Mission's **Fraser River Heritage Park** (7974 Mary Street, Box 3341, Mission, V2V 4J5; 604-826-0277). Folk festivals, car shows, children's art classes, twilight concerts, and a jam-packed **Canada Day** (July 1) keep the park humming through the warmer months. A concession booth serves light lunches and delicious home-made scones with blackberry jelly (prepared by volunteers in the fall). It's a pretty spot to stop off for a picnic, offering panoramic views of the Fraser River Valley and Mount Baker.

East of Mission, high up over the Lougheed Highway, you'll see (or hear) the distinctive bells in the tower of ◆ **Westminster Abbey** (604-826-8975). The Benedictine monks invite visitors from 2:00–4:00 P.M. Sundays and from 1:30–4:00 P.M. weekdays to see their beautiful church. Its sixty-four 22-foot-high stained-glass windows, combined with a tall dome of colored glass rising above the altar, make it an architectural beauty. To get there, turn left off Highway 7 onto Dewdney Trunk Road. If you come to the DUCKS CROSSING sign, you've passed it. It's also accessible from Stave Lake Street, just west of Mission's Heritage Park.

Leave the serenity of the monastery, and head back to Highway 7. East of Dewdney Trunk Road, at 35087 Lougheed Highway, is another kind of serenity, the ◆ **Hatzic Rock Site,** or more officially, X̱Á:YTEM **Longhouse Interpretive Centre.** This site is British Columbia's oldest dwelling—it's even older than the Pyramids and Stonehenge. The remains of a semisubterranean house, between five and six thousand years old, were discovered in 1990 by Gordon Mohs, an archaeologist employed by the Stó:lo Nation. Since then, this Coast Salish Indian group and scientists from the University of British Columbia have uncovered tens of thousands of artifacts, some radiocarbon-dated 9,000 years, revealing a long-term Stó:lo presence and evidence of a ceremonially inclined trader people.

The rock, or X̱Á:YTEM, (pronounced *háy-tum*) is associated with an early period in Stó:lo history when X̱exá:ls threw three chiefs into a heap and transformed them to stone for not teaching the people the written language he gave them. Hands-on interpretive programs are operated by the Stó:lo Heritage Trust. Drop in or phone (604) 820-9725 for visiting times and admission prices.

The Lougheed Highway curls 28 miles (45 km) east along the Fraser toward **Agassiz,** billed the Corn Capital of BC. At Harrison Mills, 23 miles (37 km) east of Mission, the ◆ **Kilby General Store Museum** (604-796-9576) is a must-stop attraction, especially if the kids want to "play shop" in the basement store, where weigh scales and goods are set up as they were back in the twenties. It's open 11:00 A.M. to 5:00 P.M. daily July and August, and Thursday to Monday mid-May to mid-October.

BRITISH COLUMBIA TRIVIA

Sasquatch (from the Coast Salish word *Sesqac*), British Columbia's infamous hairy giant, was not a very popular fellow. His trick was to come down from the mountains, seize young Indian maidens, and seal their eyes with pitch, thus preventing them from knowing their whereabouts. What he did with them is anybody's guess. Keep your eyes peeled (or pitched!) for him in the Harrison Bay area, west of Agassiz in the Fraser River Valley. Every May, eyewitnesses, scientists, believers, and nonbelievers gather in Harrison Hot Springs at the Sasquatch Forum to examine the latest evidence. Sasquatch Hikes, Sasquatch Golf, Bigfoot Races, and Sasquatch Parades all add to the craziness.

Continue enjoying the "days of yore" at the small museum run by the **Agassiz–Harrison Historical Society** (6947 Lougheed Highway, Agassiz, V0M 1A0; 604-796-3545). It's housed in the oldest wooden railroad station (1893) still in existence in BC, and is open 10:00 A.M. to 4:00 P.M. daily mid-May to mid-September.

The village of **Harrison Hot Springs** lies 4 miles (6.5 km) north. Idyllically set on Harrison Lake, southwestern British Columbia's largest lake, below snow-covered 7,825-foot (2,385-m) Mount Breakenridge, Harrison Hot Springs, with fabulous **Sasquatch Provincial Park** just 4 miles (6.5 km) beyond, is a popular spot for a beach holiday.

Every September Harrison hosts the **World Championship Sand Sculpture Competition** (604-796-3425), when international teams pit their skills against each other. The *Guinness Book of Records* gives Harrison Hot Springs a mention as the site of the world's tallest hand-built sand castle (a 21.5-foot [6.5-m] Christmas tree). With no tides to wash them away, the fantastic sand creations are on display until early October.

Half a block back from the sandy beach, ◆ **Harrison Heritage House and Kottage Bed and Breakfast** (312 Lillooet Avenue, Box 475, Harrison Hot Springs, V0M 1K0; 604-796-9552) has lacy rooms in the $50–$70 range. There's also a huge honeymoon suite, complete with a private hot tub and fireplace for $115, or a separate cottage for $105 ($600 weekly). The filling breakfasts are a great start to the day.

Nearby, meals at **The Old Settler Pub** (222 Cedar Avenue, 604-796-9722) are also filling, if you can handle the smoky pub atmosphere. My

$10.95 salmon dinner was delicious. Humorous chain-saw carvings decorate the log building.

Log carvings also decorate **Hope,** dubbed the Chain-saw Capital of British Columbia, 20 miles (32 km) east of Agassiz on the south side of the Fraser River. It's an incredibly pretty spot, set on a large flat plain deep in among the mountains.

Hollywood has discovered Hope's beauty, too. *First Blood* (first of the Rambo series), is the best-known of the movies to emerge from Hope. The Chamber of Commerce (919 Water Avenue, V0X 1L0; 604–869–2021) has developed a walking and driving tour of the film's key locations.

One of these is in the **Coquihalla Canyon Recreation Area** at the ⬧ **Othello–Quintette Tunnels,** an amazing engineering feat, which, at a cost of $300,000 in 1914, is perhaps the most expensive mile of railway track in the world. Look for the cliff above the stump at Tunnel No. 2 where Rambo's spectacular canyon jump took place. To get there, take Kawkawa Lake Road from the ball park on 6th Avenue passing the cemetery and Kawkawa Lake to Othello Road, a distance of about 3 miles (5 km). Turn right to a parking lot. Private campgrounds, such as **Othello Tunnels R.V. Park Campground** (604–869–9448) operate in summer.

Back in Hope, forget movie-mania and spend a quiet minute in **Christ Church** at the corner of Park and Fraser Streets. Consecrated in 1861, this Anglican church is the oldest continuously active church on the mainland still on its original foundations.

With so much to do in this area, stay a while in one of Hope's many motels (check the glass case outside the Info-Centre), or book into the **Evergreen Bed and Breakfast** (1208 Ryder Street, Box 811, Hope, V0X 1L0; 604–869–9918), with its lovely mountain views. It operates year-round and is at the corner of Old Hope–Princeton Way and Ryder. Rates are $59–$69. A block away there's

> ## BRITISH COLUMBIA FACT
>
> BC lies between 114° 03' 12" and 139° 03' 40" west of the prime meridian, and between 48° 17' 34" and 60° north of the equator.

a popular cafe called **Home Restaurants** (604–869–5558), where I had a big bowl of thick clam chowder and a bun for $3.25.

From Hope you can either head north through the Fraser River Canyon via the Trans-Canada, northeast via the Coquihalla Highway 5 to Merritt and Kamloops, or east to ⬧ **Manning Provincial Park** along the Crowsnest Highway, a beautiful but winding extravaganza through the Cascades that leads to Princeton and the Okanagan.

This is Canada! were my thoughts after taking the latter choice. I was passing snow-powdered alpine larch at the 4,400-foot (1,341-m) Alison Pass, and had read there were 175,440 acres (71,000 ha) more of this delightful park. If you're there in June, take a twenty-minute walk through colorful **Rhododendron Flats,** close to the highway about 6 miles (10 km) east of the marmot carving at the west gate. For park information, contact BC Parks, Box 3, Manning Park, V0X 1R0; (250) 840–8836.

THE FRASER CANYON

At the WELCOME TO HISTORIC YALE sign, 15 miles (24 km) north of Hope, in the Fraser Canyon, a steep hike called the ◆ **Spirit Caves Trail** begins. The round-trip is about 3 miles (5 km), and the elevation gain is 1,640 feet (500 m). It's worth the climb for the great views of Yale and the Fraser River. Allow about three hours to enjoy it. But if you prefer to just amble through a lush meadow loaded with history, the **Pioneer Cemetery,** directly across from the trailhead, is one of the prettiest old cemeteries in the province. The ages on many headstones (dating to 1862) hint at stories of lives prematurely taken.

At the tiny, but classy ◆ **Yale Museum** (open late March to November, 604–863–2324), you'll learn of the lives of these pioneers who sought their gold fortunes between the 1850s and the 1880s, when Yale was the head of navigation for the Fraser. The costumed museum staff show a thirty-minute film on Yale's history and do guided tours of the town and mainland BC's oldest church, the 1860-built **Church of Saint John the Divine.** The tour and movie costs range from $2.00 to $4.00.

At Yale, you're into the spectacular **Fraser Canyon** tunnels. Between Yale and Boston Bar, 26 miles (42 km) north, you'll remove your sunglasses seven times as you pass through these fantastic tunnels with names such as Saddle Rock, Sailor Bar, Hell's Gate, and the 2,000-foot (610-m) China Bar Tunnel, one of North America's longest. Here, enterprising Chinese found their golden mother lode after reworking an old, supposedly exhausted, area.

There's little gold today other than that in the glint of the turbulent rapids seen from the airtram at **Hell's Gate,** the narrowest (110 feet [33 m]) point of the Fraser River. The canyon reminded early explorer Simon Fraser of "The Gates of Hell." It was hell, indeed, for millions of salmon when, in 1914, with the building of the second railroad, the canyon wall slid into the river, causing British Columbia's worst environmental disaster. It almost destroyed the Fraser River run. Several gigantic fishways now assist approximately two million sockeye salmon yearly to reach their spawning grounds.

You can look down on these fishways from the ◆ **Hell's Gate Airtram** (Box 129, Hope, V0X 1L0; 604-867-9277), which runs early April to November. At the lower terminal there's the **Salmon House Restaurant** (excellent salmon steaks), the **Fudge Factory** (thirty flavors of homemade fudge), gift shops, and a fisheries display. Adult fare is $9.00, and if you watch all three movies, you can easily spend two hours on the *other side*.

The tunnels end at Boston Bar, but from here, there's another 26 miles (42 km) of Fraser River views to Lytton. Just before Lytton, the Siska (meaning *uncle)* Community Hall houses a small museum. Next door, the ◆ **Siska Art Gallery** (Box 519, Lytton, V0K 1Z0; 250-455-2219, E-mail: siskaib@mail.netshop.net) displays soapstone carvings, wooden masks, beaded crafts, drums, and dreamcatchers. They're open year-round. You can't miss the yellow SISKA MUSEUM sign up on the highway.

We leave the Trans-Canada at Lytton, often named on weather broadcasts as Canada's *hotspot.* It's here that the earthy Fraser meets the pretty, aqua green Thompson River, and where we discover another hotspot, the ecologically important Stein Valley, the spiritual home of the Nlaka'pamux Nation. In past years environmentalists and First Nations people have fought to preserve this wilderness area from the logger's ax. In 1995, the 264,393 acres (107,000 ha) of the Stein Valley were permanently protected as the **Stein Valley Nlaka'pamux Heritage Provincial Park.** For day-hikers, there's some good hiking in the lower Stein Valley near Lytton. Pick up maps at the **Lytton InfoCentre** (400 Fraser Street, Box 460, Lytton, V0K 1Z0; 250-455-2523). Information on the 47-mile (75-km) Stein Valley trail through to the Pemberton area is available from **BC Parks** (1210 McGill Road, Kamloops, V2C 6N6; 250-851-3000).

If you prefer the excitement of water over walking, ◆ **Kumsheen Raft Adventures** (Box 30, Lytton, V0K 1Z0; 250-455-2296, 1-800-663-6667), located on the Trans-Canada Highway, 4 miles (6 km) northeast of Lytton, runs thrilling rafting trips that range from three hours to five days long. Recently, the headquarters have been improved to include a hot tub, restaurant, volleyball courts, waterfront campsites ($6.00 per person), and uniquely decorated wood-floor tent cabins. These contain two double beds, all linen, and cost $69. In true rafting fun, games boards and ironing boards (must look neat in the rapids!) are set up, ready to use. And the Kumsheen coffee! Stop off for a fifty-cent cup of the best Colombian, and maybe sign up for a rip-roaring trip down a raging river.

THE SEA TO SKY HIGHWAY

Highway 12 (from the green bridge at the north end of Lytton) follows the dizzying, murky Fraser River, past black trampoline-like tarps shading the world's largest ginseng farms for 40 miles (65 km) north to **Lillooet** (see section on Cariboo–Chilcotin). Here we leave the Fraser River and join Highway 99 (previously the rough-and-ready but now paved Duffey Lake Road), where stunning views of emerald lakes and icy glaciers lead toward Pemberton and eventually to Horseshoe Bay, just north of Vancouver along the Sea to Sky Highway.

This Duffey Lake Road is rugged and remote. The only radio station I could raise was in Mandarin! But, as attested to by movie crews shooting Subaru advertising, its beauty is being broadcast. It follows the fast-coursing Cayoosh Creek, steeply down to Duffey Lake, Joffre Lakes, and Lillooet Lake, over one-lane wooden bridges to Mt. Currie and Pemberton.

At Mt. Currie, stop off at ◆ **The Spirit Circle, Art, Craft and Tea Company** (212 Sea to Sky Highway, Mt. Currie, V0N 2K0; 604–894–6336) to drink medicinal teas and organic coffees, or eat healthful food on the pleasant patio. Traditional medicines and local native handicrafts are sold.

Nearby at the ◆ **Rainbow Valley Inn Bed and Breakfast** (1864 Sea to Sky Highway, Box 483, Pemberton, V0N 2K0; 604–894–3300; E-mail: flanagan@whistler.net) you can rest awhile, surrounded by towering alpine peaks, cedar groves, a duck pond, and a horse barn. Jim and Dorothea Flanagan's farmland home has a huge fireplace and three guest rooms with lovely, rural mountain views. Each room has queen-size beds and Shaker-style pine furnishings. Dorothea is a professional chef and begins her day by making fresh bread and squeezing the oranges. Eggs Benedict with smoked salmon is a favorite, but for a spicy change she serves breakfast burritos with salsa made from a secret family recipe. The Rainbow Inn is well signed on the south side of the highway, halfway between Pemberton and Mt. Currie.

In 1967, Pemberton became the first commercial seed potato area in the world to grow virus-free seed potatoes. With that in mind I had to try out the fries in **Willie G's.** It's at the top end of Aster Street. The Caesar salad and pasta on the outside deck were fine, too.

But I didn't come just for the potatoes. There's so much to do in the area. If you're into seeing things from above, and this area warrants it, call the **Pemberton Soaring Centre** (604–894–5727). A Valley Flight costs $70 for a fifteen- to twenty-minute glide over paradise.

To find out about other flights, as well as white-water rafting, horse-back riding, jet-boat tours, parasailing, fly-fishing, canoeing, and golfing, stop off at the **Pemberton InfoCentre** at the junction of Highway 99 and Portage Road, open daily July and August, or write the Chamber of Commerce (Box 370, Pemberton, V0N 2L0; 604-894-6175). There's a good leg-stretch just south of Pemberton. It's a pleasant, short walk along a track to the falls in **Nairn Falls Provincial Park.**

Pemberton is just twenty minutes from North America's number-one ski resorts at **Whistler** and **Blackcombe,** 62 miles (100 km) north of Vancouver.

BRITISH COLUMBIA FACT

It would take all of Washington, Oregon, California, and Tennessee to fill BC's land mass.

Even in summer you can ski and snowboard at **Blackcombe** on Horstman Glacier. If you need accommodation here, call 1–800–WHISTLER in North America or (604) 664–5625. **Whistler Resort Association**'s address is Box 1400, Whistler, V0N 1B0.

The Sea to Sky Highway continues south past the western edge of **Garibaldi Provincial Park.** To see what "sea to sky" really means, take a drive in the Diamond Head area in the southwest tail of the park. South of Alice Lake, and 2.5 miles (4 km) north of **Squamish,** turn onto Mamquam Road, marked as DIAMOND HEAD (GARIBALDI PARK). It's paved for 2.5 miles (4 km). Finally, after the last switchback and about 10 miles (16 km), you'll get breathtaking views of the Squamish River Valley, the Stawamus Chief, and Howe Sound. From here, if you are equipped (and fit!), there is a two- to three-hour hike to Elfin Lakes, with good views of Diamond Head. The park office (Garibaldi/Sunshine Coast District Office, Alice Lake Provincial Park, Box 220, Brackendale, V0N 1H0; 604–898–3678/9313) has hiking and camping information on this fabulous area just 40 miles (64 km) north of Vancouver.

At nearby Brackendale, the winter home of the bald eagle, every January hundreds of eagle-eyes gather, cameras and binoculars to the ready, for the annual eagle count. In January 1994, a world-record 3,766 were counted. Enthusiasts leave from the ◆ **Brackendale Art Gallery Theatre and Teahouse** (604–898–3333). Eagles or not, stop off here to sample the first-class soups and croissant sandwiches. Located behind a large white unicorn at 41950 Government Road, near the corner of Depot Road, it's open weekends and holidays from noon–10:00 P.M. And don't miss the famous bells made from recycled steel in the rickety upstairs gallery.

Brackendale Art Gallery Theatre and Teahouse

You're soon in Squamish (6 miles [10 km] south), where there are so many recreational activities that it's hard to know where to start. Rock climbers go nuts here. They love the cracks and chimneys in the 2,139-foot (652-m) ♣ **Stawamus Chief,** the second-largest granite monolith in the world (only Gibraltar is larger). It was formed during volcanic activity thousands of years ago and left exposed for glaciers to scour over its top. You can view it and, if your lens is long enough, capture some colorful climbing photos from the parking lot on Highway 99. The Squamish Chamber of Commerce (37950 Cleveland Avenue, Box 1009, Squamish, V0N 3G0; 604-892-9244) will help with more information.

Don't leave Squamish without trying the restaurant (and the beer!) at the **Howe Sound Inn and Brewing Company** (1-800-919-ALES [2537] at 37801 Cleveland Avenue. It opened in 1996, and serves both pub-style meals and moderately priced restaurant meals. The inn's rooms (rates from $95 double) all have panoramic views of Stawamus Chief and the Coast Mountains.

At the **BC Museum of Mining** (604-896-2233, or 688-8735 if you're in Vancouver), 7.5 miles (12 km) south of Squamish, the views are all underground. An electric train takes you into the mountain on a tour of what was once the largest copper producer in the British Empire. Its history has not all been happy though. Back in 1915, the mine was struck by an avalanche, killing thirty-two miners. It's open May to October; adult admission is $9.50, students and seniors $7.50, kids under five are free, and there are family discounts.

If you want to see this area but have no vehicle, consider chugging past Howe Sound and through the Coast Mountains by train. The **Cariboo Prospector** leaves North Vancouver at 7:00 A.M. daily, arriving in Lillooet at 12:35 P.M. The return trip leaves Lillooet at 3:20 P.M., returning to Vancouver at 8:55 P.M. The round-trip cost including breakfast and dinner is $126. And think of all the gas you'll save!

But if you only have one evening to enjoy this gorgeous part of British Columbia, the **Pacific Starlight Dinner Train** leaves North Vancouver June to October, Wednesday through Sunday at 6:15 P.M. Gourmet meals, fabulous scenery, and a forty-five-minute walk in **Porteau Cove Provincial Park** (between dinner and dessert) are what

FINDING AN OLD FRIEND

I'm addicted to dock strolling. Barely a week goes by that I don't wander down to the local marina to sniff out the new arrivals. From Vancouver recently, I sailed on BC Ferries' *Queen of Capilano* to Snug Cove on Bowen Island, and headed for the Union Steamship Company's docks. Back in the 1920s, when the Company's grand ships cruised these waters, humming with the summer sounds of dancers and drinkers, this waterfront buzzed. I wasn't looking for the ghosts of the booze cruises though, but for my old mate, the sloop *Zeevogel*, our family home for three exciting years in the late eighties. From Victoria, she had safely sailed to exotic destinations like Tonga's Niuatoputapu, French Guiana's Devil's Island, and Ecuador's mysterious Galapagos. And now, there she lies, snugly protected on Bowen Island, while a new young family pampers and primes her, readying the sweet ship for more exciting discoveries ahead.

it's all about. You'll pay $69 per person, plus drinks and tips in the lower seating area, and $84 in the 360-degree-view dome cars. Call **BC Rail** (1-800-663-8238 outside BC, 1-800-339-8752 inside BC) for information on both trips.

THE SUNSHINE COAST

Highway 101, the Sunshine Coast Highway, connects pretty coastal communities with attractive names such as Secret Cove, Smuggler Cove, Sechelt, Halfmoon Bay, Garden Bay, Earl's Cove, and Saltery Bay, sprinkled along the sheltered coastline between Howe Sound and the sparkling waters of Desolation Sound.

The ferry from the terminal at Horseshoe Bay at the western end of the Upper Levels Highway in Vancouver takes forty minutes to cross to Langdale, the southern entrance to the Sunshine Coast. Phone BC Ferries (1-888-BCFERRY, 604-669-1211) for information.

A few minutes west of Langdale (take the scenic Marine Drive instead of the bypass), fans of *The Beachcombers* will want to stop off in **Gibsons**

Kayaking in the Strait of Georgia

to see some of the haunts made famous by the old television series. ◆ **Molly's Reach** (the main set), since 1995 a seafood restaurant (604–886–9710), sits kitty-corner from the **Gibsons InfoCentre** (Box 1190, Gibsons, V0N 1V0; 604–886–2325).

The stores and cafes at Gibsons Landing tend to be unusual. South Africans Ruth Opperman and Phillip Du Preez came to Gibsons from their studio near the Cape of Good Hope and opened ◆ **Ruphi Fabrics and Ceramics** (449 Marine Drive, 604–886–ARTS, E-mail:

> **BRITISH COLUMBIA FACT**
>
> BC's coastline length is 16,902 miles (27,200 km).

ruphi@sunshine.net). Bright, hand-painted wall hangings, tablecloths, and checkered or polka-dotted ceramic pieces give the little hole-in-the-wall studio an eccentric look. They'll ship pieces home for you, too. Just two quaint stores away, interior designer Shannon MacDonald operates **Matthews & More—Home Body and Soul** (Box 239, 453 Marine Drive, Gibsons Landing, V0N 1V0; 604–886–8801), where if you're into the great outdoors, you'll find some pretty nifty clothing, as well as Shannon's own line of body products.

There's more funkiness up the hill from the Landing at ◆ **Aladdins Cafe** (546 Highway 101, V0N 1V0; 604–886–4898). They serve the best desserts you'll ever find and fresh Mediterranean food. A tasty, Veggie Combo entree for two costs $11.92.

The InfoCentre has dozens more eateries listed and quite a few bed and breakfasts. **Marina House** (546 Marine Drive, Box 1696, Gibsons, V0N 1V0; 604–886–7888) was built in 1931 by local medical legend Doc Inglis. It has lovely view rooms (Molly's and Sarah's) with private baths, which range from $80, including coffee in your room and a full breakfast in the library.

Before leaving Gibsons, take a look at the Charles Bedford shell collection at the **Elphinstone Pioneer Museum** (Box 766, Gibsons, V0N 1V0; 604–886–8232) at 716 Winn Road. And take a stroll down **Molly's Lane** and the **Seawalk** to bring back those *Beachcomber* memories.

Head north out of Gibsons past thick forests and sandy beaches toward Sechelt. At Roberts Creek (turn at the Fire Department) take a walk out along the pier at Rock Point, where unsightly propane tanks used to sit. If you haven't seen it lately, you're in for a surprise. It's now a scenic area with driftwood "armchairs" and wonderful sunsets. Nearby the **Gumboot Garden Cafe** (1057 Roberts Creek Road, 604–885–4216) serves ever so rustically fresh wholesome foods, in keeping with a back-to-the-sixties Roberts Creek atmosphere. They're open daily from whenever till 8:30 P.M., and *casual* is the key word. Try the vegetarian spaghetti or the anchovy-rich Caesar salad.

North past the sandy beach at Davis Bay, you'll come to Sechelt, home of artists, writers, and retirees. Every August, the nationally acclaimed **Festival of the Written Arts** is held at the **Rockwood Centre** (at the top of Cowrie Street, 604-885-9631 or 1-800-565-9631; E-mail: writtenarts@sunshine.net), up from the **Sechelt Travel InfoCentre** in the Trail Bay Mall (Box 360, Sechelt, V0N 3A0; 604-885-0662). Visit the galleries and shops in town, and pick up some local artists' works at the **Sunshine Coast Arts Centre** (corner of Medusa Road and Trail Avenue, 604-885-5412). There's native artwork at the Indian Band Complex, **House of Hewhiwus,** on the south side of the highway opposite St. Mary's Hospital as you enter Sechelt.

Sechelt's best restaurant is reputedly ❦ **The Blue Heron** (604-885-3847 or 1-800-818-8977), on the waterfront north of town on Sechelt Inlet Road. It's open Wednesday through Sunday, and you should make reservations.

And for a place to stay, why not right on the beach. ❦ **Beachcomber Bed and Breakfast** at 6487 Sunshine Coast Highway (RR 2 Mason Site, C12, Sechelt, V0N 3A0; 604-885-1990; E-mail: alex_baggio@sunshine.net) is a striking home about a mile north of Sechelt, just before the Wakefield Inn. After leaving Sechelt, take the first turn left toward the beach (Mason Road) and meet Alex and Susan Baggio, friendly Aussies who have built a dream home on the water. This artist couple can tell you the best galleries to wander through, the best places to eat, and the best hiking trails on the Sunshine Coast. You can launch your canoe or kayak from the backyard, or beachcomb while enjoying sensational sunsets over the Trail Islands. Then after Susan's casually delicious breakfast, take a five-minute drive to one of the coast's eighteen-hole golf courses. Rates are $80 double, $120 for a party of four, and $25 for each additional person.

One place they suggested to hike was **Smugglers Cove Marine Park** (604-885-9019), just past Halfmoon Bay. About 5.5 miles (9 km) northwest of Sechelt, go up a long hill and turn left at Brooks Road, following this almost to the end, where there's a parking lot. The cove, named for

BRITISH COLUMBIA FACT

Highest mountain: Fairweather (near Alaskan border in the Coast Mountains): 15,299 feet (4,633 m).

the illegal traffic of Chinese workers to the United States, is an easy 1-mile hike in.

The highway continues north to ◆ **Pender Harbor,** a puzzling jigsaw of inlets and bays, with a few lakes, islands, and reefs thrown in. Here you'll find tiny fishing communities such as Madeira Park, where I saw a BEWARE OF ATTACK SQUIRREL sign and had great sandwiches in a cafe called **Madeira Mercantile.** Many of the harbor's community-proud residents are there for the good fishing, both saltwater and fresh. Dozens of boat charters and rental facilities are available. To make it easy for you, the Gibsons Chamber of Commerce (604–886–2325) has compiled a comprehensive list.

The chamber also has a list of chamber members who run bed and breakfasts. One in the Pender Harbor area is **Beaver Island Bed and Breakfast Inn** (RR 1, S4, C6, 4726 Webb Road, Madeira Park, V0N 2H0; 604–883–2990). It's a casual, self-contained bachelor suite on the waterfront at Bargain Harbor. To get there from the south, take the first Pender Harbor turnoff (Francis Peninsula Road) and stay on this for 2 miles (3 km) till you reach Webb Road. There's a sign right at the corner. You'll share this neat hobby farm with a very believable African gray parrot, two goats, a duck, and two ferocious-looking but friendly pigs. Go past the beasts to stairs that eventually reach a private dock, where you can cast your line. Rates, including breakfast, start at $50.

Highway 101 leads north to the ferry at Earl's Cove, but before leaving the peninsula, take a look at the thrilling ◆ **Skookumchuck Narrows.** Many a sailor has met his Waterloo when his boat was sucked into these treacherous waters. Before the ferry terminal, take the turnoff to Egmont, which is about 4 miles (6.5 km) west. Signs lead you to a 2.5-mile (4-km), well-built trail. Check tide tables and local papers for the best viewing times and places.

The ferry takes you to Saltery Bay, 19 miles (30 km) from Powell River. In **Saltery Bay Provincial Park,** a 10-foot (3-m) bronze mermaid lies at 66 feet (20 m) and seems to reach out to the many scuba divers who believe this area to be the best diving in the world.

We're almost at the end of the road as we approach Powell River, the first pulp and paper town in Western Canada. Despite log booms and spewing chimneys, there's a pleasant **Heritage Townsite** that in 1995 was awarded historic district status. At the **Powell River Visitor's Bureau** (4690 Marine Avenue, 604–485–4701; E-mail: prvb@prcn.org) pick up "Heritage Walk" material for a self-guided tour. There are quite a few interesting eateries, including **Jungle Java Cafe** (4670 Marine

Avenue, 604-485-5687) just south of the visitors center. Sip good, refillable coffee, enjoy homemade desserts and sandwiches, and wonder at the decor of ostriches running across walls covered with coffee bags.

There are no jungle creatures at ◆ **Willingdon Beach Campsite** (604-485-2242) just north of town, but the lovely sunsets make up for that. You can sit on a driftwood beach to soak up the final rays, eating fresh-out-of-the-sea fish and chips from **Kathy's Kitchen** next door.

But if you prefer the comfort of a hot tub and a massage, stay at **Beacon Bed and Breakfast** (3750 Marine Avenue, Powell River, V8A 2H8; 604-485-5563), a waterfront home where Bodywork Technician and Healing Touch Practitioner Shirley Randall knows how to pamper guests. You can't miss the red-and-white beacons on the fence 3 miles (5 km) south of Powell River. Rates are from $65, including a healthful breakfast. Bodywork is extra ($40 per hour).

Highway 101 continues north to the coastal village of Lund, the last frontier before Desolation Sound. **Cedar Lodge Resort** (C-8, 9825 Malaspina Road, RR 2, Powell River, V8A 4Z3; 604-483-4414), in Okeover Arm Provincial Park, has hiking trails. Accommodation with full breakfast starts at $45. Nearby at 2694 Dawson Road, ◆ **Desolation Resort** (C-36, Malaspina Road, RR 2, Powell River, V8A 4Z3; 604-483-3592) is a luxurious, dramatically simple resort hidden in the woods; the chalets and apartments seem to hang over the water. A one-bedroom, fully furnished apartment that sleeps three is $140 per day. There are canoes and kayaks to use, and the eagles, whales, seals, and sea lions come free.

A few minutes away is the quiet fishing village of Lund, gateway to Desolation Sound, a sailor's paradise, and a water-taxi away (604-483-9749, cell phone: 483-8078) from British Columbia's biggest arbutus tree and the white sand beaches on what I feel is the prettiest of the Gulf Islands: **Savary Island.**

WHERE TO STAY:

1. **Locarno Beach Bed and Breakfast** (4550 N.W. Marine Drive, Vancouver, V6R 1B8; 604-224-2177) across from a beach, park, close to university. Rates are $80-$90.

2. **Harrison Heritage House and Kottage Bed and Breakfast** (Box 475, Harrison Hot Springs, V0M 1K0; 604-796-9552) at 312 Lillooet Avenue. Rates are $50-$115.

3. **Evergreen Bed and Breakfast** (1208 Ryder Street, Box 811, Hope, V0X 1L0; 604-869-9918).

4. **Rainbow Valley Inn Bed & Breakfast** (1864 Sea to Sky Highway, Box 483, Mount Currie, Pemberton, V0N 2K0; 604-894-3300; E-mail: flanagan@whistler.net). Rates are $65-$99 year-round.

5. **Beachcomber Bed and Breakfast** (6487 Sunshine Coast Highway, RR 2, Mason Site, C12, Sechelt, V0N 3A0; 604-885-1990; E-mail: alex_baggio@sunshine.net). On the beach, rates from $80.

6. **Cedar Lodge Resort** (C-8, 9825 Malaspina Road, RR 2, Powell River, V8A 4Z3; 604-483-4414) in Okeover Arm Provincial Park.

WHERE TO EAT:

1. **Harry's Take Out** (1087 Robson Street, Vancouver; 604-331-0046). Pizzas.

2. **Raku Kushiyaki** (4422 West Tenth Avenue, 604-222-8188). Near Forty-second Street in Vancouver. Japanese-style, classy, reasonable prices. Reservations recommended.

3. **The Black Forest Restaurant** (180 Esplanade Avenue, Harrison Hot Springs, V0K 1K0; 604-796-9343). Open 5:00-10:00 P.M. year-round and for lunch in the summer. Bavarian food, seafood, pasta. Moderately priced.

4. **The Spirit Circle, Art, Craft, and Tea Company** (212 Sea to Sky Highway, Mt. Currie, V0N 2K0; 604-894-6336). Light, healthful foods.

5. **Howe Sound Inn and Brewing Company** (37801 Cleveland Avenue, Squamish, V0N 3G0; 1-800-919-ALES [2537]). Moderately priced restaurant and pub meals.

6. **Aladdins Cafe** (546 Highway 101, Gibsons, V0N 1V0; 604-886-4898). Great desserts, Mediterranean food. Moderately priced.

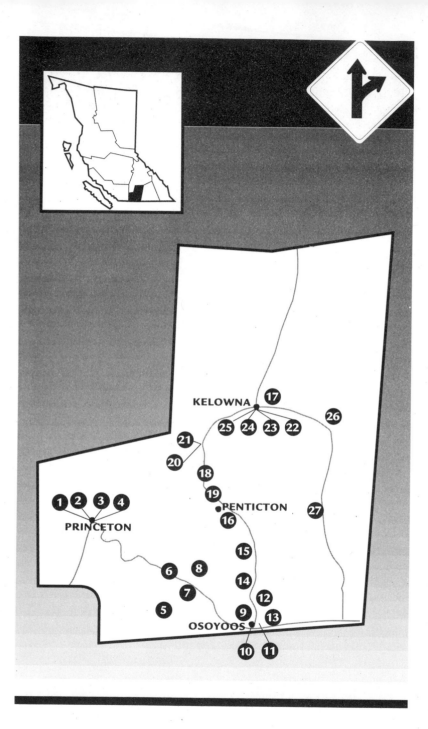

THE OKANAGAN–SIMILKAMEEN

1. The Mini Chef Restaurant
2. Princeton Museum and Archives
3. Pony Express Ride
4. Princeton Castle and R.V. Park
5. Cathedral Provincial Park
6. Login Bed and Breakfast
7. Orchard Blossom Honey House
8. The Grist Mill
9. Spotted Lake
10. Haynes Point Lakeside Guest House
11. Haynes Point Provincial Park
12. Desert Ecological Reserve
13. Inkameep Campground and R.V. Park
14. Carriage House Wines
15. Dominion Radio Astrophysical Observatory
16. Okanagan Game Farm
17. Okanagan Spring Wine Festival
18. Kettle Valley Steam Railway
19. Summerland Museum
20. Okanagan Pottery Studio
21. Hainle Vineyards Estate Winery
22. Ogopogo
23. Myra Canyon
24. A View to Remember Bed and Breakfast
25. The Gathering Room
26. Big White Ski Resort
27. Beaverdell Hotel

THE OKANAGAN-SIMILKAMEEN

Apples and wine, watersports, and lots of sunshine are images that prevail on hearing the words *Okanagan–Similkameen*. Here in Canada's warmest, driest climate, we'll travel through just 3 percent of British Columbia's 366,275 square miles (948,596 sq km), but our diverse journey will lead us from Princeton, in the foothills of the Cascades, along the once gold-rich Similkameen River, past eccentrically shaped mountains and turquoise lakes in Cathedral Provincial Park, through orchards of cherries, peaches, pears, apples, apricots, and grapes. Down close to the U.S. border, we'll see painted turtles and rattlesnakes lurking in Canada's only desert. We'll meet the mystical Ogopogo in the 90-mile-long (145-km) Okanagan Lake, one of more than 250 lakes in the region. And in the fall we'll enjoy world-class wine at the Okanagan Wine Festival, for which this land of plenty is fast becoming famous.

PRINCETON

Starting in the east at the Manning Park border, the mountainous Crowsnest Highway 3 winds north to **Princeton,** a town *mother-loded* with a history of gold and copper mining from the 1880s. Originally called Vermilion Forks after the nearby bluffs of red ocher, a substance prized by the Similkameen Indians for trading and face painting, Princeton, the southern gateway to the populous BC interior, sits quietly in the foothills of the Cascade Mountains, where the Tulameen and Similkameen rivers meet.

On the main street, ❖ **The Mini Chef Restaurant** at 161 Vermilion Street (250-295-7711) serves inexpensive homemade pies, soups, and delicious full meals. Unique in BC, it is run as a training center for the developmentally impaired, and employs about ten Princeton-area residents. The elegantly renovated and bright restaurant is as spotlessly clean as the proverbial whistle.

Two doors down, the ❖ **Princeton Museum and Archives** (167 Vermilion, 250-295-7588) is a credit to this population of just three thousand. Curator and archivist Margaret Stoneberg, a Princetonian since the fifties, has had a predominant influence in setting up and maintaining the chock-full museum. It features one of Princeton's more infamous characters, the likable train robber and prison escapee, Bill Miner. After doing time in the U.S. for Pony Express robberies, he moved his talents to the Princeton area and, in upwardly mobile fashion, started on the trains, where as *The Gentleman Bandit* he restricted his robberies to the baggage cars, taking the payrolls, but never the ladies' jewelry. One daring robbery near Kamloops ended in his capture and imprisonment. He escaped and fled to the United States where, after recapture, he died in a Georgia prison.

The basement of the museum houses a vast collection of rocks and petrified wood, and one of the largest collections of fossils in British Columbia. The museum is open from 9:00 A.M. to 6:00 P.M. daily in July and August, and afternoons during the rest of the year. If no one is around, ask at the library next door for information, or you can call Margaret Stoneberg at home at (250) 295-3362. That's the kind of friendly place it is.

Every summer since 1988, Princeton has celebrated a ◆ **Pony Express Ride** with her Washington State twin city, Tonasket. Flag-bearing riders (five Canadian and five American) carry 200 envelopes (sold for $5.00 each) in authentic U.S. Postal Service mailbags along a 100-mile route between the two towns. Each letter is stamped at post offices along the way. It's a means of promoting the annual (August) **Princeton Rodeo,** where barrel racing, bull riding and mutton bustin' have promoted the rodeo to "Best Rodeo in BC" status.

If you're needing a place to bed for the night, ◆ **Princeton Castle and R.V. Park** (5 Mile Road, RR 1, Site 1, Comp. 10, Princeton, V0X

A PRINCETON TREASURE

The Princeton Museum was closed, so I inquired at the library.

"Find Margaret Stoneberg," was the answer. "She's usually around somewhere."

I found dear Margaret Stoneberg, a wool hat pulled tightly on, a stuffed bag of books by her feet, and her eyes close to a newspaper she was reading. She parted a ring of keys, selected one, rose slowly from her paper, and shuffled me in to the museum.

"At first there was just trees and the mountain," she began.

Two hours later, I was still listening eagerly to stories from the gold and copper heydays, learning how during the war all the beer *from here to Alaska* was Princeton beer, and hearing how things haven't always changed for the better. As we left the museum, she was still pointing out artifacts.

"That organ was $29.50 in the 1903 catalogue," she whispered, a note of nostalgia in her tiny voice.

1W0; 250-295-7988) is a good choice, no matter what the budget. A new log lodge, cabins, and an R.V. park are set behind the racetrack off Highway 40 (Osprey Lake Road) on the site of an intended cement plant and power house. For some unknown reason, the massive architectural venture didn't pan out (possibly they ran out of limestone), and what is left looks like the ruins of a medieval castle. You may want to spend some time searching for the notorious Bill Miner's lost treasure, rumored to be hidden in his hideout in the hills near the castle. Locals tell me you'll have more luck panning for gold in the creek, though. Or perhaps flying to the moon!

THE SIMILKAMEEN VALLEY

Leaving Princeton, the Crowsnest Highway 3 follows the Similkameen River 41 miles (67 km) east to Keremeos. Three miles (5 km) before Keremeos, a 16-mile (25-km) southern side trip on the gravel Ashnola River Road brings you into ◆ **Cathedral Provincial Park.** California bighorn sheep, mule deer, porcupines, and black bears range in this 81,000-acre (33,000-ha) mountain wilderness, the setting for the movie *Clan of the Cave Bear.*

The bridge at the start of the road into the park is privately owned, so unless you are using the jeep service provided by the **Cathedral Lakes Lodge** owners (250-226-7560), park at the footbridge and hike in. From the center of the park, try the 6-mile (10-km) hike from Quiniscoe Lake to the 8,622 feet (2,628 m) Lakeview Mountain. It's quite a climb, but on a clear day you can see across the Cascades to Washington's Mount Baker. The wildflowers (mainly heather and lupine), jagged peaks, and turquoise Cathedral Lakes make the area a wilderness heaven. It's a "Be Prepared" park, with no commercial facilities other than the private lodge. Contact Okanagan District Office, Okanagan Lake Provincial Park, Box 399, Summerland, BC, V0H 1Z0, or phone (250) 499-5848 for information and the Ministry of Parks brochure. If you're already in the area, Keremeos and District Chamber of Commerce (414 Seventh Avenue, Box 490, Keremeos, V0X 1N0; 250-499-5225) can help. More detailed topographic maps (sheets 92H/1E½ and 1W½) are available for a fee from Maps BC, (Parliament Buildings, Victoria, V8V 1X5; 250-387-1441).

At the route map information sign on Highway 3, 3 miles (5 km) west of Keremeos, the ◆ **Login Bed and Breakfast** (C1, Site 27, Highway 3 West, RR 1, Keremeos, V0X 1N0; 250-499-2781; E-mail: loginbnb@kere-meos.com) caters to people and horses too at this pleasant B&B, a short hike away from the Ashnola wilderness. The rooms have lovely views of the Similkameen scenery, and you should see plenty of bighorn sheep right outside your window. Breakfasts are excellent, with enough leftovers to stuff your packs for the hike snack. There's a kitchen for your use and a lovely log fireplace. Rates are moderate, and the hosts, Helen and Eric Falkenberg, will even let you use their Internet access. Ask them about rides or hikes outside the park to spots like Crater Lake, Barcelo Canyon, and the Columns.

Keremeos, where fruit stands and mountains dominate the horizon, is the epitome of the word *nestled*. And nestled in this lovely Similkameen Valley you'll find lots to see and do, including the ◆ **Orchard Blossom Honey House** (250-499-2821), with its historic beekeeping equipment, and **Carriage 'n' Works** (250-499-7738), where old wagons and carriages are restored.

But the valley's best known attraction is British Columbia's only water-powered flour mill, built in 1877. ◆ **The Grist Mill** (RR 1, Upper Bench Road, Keremeos, V0X 1N0; 250-499-2888) is well signed and off Highway 3A (the quick way to Penticton) on Keremeos Creek and features restored, rare, original machinery driven by a 12-foot waterwheel, a Heritage Gardens showing the agricultural history of the Similkameen Valley, and hands-on displays about this historic milling process. Pioneer lifestyle activities, enacted by costumed interpreters, give you that 1880s atmosphere.

BRITISH COLUMBIA FACT

BC's dimensions are about 780 miles (1,250 km) from north to south and about 650 miles (1,050 km) from east to west.

At the Tea Room, you can enjoy light lunches featuring fresh-baked goods made from flour milled as it was in 1877 and organically grown heritage vegetables and flowers from the Heritage Gardens. In the Mill Shop you'll find seeds and plant-starts from the Heritage Gardens, wheat-straw weavings, corn dolls, dried gourds, and, of course, milled flour. Topical books are a nice addition. The Grist Mill is open formally from May to October and informally the rest of the year. Admission prices are reasonable, with tour discounts available.

THE OKANAGAN VALLEY

The Similkameen River winds south to the border, and the highway leaves it to take a northeastern route. Just 5.5 miles (8.8 km) west of

Osoyoos, the strange ◆ **Spotted Lake** (called *Klilok* by the Okanagan Indians) can be seen from the highway. Evaporation and crystallization cause the formation of salty, white circular plates on the surface, hence its name. If it weren't on private land, you'd be able to soak away your arthritic pains in this muddy paradise of Epsom salts, calcium, and magnesium, as did the First Nations people in centuries gone by. Instead be content to enjoy the unusual view from the highway.

Osoyoos Lake, named from *Soi'yus,* an Inkaneep Indian word meaning roughly *gathered together* or *where the water narrows,* comes into view. "Seems a zealous Irishman added the 'O'," explained former schoolteacher John Wallace who, with his wife June, was my host at ◆ **Haynes Point Lakeside Guest House** (3619 Jasmine Drive, Osoyoos, V0H 1V0; 250-495-7443). The Wallaces know and share a remarkable amount of information about the area, even to preparing handouts on birding or arranging golfing or winery tours (there are five fine golf courses and ten wineries within thirty minutes), or you can simply enjoy June's delicious breakfasts (where I learned to put cardamom in my coffee for that special flavor) and unwind in one of the hammocks overlooking the lake. Their three guest rooms are distinctively decorated to a theme, and the view over the lake and hills is wonderful. In summer, boating and swimming in "Canada's warmest lake" is popular. To get there, turn south from the Crowsnest onto Highway 97, and after 2 miles (3 km) follow the Haynes Point Provincial Park sign onto Thirty-second Avenue. Jasmine Street is a left turn just before the lake. Rates are between $70 and $85; the pampered feeling you come away with makes these rates quite reasonable.

Less than five minutes away at the ◆ **Haynes Point Provincial Park** (250-494-0321), a strip of land stretches out into the middle of the lake, narrowing to just over 60 feet (18 m) wide in spots. Forty-five waterfront, forested campsites are at the end. The park offers walks, audiovisual programs, and other activities related to the history of the area. Red-winged blackbirds, ospreys, and eagles are seen regularly. If you're particularly lucky, you may hear the hum of a hovering Calliope hummingbird, Canada's tiniest bird. The park is extremely popular, though, so reserve a spot ahead of time by calling 1-800-689-9025 (the Discover Camping Campgrounds Reservation Service), which operates between March 1 and September 15.

Seven miles (12 km) north of Osoyoos along Highway 97, take Road 22 (298th Avenue) across a rickety wooden bridge over an irrigation canal (*The Ditch*) onto Black Sage Road, a paved but quiet road that passes the old **Haynes ranch house** and barn, where you'll find excellent photo opportunities at a historic site.

A little farther north, at the ◆ **Desert Ecological Reserve,** you'll see prickly pear cactus, rock rose, antelope bush, and desert creatures such as the endangered burrowing owl, Northwestern Pacific rattlesnakes, western painted turtles, black widow spiders, and scorpions, all defying man's intrusion. Creatures found nowhere else in Canada include kangaroo rats, praying mantises, a bird called the sage thrasher, and the Great Basin spadefoot toad. Controversy hovers over whether this is a true desert, and whether this "vest-pocket desert" is the tip of the Sonoran Desert extending up from Mexico into Canada. The truth is that because of the variation in ideas on what a desert is, or isn't, there will always be this confusion. Xerophytic vegetation of a type rare in Canada exists here, but this alone does not a desert make. It's located on the Inkaneep Indian Reserve and covers approximately 247 acres (100 ha). Contact the Osoyoos Chamber of Commerce (Box 227, Osoyoos, V0H 1V0; 250-495-7142), or the Inkaneep (Osoyoos) Administration (RR 3, Site 25, C-1, Oliver, V0H 1T0; 250-498-3444), for permission to visit this unique area.

The best access is via ◆ **Inkameep Campground and R.V. Park** (250-495-7279), a family campground right on Osoyoos Lake's east shore. Turn off Highway 3 East (Main Street) at Forty-fifth Street just past the **Little Duffer Ice Cream Parlor and Mini Golf** (250-495-6354) and drive north toward the lakeshore. En route you'll pass the **Indian Grove Riding Stable** (250-495-7555), where rides through the desert to see rattlesnakes, coyotes, and underground waterfalls can be arranged.

In dramatic contrast, vineyards replace the desert. The Okanagan has entered the world arena in wine growing, with many high-quality wines winning national and international awards in recent years. One little gem of a winery, farther north on Black Sage Road toward Oliver, is ◆ **Carriage House Wines** (Black Sage Road, Oliver, V0H 1T0; 250-498-8818). Here David Wagner, the "only home grown vintner in the area," works an eight and a half acre "farm-gate" winery with his wife Karen, producing pinot blanc, chardonnay, and cabernet sauvignon. Savoring the aroma of a 1996 Kerner, a mandatory prelude before the sip, swirl, and swallow, even my inexpert nose told me I had found something special. Carriage House Wines, where they *pride themselves on being small,* is open daily for tours from 10:00 A.M. to 6:00 P.M., or anytime by appointment.

From the winery there's a lovely view across the Okanagan River Dike to other larger vineyards, notably **Tinhorn Creek** and **Gehringer Brothers Estate Wineries,** which leads me to understand that there is some truth to the rumor that the Oliver postal code, V0H 1T0, really does stand for "View of heaven in the Okanagan."

From Oliver, take the Fairview–White Lake Road, which runs northeast from the gold-rush town of Fairview into the next millennium at the ✦ **Dominion Radio Astrophysical Observatory** (P.O. Box 248, Penticton, V2A 6K3; 250–493–2277). If you're coming from Penticton, turn off Highway 97 at Kaleden junction onto White Lake Road, and should you then get lost, simply ask a friendly local where the observatory is.

A tour of the complex (which is part of the National Research Council of Canada) takes you past a row of seven antennae that work together to simulate a giant 1,969-foot (600-m) telescope. The most prominent "dish" antenna is 85 feet (26 m) across. At the visitors center, displays explain how images from these telescopes are used to probe the invisible gases between the stars. Canadian scientists here are working to understand how stars are born, how they die, and how stars and gas are interrelated in the Milky Way. Beyond the visitors center is a smaller radio telescope that monitors the radio output from the sun. From these data, scientists can research global climate change. Because ignition systems can emit radio waves that interfere with the astronomers' observations, you must leave your car in a parking lot and walk about 600 yards to the observatory

BRITISH COLUMBIA FACT

Of U.S. states, only Alaska is larger.

grounds. Canada's only radio observatory is open all year during daylight hours. Lectures and demonstrations are held on Sundays in July and August from 2:00–5:00 P.M. They're free too!

Overlooking Skaha (Dog) Lake on Highway 97, about 5 miles (8 km) south of Penticton, if you keep a sharp eye out to the west you may think you've traveled from space into Africa. The ✦ **Okanagan Game Farm** (250–497–5405) is open year-round daily from 8:00 A.M. to dusk and sprawls over 650 acres (263 ha), with more than 100 species of animals, including lions, zebras, and camels.

From game farms to vineyards, the Okanagan has it all. For four days during the first weekend of every May, the ✦ **Okanagan Spring Wine Festival** takes place when valley vintners release their new wines. If you

BRITISH COLUMBIA TRIVIA

At the Summerland Research Station in the Okanagan, many different varieties of apples are developed. Some of these include Spartan, Sunrise, Starkcrimson Red Delicious, Sumac, Sinta, Shamrock, Summerred, and Spur Mac. A simply splendid selection of sobriquets.

time your visit for early October, you'll be inundated with bacchanal choices at the **Annual Fall Okanagan Wine Festival,** a hopping event with more than 100 diverse choices, from grape stomps, wine biking tours, and pig roasts, to a chocolate and port buffet. Contact the Okanagan Wine Festival Office (1030 McCurdy Road, Kelowna, V1X 2P7; 250-861-6654 or 1-800-972-5151) for information and bookings.

Okanagan summers are the warmest in British Columbia, so cooling-off spots between Penticton and Summerland (like **Kickinninee** and **Sun-Oka** beaches on Okanagan Lake) deserve a check mark in the book. With more hours of summer sunshine than Hawaii, though, make sure you're well protected.

Summerland is a major fruit-processing center, an industry that was helped in its early days by steam trains. A ride on the ♦ **Kettle Valley Steam Railway** (Box 1288, Summerland, V0H 1Z0; 250-494-8422; E-mail: KVR@summer.com) will help transport you back to this time. Tickets are sold at the Summerland Chamber of Commerce Office (Box 1075, Summerland, V0H 1Z0; 250-494-2686). Park-and-ride tickets for adults are $9.75, seniors $8.75, and youths four to twelve $6.50. Look for the clearly marked shuttle bus pickup points.

In town, the ♦ **Summerland Museum** (Box 1491, Summerland, V0H 1Z0; 250-494-9395; E-mail: smuseum@summer.com) has some railway memorabilia with a collection of historical photographs. As well, it displays pioneer tools used in fruit growing and holds slide and video presentations. Upstairs is an art gallery operated by the Summerland Arts Council. The museum is open year-round with hours in June, July, and August, Monday–Saturday from 10:00 A.M. to 4:00 P.M., and September to May, Tuesday–Saturday from 1:00–4:00 P.M.

The winding highway climbs through Summerland past vineyards and rocky cliffs bordering Okanagan Lake to Peachland, 13 miles (21 km) north. Here Peter and Daphne Flanagan and Daphne's parents, Des and Peg Loan, operate a small, bright, family business,

◆ **Okanagan Pottery Studio** (6030 Highway 97S, Peachland, V0H 1X0; 250-767-2010). Here you'll see strong purples and greens, and grape-leaf designs inspired by the beauty of the Okanagan in many of the artists' works. The studio was built by the Loans in 1968, and their original kiln is still in operation. Peter's work has been honored with the Special Judges' Award at Mino, Japan. Look for his neat French butter dishes. The butter sits in the "lid." Water in the bottom forms a seal, preserving the butter without refrigeration. The dishes are small, practical, and inexpensive if you're looking for an Okanagan souvenir.

Another interesting stop heading north along Highway 97, just past the huge Golf Ball on the roadside, is ◆ **Hainle Vineyards Estate Winery** (5355 Trepanier Bench Road, Peachland, V0H 1X0; 250-767-2525; E-mail: tilman@hainle.com), a small, family-run winery producing naturally dry, fully fermented wines. In addition to a tasting room, wine shop, and bistro, where yummy lunch specials both complement and compliment their wines, the winery offers a spectacular view of the valley. Their Icewine, the first of its kind in Canada, is a rare wine made by allowing the fruit to freeze on the vine to at least 17°F (−8°C). This requires an early morning workforce frantically picking, crushing and pressing before the warm sun thaws the grapes. The frozen water from the fruit remains in the press, and from the concentrated juice, wines result that range from sherry-like to fruity, and from almost dry to rich and sweet. It's the first BC winery to have its own Web site (http://www.bcwine.com/hainle/) and the first to label its bottles *certified organic*.

From the west, your introduction to **Kelowna** (population 87,000 and growing fast) is via a 2,000-foot (640-m) floating bridge, North America's first and largest. As you cross Okanagan Lake, keep an eye out for ◆ **Ogopogo.** Long before the first mission settlement by Father Pandosy in 1860, Interior Salish folklore told of a mysterious monster called N'ha-a-itk, the Devil of the Lake. According to the favored tale, if you see a long, snake-like, humpy, greenish oddity with a horse-like head, you'll be the next believer. Could this be the reason Kelowna is labeled *City of Smiles?*

For a panoramic view of this smiling city, hike or bike on a route created by the Kettle Valley Railway through the horseshoe-shaped ◆ **Myra Canyon.** A one-hour bike trip over sixteen trestle bridges and through two tunnels will reveal breathtaking views of the canyon and Kelowna below. If you prefer a one-way ride, **Air-Hart Floatplane Tours** (Box 24078, Lake Front Post Office, Kelowna, V1Y 9P9; 250-769-8060) will

> # BRITISH COLUMBIA TRIVIA
>
> The government of British Columbia announced in 1926 that the new ferry being constructed for Okanagan Lake would be equipped with monster-repelling devices. The threatening monster, Ogopogo, was named after a music hall song popular in the twenties.

fly you and your bike to nearby Idabel Lake. Contact the Chamber of Commerce/InfoCentre (544 Harvey Avenue, Kelowna, V1Y 6C9; 250-861-1515) for directions and information.

After a strenuous hike you'll need a restful night. ◆ **A View to Remember Bed and Breakfast** (1090 Trevor Drive, Kelowna, V1Z 2J8; 250-769-4028; west of the floating bridge off Boucherie Road) has just that. Australians Celia and Robin Jarman have decorated their elegant home with antiques inside and lovely gardens outside. You'll eat fruit from their own trees on a patio with a great view of the lake and mountains.

Before leaving Kelowna, visit the **Tutt Street Square** (3045 Tutt Street, south of the city just off the KLO Road near Pandosy Street), where a quaint (there's no other word for it) teahouse called ◆ **The Gathering Room** (250-861-4188) serves wonderful homemade soups and herb breads, English and herbal teas, chocolates, Caesar salads, lattés, cappuccinos, award-winning cheesecakes, and lemon curd tarts - such a deliciously eclectic array of food. Occasionally you may be treated to a fashion show as you eat. A stained-glass division separates the tearoom from its small gift shop. The Gathering Room is open Mondays–Saturdays 9:30 A.M. to 4:30 P.M. and Sundays 11:00 A.M. to 3:00 P.M. Across from the Gathering Room at the **Tutt Street Gallery** (250-861-4992), watercolors, oils, raku, and some notable Ken Curley bronzes, all top-quality works by Canadian artists, are displayed for sale.

THE NORTH OKANAGAN

Leaving Kelowna, Highway 97 hugs the east coast of Okanagan Lake for 29 miles (46 km) north to **Vernon. Agri-tourism** is a word often heard in this area, and it refers to the many specialty livestock and fruit and vegetable operations open to the public. A few miles north of Vernon at Armstrong, you'll find **Llama Farm** (250-546-3038) and **Little Mountain Peruvians** (250-546-3320). Farther north, at Enderby, **Fink Trout and Deer Farm** (250-838-7621) is a fun place to visit, with its

U-Catch trout pond and deer, elk, and bison farm. And if you've never seen alpacas, Canada's largest herd can be found at **Okanagan Alpaca Company** (250-838-9559), just east of Enderby. West of Vernon at Lavington, there's a **Fallow Deer Farm** (250-545-3168), and near tiny Cherryville, the **Big Bird Ostrich Ranch** offers tours by appointment (or else just pull up by the roadside and take a peek).

"U-pick" farming is becoming popular in the North Okanagan. At **MacDonald's Pure Beeswax** (250-546-3237), between Vernon and Armstrong on North Grandview Flats Road, you'll find apricots and cherries ripe for the picking. If you'd prefer to pick apples, pears, or plums, call **Cayford's Orchard** (250-546-3411) on Hallum Road in Armstrong. Of course, you have to be there in season. Contact Vernon Tourism (Box 520, 6326 Highway 97 North, Vernon, V1T 6M4; 250-542-1415) for information on fruit growing seasons, and to find out about other farms involved in this fast-growing agri-tourism industry.

KETTLE RIVER VALLEY

Four miles (6.5 km) east of the Kelowna floating bridge, the lonely Highway 33 winds south from Highway 97 for 80 miles (129 kms), following the course of the Kettle River through pretty, pastoral landscapes. A side road brings you to the ◆ **Big White Ski Resort,** 34 miles (55 km) from Kelowna and on the edge of the Monashees. With over 19 feet (6 m) of pure powder annually, expect some great skiing here. Phone 1-800-663-2772 for information and reservations. Watch out for deer on the roadside, as they seem to be everywhere.

Halfway along Highway 33 at Beaverdell, you'll find the antiquated ◆ **Beaverdell Hotel,** where a wall inscription in The Ladies Parlour reads: "Oh what stories she could tell," and promenades us back to an exciting era invoking memories of the heady days of old. The hotel, built in 1900, claims significance as the oldest operating hotel in British Columbia. Check out the old car in the yard beside the hotel (there isn't much more) and then get ready to explore the Kootenays when you reach tiny Rock Creek (population 51) just north of the Canada-U.S. border on Highway 3. We're back on the Crowsnest.

WHERE TO STAY:

1. **Princeton Castle and R.V. Park** (5 Mile Road, RR 1, Site 1, Comp. 10, Princeton, V0X 1W0; 250-295-7988).
2. **Cathedral Lakes Lodge** (RR 1, Cawston, V0X 1C0; 250-499-5848). Full accommodation $140.

3. **Login Bed and Breakfast** (C1 Site 27, Highway 3 West, RR 1, Keremeos, V0X 1N0; 250-499-2781; E-mail: loginbnb@keremeos. com).

4. **Haynes Point Lakeside Guest House** (3619 Jasmine Drive, Osoyoos, V0H 1V0; 250-495-7443). Bed and breakfast; rates $60-$85.

5. **Inkameep Campground and R.V. Park** (Forty-fifth Street, Osoyoos) RR 3, Site 25, Comp. 1, Oliver, V0H 1T0; (250) 495-7279. Open June– September. Serviced sites, store, washrooms with showers, playground.

6. **A View to Remember Bed and Breakfast** (1090 Trevor Drive, Kelowna, V1Z 2J8; 250-769-4028). Rates are $50-$75.

WHERE TO EAT:

1. **The Mini Chef Restaurant** (161 Vermilion Street, Princeton, V0X 1W0; 250-295-7711). Inexpensive.

2. **The Grist Mill Tea Room** (RR 1, Upper Bench Road, Keremeos, V0X 1N0; 250-499-2888). Inexpensive.

3. **The Gathering Room Tea House** (3045 Tutt Street, Kelowna, V1Y 2H4; 250-861-4188). Inexpensive.

4. **Hainle Vineyards Estate Bistro** (5355 Trepanier Bench Road, Peachland, V0H 1X0; 250-767-2525; E-mail: tilman@hainle.com).

5. **Nicola's Italian Restaurant** (795 Westminster Avenue West, Penticton, V2A 1K9; 250-493-3012). Pastas, moderately priced.

6. **Water Street Grill** (1346 Water Street, Kelowna, V1Y 9P4; 250-860-0707). Casual, interesting menu. Open daily from 11:30 A.M.

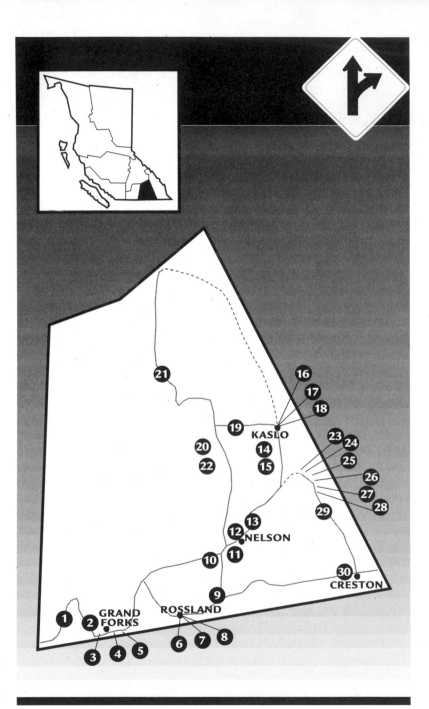

KOOTENAY COUNTRY

1. Windsor Hotel and Saloon
2. Phoenix Forest and History Tour
3. Chef's Garden Restaurant
4. Grand Forks Boundary Museum
5. Golden Heights Inn and Restaurant
6. Red Mountain
7. Leroi Mine
8. The Cellar Fibre Studio
9. Cominco lead–zinc smelter
10. Spinning Wheel Vegetarian Eatery
11. Doukhobor Village Museum
12. Grohman Narrows Provincial Park
13. Car #23
14. Silver Ledge Hotel
15. Ainsworth Hot Springs Resort
16. SS *Moyie*
17. Langham Cultural Centre
18. The Rosewood Café
19. Sandon ghost town
20. Valhalla Provincial Park
21. Nakusp Hot Springs
22. Lemon Creek Lodge
23. Yasodhara Ashram
24. Kootenay Forge
25. North Woven Broom Company
26. Weavers' Corner
27. Wedgewood Manor
28. Gray Creek Store
29. The Glass House
30. Creston Valley Wildlife Management Area

KOOTENAY COUNTRY

The Monashee, Selkirk, and Purcell ranges straddle glacier-fed rivers and lakes to form this area of British Columbia's interior, where the Ktunaxa people trace their unbroken presence back to before the last ice age. In the late 1800s, a frenzied rush for precious metals brought newcomers. Many of the towns they built are now but ghostly remnants, but some grew, and today, joined by a system of highways and free ferries, serve travelers wanting to explore this mountainous wilderness.

Our trek through the Kootenays starts close to the U.S. border in historic Greenwood, and follows the Crowsnest Highway to Rossland, where a tour of a hardrock gold mine gives us a taste of the fever that shook those early immigrants. We'll experience the Russian influence in the south as we enjoy borscht near a Doukhobor museum, then relive the mining past in a ghost town. We'll meet the interesting people on east Kootenay Lake, where ashrams, weavers, broom makers, blacksmiths, and an embalming-bottle house will arouse our curiosity.

BOUNDARY COUNTRY

After leaving the Kettle River and the Okanagan behind, we rejoin the Crowsnest (Highway 3) and travel east to **Greenwood,** Canada's smallest incorporated city. Close to the Washington State border, Greenwood features many historic buildings and sites. Just before the city, you'll see an old chimney on the north side of the highway. This marks the ruins of the **BC Copper Company Smelter** that operated between 1901 and 1918. A sign indicates a track to the 120-foot (40-m) chimney near **Lotzkar Memorial Park,** where an abandoned underground shaft evokes images of dusty miners. To get there, turn north at the Mother Lode Store and Laundromat on Washington Street.

BRITISH COLUMBIA FACT

BC entered the Canadian Confederation on July 20, 1871.

On Main Street, check out the ◆ **Windsor Hotel and Saloon,** and right next door, the restored **Greenwood Inn,** where historic photos depict Greenwood at the turn of the century. In those days, the city supported 100 businesses, including fourteen hotels, two newspapers, two banks, and a thousand-seat opera house. Today its population is just 900, and there's certainly no sign of an opera house.

If you do a city walking tour, take a look at Hammersly House, the City Hall (excellent stained glass upstairs), the Sacred Heart Catholic church (high up on the hill), and the red-brick, towered Post Office, with its antique, hourly chiming clock. Ask at the **Greenwood Museum** (250-445-6355) in front of City Hall for directions. The museum is open daily in summer from 10:00 A.M. to 4:00 P.M. and is worth a visit for its interesting collection of mining relics and photos of nearby Phoenix, now defunct but once the highest city in Canada and home of the first Canadian professional hockey team.

The ❖ **Phoenix Forest and History Tour** is a two-hour, self-guided driving tour that takes you past the old **Phoenix Cemetery,** where towering Douglas fir trees now grow beside graves of young miners and victims of the 1918-1919 influenza epidemic. A detailed brochure that makes the tour much more interesting is available from the Ministry of Forests, Boundary Forest District, 136 Sagamore Avenue, Grand Forks, V0H 1H0 (250-442-5411), or at either the Greenwood or Grand Forks Museums. The drive starts (or ends) in Greenwood at the junction of Highway 3 and Phoenix Road, covering 13.6 miles (22 km) of well-maintained road. You'll pass an area around Marshall Lake that is today a cross-country skier's dream, with more than 10 miles (17 km) of trails. Alpine skiing is nearby at the **Phoenix Ski Hill** (250-442-2813), where runs are named after the old copper mines.

Six miles (9.5 km) west of **Grand Forks** along Highway 3, keep an eye out for the abandoned two-story, red-brick **Doukhobor houses** and barns on the south side of the highway. The Doukhobors (or "spirit wrestlers") were a group of Russian pacifists who fled from persecution in Russia to Saskatchewan and Manitoba, only to be evicted again when they rejected the oath of allegiance. They arrived in the Grand Forks area in 1908, where they farmed simply and were self-sufficient in almost every way. Although the communes are now deserted, the religion lives on.

As does the cuisine! Try a typical Russian meal at the ❖ **Chef's Garden Restaurant** (4415 Highway 3, 250-442-0257), which is 3 miles (5 km) west of Grand Forks at Rilkoff's General Store. They serve tasty Russian sandwiches and borscht and also sell Russian souvenirs. Nearby, off Reservoir Road, enjoy country hospitality and homemade preserves at the **Orchard Bed and Breakfast** (5615 Spencer Road, RR 1, S850C, C3, Grand Forks, V0H 1H0; 250-442-8583).

Continue along Reservoir Road to Hardy Mountain Road, where you'll learn more about the Doukhobor culture at the **Mountain View**

Doukhobor Museum. Displayed here are handmade household articles, tools, costumes, and photographs. It's open June 1–September 30, 9:00 A.M. to 7:00 P.M. Phone curator Peter Gritchen (250-442-8855) for information.

BRITISH COLUMBIA FACT

BC is bordered by the Yukon in the north, Alberta in the east, the Pacific Ocean and Alaska in the west, and the states of Washington, Idaho, and Montana in the south.

Continue down Hardy Mountain Road into **Grand Forks,** once a lively (perhaps raunchy) hub, with a colorful red-light district and a Chinatown. Rum running, logging, mining, and railroading ruled "The Forks," where the Granby and Kettle rivers meet. Today the railways are gone, as are the smelters, but you can relive its history at the ◆ **Grand Forks Boundary Museum** (7370 Fifth Street, V0H 1H0; 250-442-3737; E-mail: boundmuseum@mail.awinc.com) on the main street through town. It's open Monday–Friday, 8:00 A.M. to 4.30 P.M. and daily in summer.

Beside the museum at the **Visitor Information Centre** (7362 Fifth Street; 250-442-2833) pick up a pamphlet to guide you on an 18-mile (30-km) drive or bike ride to the former **Granby Mining and Smelter Company,** once the largest nonferrous copper smelter in the British Empire. Today a couple of slag heaps (now processed as Kleen Blast and used in sandblasting and roofing) are all that remain of the Granby smelter. To get there, take the steel bridge over the Granby River (Granby Road) north to the **Hummingbird Bridge** (a fishing and swimming spot). Cross the bridge and take North Fork Franklin Road, which brings you back south to Grand Forks, past an old Columbia and Western Station, now the **Grand Forks Station Pub** (7654 Donaldson Street; 250-442-5855), where you can enjoy pub-style meals.

Up on Rattlesnake Hill overlooking Grand Forks (as you head east out of town) sits a grand Victorian mansion. The ◆ **Golden Heights Inn and Restaurant** (7342 Bluff Street; 250-442-0626) was shipped in pieces from California at the turn of the century by a wealthy dentist-cum-mining-speculator, Dr. A. W. Averill, whose specialty was diamond fillings! His Golden Heights home featured a ballroom, a guest cottage, six fireplaces, and a stable. Even if you don't stay overnight or come for a gourmet meal, take a walk in the park-like gardens.

The Crowsnest Highway leaves the Kettle Valley, and 13 miles (20 km) beyond Grand Forks, it heads north, hugging the long and lovely

Christina Lake. The residents here claim their lake is the warmest in British Columbia, but similar claims from Wasa Lake in the Rockies and Osoyoos Lake in the Okanagan occasionally lead to hot debates.

KOOTENAY SOUTH

Fifteen miles (24 km) east of Christina Lake on Highway 3, the road cuts through mountains of scenic forests. Cedar, birch, fir, and hemlock stands lead to the Paulson Bridge, where the views down into McRae Creek are spectacular. **Bonanza Pass,** 6 miles (10 km) farther, cuts through the Monashees at 5,036 feet (1,535 m) shortly before the highway meets the 3B south to Rossland. At the junction, the **Nancy Greene Provincial Park** features a subalpine lake with 90 miles (145 km) of great hiking or skiing trails.

The Crowsnest follows Blueberry Creek to Castlegar, but first visit **Rossland,** 17 miles (28 km) south on Highway 3B. It sits at 3,398 feet (1,036 m) above sea level in the crater of an ancient volcano. In all seasons it erupts with life. In winter, just ask any Red Mountain ski bum, and in spring, summer, or fall ask a mountain-biker blazing down one of the trails. Of the 3,700 folks who live in Rossland, more than 50 percent are under thirty-four, which might explain its lively, small-town feel.

MY PERSONAL TOUR GUIDE

Years ago I lived in the Eastern Arctic, where I knew Richard and Trish Exner. Today they live in a pretty, blue-roofed house on a hilltop in Rossland. Twenty-one Christmas cards later, we strolled over Rossland's San Francisco–like hills, remembering our Baffin days. Trish introduced me to some of the town's colorful characters. I met Lee Flanders, the barber, who joked he'd *rather be a barber than one of those schlubs down in the mine.* We said hello to Jack McDonald, Rossland's historian, and Harry Lefebvre, who used to be the Mayor. Maurice Samuelson ambled by; he used to be the postman. Trish was the consummate tour guide, taking me from hot pools to osprey nests, to beautiful lookouts in the Silvery Slocan, and finally back to the Exner cabin on Kootenay Lake, which was mine "for as long as I liked." The northern hospitality I remember well is alive and kicking in Rossland.

Rossland is Nancy Greene country. A nationally recognized name for Olympic Gold success in alpine skiing, Nancy Greene has had named for her a lake, a mountain, a provincial park, and a recreation area. She started her climb to fame back in the sixties at the fabulous ◆ **Red Mountain** (1–800–663–0105), home of Western Canada's first chairlift. The mountain itself is legendary among skiers for its steep, challenging terrain. Just a mile north of town, it towers over Rossland with its full-tilt diamond runs.

A favorite hangout of the ski set when tummies start rumbling is **Elmers Corner Cafe** (250–362–5266) up the hill on the corner of Second Avenue and Washington Street. On Thursday nights their "all-you-can-eat" pasta with Caesar salad and garlic bread is a winner at $7.95. They're open from noon to 9:00 P.M. daily except Tuesdays.

There's no need to pay a mother lode for accommodation in Rossland. In 1996, a new hostel opened on Columbia Avenue just west of the Chamber of Commerce. **Mountain Shadow Hostel** (250–362–7160) is but $17 per night for a basic bed, shower, kitchen facilities, and storage area. A little more comfortable is **Angela's Place Bed and Breakfast** (1520 Spokane, Box 944, Rossland, V0G 1Y0; 250–362–7790). It's renowned for its great food, hot tub, and warm atmosphere. The suites range from $30 to $90, depending on number of people.

As you enter town at the junction of Highways 22 and 3A (in summer the InfoCentre site), the **Rossland Historical Museum** (Box 26, Rossland, V0G 1Y0; 250–362–7722) features a collection of mining paraphernalia and houses the **Western Canada Ski Hall of Fame** (where local champions Nancy Greene and Kerrin Lee-Gartner are honored). Open from mid-May to mid-September, it's the site of the ◆ **Leroi Mine,** the only hardrock gold mine in Canada offering public tours. After being sold for a $12.50 recording fee, the Leroi eventually grossed more than $30 million. In the late 1890s, it produced 50 percent of Canada's gold at a time when Rossland's population was around seven thousand. It ran dry in 1929, a black year for Rossland, as it was also the year of a disastrous fire.

Despite fires, in Rossland you'll get that turn-of-the-century feel when you see its heritage buildings. The city has produced a brochure (*Historical Heritage Walking Tour*) to guide you through its architectural history. Contact the Chamber of Commerce in Rossland (250–362–5666; E-mail: rossland.chamber@resonet.com) to find out more about these thirty designated heritage buildings.

One of the grandest, the **Bank of Montreal,** on the corner of Washington Street and Columbia Avenue, was designed by Francis Mawson Rattenbury. The restored wooden counters and ornate plaster

Leroi Mine

BRITISH COLUMBIA TRIVIA

Francis Mawson Rattenbury designed the impressive British Columbia Legislature building and the Empress Hotel in Victoria. His private life was also impressive. A married man, he openly courted his mistress, Alma Packenham. After the death of his wife, he married Alma and left Victoria to settle in Bournemouth, England. Alma soon had designs on the family chauffeur though, and the pair were charged with murdering Rattenbury. She was acquitted, but her lover, George Stoner, was sentenced to death. Unable to go on, Alma committed suicide. Stoner had his sentence commuted to life imprisonment and was eventually released.

ceilings sit above the **Golden City Barber Shop,** where many tales of fortunes won or lost must have been heard. Once a telegraph office, you can still have your hair cut (and talk about lost fortunes) in an original 1926 porcelain revolving chair that was reupholstered with Naugahyde from the old Rossland theater seats.

Next door to the barbershop on Washington Street was once the town bathhouse. It's now ◆ **The Cellar Fibre Studio** (Box 1575, Rossland, V0G 1Y0; 250-362-7600) and features kids' clothes, weaving, and pottery, mostly work of Kootenay locals. Drop in and hear tales of miners who hid their gold under the floorboards.

On the other side of Washington Street is a newly renovated restaurant with yummy, homemade delectables. **Gold Rush Books and Espresso** (open seven days per week at 2063 Washington Street; 250-362-5333) serves delicious coffees, homemade muffins and cookies, soups, and gourmet teas. An eclectic book selection covers everything from philosophy to cooking.

Other buildings of historic note are the **Post Office,** built in 1910 on the corner of Queen Street and Columbia Avenue, and the **Courthouse** on the corner of Monte Cristo Street and Columbia Avenue. Completed in 1901 at a cost of $53,000, the stained glass and woodwork in the courtroom are exquisite. It holds National Heritage status. Then take a look at Saint Andrew's United Church and the **British Columbia Firefighter's Museum** (Box 789, Rossland, V0G 1Y0; 250-362-5514), on opposite corners at Queen Street and First Avenue. The museum features a hose tower, horse-drawn hose-and-reel wagons, uniforms, and old fire trucks. Unfortunately, it's open only in July and August.

When you've had your fill of Rossland, and that isn't easy, head down Highway 3B east to **Trail.** Here, the road drops 2,000 feet (610 m) in 7 miles (11 km) into one of BC's major industrial cities. This is the home of **Cominco,** and the world's largest integrated **lead–zinc smelter.** Retired Cominco employees give two- to three-hour tours of the Cominco complex Monday–Friday at 10:00 A.M. Phone the **Trail Chamber of Commerce** (250-368-3144; E-mail: tcoc@ciao.org) for year-round reservations. Children under twelve are not admitted, and you must wear long-sleeve shirts, slacks, and covered shoes, and leave your camera at home.

After the smelter tour, enjoy a spaghetti dinner at the **Colander Restaurant** (1475 Cedar Avenue, Trail, V1R 4C5; 250-364-1816), where all the pasta you can eat, chicken jo-jo's, salad, plus a bun cost $10.95. Italian food is not uncommon fare in Trail, a city with a long Italian heritage. It proudly maintains the only Italian archives in North America at Colombo Lodge (584 Rossland Avenue, 250-368-3144).

Highway 22 travels north from Trail beside the Columbia River for 16 miles (26 km) to **Castlegar,** where the Columbia meets the Kootenay River and, as in Grand Forks, where the Doukhobors have left their mark.

For a taste of this Russian influence, travel north from Trail on Highway 22. At its junction with Highway 3, cross the Columbia River Bridge and then turn left onto Highway 3A. Directly opposite the Castlegar Airport on Heritage Way, stop at the **Spinning Wheel Vegetarian Eatery** (250-365-7202) where the borscht is fabulous and the service equally impressive. A small bowl of borscht with homemade bread is $2.99, a large bowl, $3.99. There's also an "All you can eat bottomless bowl for $8.88." Other tasty Russian offerings are Bolshoi cheese, Pirahi, and for the kids, there's Peter Wabbit, Tiger Treats, and Duffy Ducks, all at undersized prices, too! It's open seven days a week.

See Castlegar's roots right next door on Heritage Way at the **Doukhobor Village Museum** (250-365-6622). It's easy to appreciate the turn-of-the-century hardships when you see this reconstructed Doukhobor community. Check out its bread oven, blacksmith shop, and wood-fired bathhouse. The museum is open daily May to September from 9:00 A.M. to 5:00 P.M. Admission is $3.00 for adults and $2.00 for students.

Twenty-three miles (38 km) northeast of Castlegar along Highway 3A, **Nelson** graces the West Arm of Kootenay Lake in the heart of the Selkirk Mountains. As you approach from the south, keep an eye out for **osprey nests** on the bridge pylons at Taghum about 3 miles (5 km) before **Grohman Narrows Provincial Park.** The park is a pleasant picnic spot just as you enter Nelson. Plan on doing the thirty-minute walk around the nature trail.

Nelson is in a picture-perfect setting. It's long been appreciated for movie backdrops, the Steve Martin film *Roxanne* being one. Martin's character Cyrano, with his long nose, would have appreciated the clean mountain air of this lovely city of heritage buildings, artisans, and steep streets overlooking Kootenay Lake's West Arm.

To appreciate it yourself, take a ride in the restored ◆ **Car #23,** built in 1906 for service in Cleveland, Ohio. It was used in Nelson from 1924 to 1949. Car #23 runs daily from July 1 to Labor Day, noon–9:00 P.M. and costs $2.00 for adults and $1.00 for children. For information, contact the **Nelson Chamber of Commerce** (225 Hall Street, 250–352–3433). While there, pick up a self-guided tour brochure for an **architectural heritage walking (or driving) tour** to view some of the 350 heritage buildings the city boasts.

KOOTENAY LAKE WEST

A 21-mile (34-km) drive northeast from Nelson along Highway 3A beside the Kootenay River brings you to Balfour and the world's longest free ferry ride, but first we'll take Highway 31 north along the west shore of **Kootenay Lake,** renowned for its good fishing. Drop the hook for Dolly Varden, Kokanee, and rainbow trout. A few miles along, you'll see an odd sight. Near Toad Rock turnoff, dozens of men's ties, neatly knotted, hang high on light poles, apparently put there by students some years ago. Grads take their pranks seriously in the Kootenays.

Nine miles (15 km) north of Balfour at Ainsworth Hot Springs is the ◆ **Silver Ledge Hotel** (250–229–4640), a 100-year-old hotel restored to its late-nineteenth-century state. It houses a collection of old photos of the Ainsworth Mining District. Once home to three thousand silver seekers, Ainsworth now has fewer than 100 permanent residents.

For a hot soak, go next door to the caves at the ◆ **Ainsworth Hot Springs Resort** (Box 1268, Ainsworth Hot Springs, V0G 1A0; 1–800–668–1171). You'll soak in 111°F (44°C) water in a 66-foot (20-m) dripping, U-shaped cave, which was originally a mine shaft. This hot springs water has reputedly the highest mineral content in Canada. Molten rock, boiling up from the earth's core, heats the water in a process different from that of all other hot springs (there are ninety-five in all) in British Columbia. In the dark patches, you may bump into a quietly meditating mortal as you drift through the steamy caves. Cost is $6.00 for adults and $4.50 for kids. Swimsuits and towels are available for a small fee. For the hardy, there's a

39°F (4°C) glacier-fed pool to alternate with the sizzling dips. The resort provides fine dining at moderate prices, and the lovely lake views are free.

Thirteen miles (21 km) north of the hot springs, the plain street names (numbers and letters) of **Kaslo** belie her prettiness. In 1893, when silver, galena, and gold enriched the mountainsides, Kaslo's population was three thousand. Today it's less than one thousand. Steamers helped develop the area, and to this memory the Kootenay Lake Historical Society has restored the oldest passenger sternwheeler in the world, the ◆ **SS** *Moyie* (250–353–2525). She sits majestically on the waterfront in downtown Kaslo after having steamed an estimated two million miles between 1898 and 1957. Prefabricated in Toronto and shipped in sections in 1898, the 830-ton *Moyie* is open daily mid-May to mid-September from 9:30 A.M. to 4:30 P.M.

BRITISH COLUMBIA FACT

Pacific dogwood is the provincial emblem.

Across from the Post Office at the corner of Fourth and B, the ◆ **Langham Cultural Centre** (250–353–2661), one of sixty officially designated heritage buildings in Kaslo, was once a hotel for miners in the 1890s. Now it comprises two galleries, a ninety-seat theater, and an ecomuseum. Poignant photographs on the walls tell the story of Kaslo's 1,200 resilient Japanese–Canadian internees, seventy-eight of whom were housed in the Langham during World War II.

The brick **"Fire Department"** building in the center of town next to the Mohawk gas station serves as the museum and features a log miner's cabin. It's open June–September from 10:00 A.M. to 5:00 P.M., and the cheap admission ($2.00 for adults and $1.00 for children) will give a good introduction to those booming, mining days.

Kaslo was the setting for the Mark Harmon movie *Magic on the Water.* If you stare at the lake long enough, you may see Orky, the movie's odd but genial lake monster. A walking tour of this Switzerland of the Americas village and its environs is worthwhile. It's hard to imagine that it has seen devastation in the form of fire, flood, and even hurricane.

To view Kaslo panoramically, take a walk up A Avenue and turn right on Wardner Street. After a block you'll see a trailhead on the left side. Turn right and 300 yards (275 m) up you'll come to a sharp left turn followed by some steep switchbacks. At the top you'll get a breathtaking view of Kaslo and Kootenay Lake. In fall, mountain ash trees add flaming color to the scene.

After the hike, stop at ❧ **The Rosewood Cafe** (213 Fifth Street, Box 1435, Kaslo, V0G 1M0; 250-353-ROSE.) This comfortable bed and breakfast and restaurant serves calamari, Camembert fondue, blackened Cajun shrimp, and tortellini in a curry sauce, at moderate prices. In summer, outdoor barbecue specials are popular. The overnight suite accommodates up to four adults and two children and costs approximately $85.

From Kaslo you could choose to head north along Kootenay Lake on Highway 31 for 88 miles (142 km), taking you past Duncan and Trout Lakes to Galena, over mostly unpaved road. Check in Kaslo for road conditions. From Galena, a free ferry crosses Upper Arrow Lake to Shelter Bay, 31 miles (50 km) south of Revelstoke.

Instead, we'll take the easy route and travel 29 miles (47 km) west from Kaslo along Highway 31A to Slocan Lake. A sign 24 miles (38 km) west of Kaslo indicates the turnoff to the ghost town of ❧ **Sandon.** A 3-mile (5-km) unpaved road leads to this once rowdy town that supported twenty-four hotels, three newspapers, and an opera. It had electricity even before Vancouver. Once the silver-mining capital of Canada, Sandon's population of five thousand gradually decreased, only to grow briefly again when the coastal Japanese were interned there in 1942. A collection of historic photographs and artifacts is located in the visitors center in the **Slocan Mercantile Building.** When space ran out in its early days, Sandon was enlarged by building a flume to contain the river, then planking over it to add a boardwalk "street." A washout in 1955 devastated the city center, but the City Hall and British Columbia's oldest operating hydroelectric station still remain. The visitors center is open June to October, with tours of the **Silversmith hydroelectric station** operating in July and August from 10:00 A.M. to 4:30 P.M. daily. Enjoy homemade meals at the **Tin Cup Cafe.**

BRITISH COLUMBIA FACT

Steller's jay is the official bird.

Six miles west of the Sandon turnoff is **New Denver.** Here Highway 31A meets Highway 6 at Slocan Lake on the edge of the aptly named ❧ **Valhalla Provincial Park** (250-825-4421). Access to this isolated, undeveloped wilderness is mostly by boat across the lake or via Little Slocan Lake Road, after crossing the river in Slocan. It's beautiful, but the hiking is for the experienced.

If you're a hot-springs zealot, a 29-mile (47-km) side trip from New Denver along Highway 6 leads northwest to Nakusp on Upper Arrow

Lake. Here the clear air of the Selkirks is rivaled only by the untainted waters of ❖ **Nakusp Hot Springs,** 8 miles (13 km) farther east along a paved road. It's more *off the beaten path,* but hot-springs connoisseurs insist it's number one in the Kootenays. Contact Nakusp and District Chamber of Commerce (Box 387, Nakusp, V0G 1R0; 1-800-909-8819) for information.

As an aside, Nakusp can be reached from the west (from Vernon) along Highway 6, via the 3,900-foot (1189-m) Monashee Pass and a free ferry across Lower Arrow Lake from Needles to Fauquier.

Just 3 miles (5 km) south of New Denver on Highway 6, as we wind through the beautiful **Slocan Valley,** is historic **Silverton.** You'll find a really pretty campground on the lakeshore right in town, and the outdoor museum is worth a visit. For a little more comfort, the **Silverton Resort** (Box 107, Silverton, V0G 2B0; 250-358-7157) has six log cabins right on the lake and provides canoes, mountains bikes, and windsurfers. Less than a mile (1.5 km) south is an amazing **viewpoint** on a high cliff overlooking Slocan lake. Don't miss it, or you'll miss one of the best views in British Columbia.

Slocan is 17 miles (27 km) south of Silverton, and 5 miles (7 km) south of Slocan is the turnoff to a rustic, year-round guest lodge. The front field of the ❖ **Lemon Creek Lodge** (Box 68, Slocan, V0G 2C0; 250-355-2403) was home to hundreds of Japanese-Canadian wartime internees. A photo of the internment camp in the warmly furnished living room shows how it looked in those difficult years. Located between Valhalla and Kokanee Glacier Provincial Parks, Lemon Creek Lodge offers ten neat and clean bedrooms with five shared bathrooms, three cabins, a fabulous Finnish sauna, a hot tub, a Japanese Garden, and a restaurant. Double accommodation with breakfast costs $55.

Our side trip through the Slocan Valley returns via Nelson to Balfour and back to the world's longest free ferry ride (**Kootenay Lake Ferry,** 250-354-6521). Eighteen forty-minute runs daily (twelve in winter) sail you between the Purcell and Selkirk mountains to Kootenay Bay on the eastern shore. Watch for **Canada geese** on the beach at Balfour. You can buy grain (or *cwackers*) to feed them at Lang's Restaurant near the ferry lineup.

Aboard the MV *Anscomb* or the MV *Balfour,* the ferry cafe serves inexpensive but tasty food. Nourishing soup-of-the-day is $2.50, and coffee is $1.00. Breakfast for $4.95 was more than I could eat, and the homemade apple pie—unforgettable. In winter change your watch back one hour after you disembark at Kootenay Bay. You're now in Mountain Standard

Time. Just to confuse you, though, in April, when Daylight Saving Time comes into effect, the time doesn't change, because Kootenay Bay maintains Mountain Standard Time year-round. You'll soon learn that time really does stand still on Kootenay Lake's east shore!

KOOTENAY LAKE EAST

After arriving on the east shore of Kootenay Lake, some strange, inexplicable force urged me to take the Riondel Road turnoff. Two miles (3 km) from this turnoff along a gravel road (Walker's Landing) I found ✦ **Yasodhara Ashram** (Box 9, Kootenay Bay, V0B 1X0; 250–227–9224; 1–800–661–8711; E-mail: yashram@netidea.com), a yoga study and retreat center. Here courses are offered, based on the teachings of the late Swami Sivananda Radha. There's a feeling of peace and tranquillity as you walk toward the Temple, a white, igloo-shaped center of worship on the lakefront. Residents work quietly in vegetable gardens, and chickens and cows complete the tranquil scene. If retreat isn't part of your plans, you may stay in the pleasant guest rooms (accommodation for up to eighty) as an eight-hour-a-day working guest for $25, including three healthful meals, or as a bed-and-breakfast guest for $65.

Back on Highway 3A, about 2 miles (3.5 km) south of the ferry terminal, the ✦ **Kootenay Forge** artist–blacksmiths (Box 119, Crawford Bay, V0B 1E0; 250–227–9466) produce practical gifts such as umbrella stands, magazine racks, fireplace accessories, candlesticks, and antiquated door knockers. John Smith (his real name) and his staff of traditional smiths have been forging and riveting these timeless articles in their "smithy" for fifteen years. A sign in the gift shop reads: ON THIS DAY IN 1895, NOTHING HAPPENED. Perhaps this is *black*-smith humor?

Right beside the highway, a mile or so south of the smithy, at the ✦ **North Woven Broom Company** (Box 126, Crawford Bay, V0B 1E0; 250-227-9245), a pungently sweet odor permeates everything inside an old barn. You feel the same time warp as at the blacksmith shop as you watch Janet and Rob Schwieger fashion brooms from Mexican unprocessed broomcorn. Their machinery consists of a turn-of-the-century treadle-stitcher to sew the brooms flat, and an antique vise for gripping the hand-stitched whisks and crooked-handled brooms. They spend their days listening to CBC radio, peacefully wetting and weaving, tying and treadling, as they turn out these nifty brooms. They're open daily "most of the time" from April to October and on weekdays in winter.

Yet another cottage industry in this close-knit Crawford Bay community is ✦ **Weavers' Corner** (Box 160, Crawford Bay, V0B 1E0; 250–

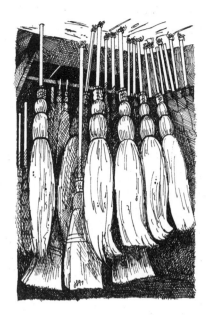

North Woven Broom Company

227-9655). Here owner Janet Wallace weaves wool, silk, and cotton on a traditional loom. Seamstresses then complete colorful vests, bags, and wall hangings. They're open May to October daily and weekdays in winter. And keeping it in the family, Ted Wallace, a teacher at the Crawford Bay school (the smallest school in British Columbia), creates visionary paintings reproduced on cards for sale at Weavers' Corner.

There's a lovely residence just over the Crawford Creek bridge, 4 miles (7 km) south of the ferry terminal. ◆ **Wedgewood Manor** (Box 135, Crawford Bay, V0B 1E0; 250-227-9233) is lavishly Victorian. Originally built in 1910 by a daughter of the English Wedgwood china family, the inn is entirely set apart for guests but the accommodation rates ($79–$110) include a hot breakfast. You'll feel you're on a country estate as you stroll through its fifty acres of woods and gardens, or perhaps as you relax by the parlor fireside, curled up with a mystery from the library shelf.

At Gray Creek, 7 miles (11 km) south of the ferry dock, a warning of what is to come is right there on the highway. The winding lakeshore road passes a sign proclaiming: POPULATION 354—METRIC FREE. So, of course, gas still sells by the gallon, and the only store is like a page out of a *Waltons* television script. But the variety of products in this overstuffed emporium is second to none. At the ◆ **Gray Creek Store** (1979

Chainsaw Avenue, Gray Creek, V0B 1S0; 250-227-9315) you're likely to trip over wheelbarrows, woodstoves, kitchen sinks, chain saws, and the best darned collection of books on British Columbia this side of Vancouver. Oh, and you can resupply your food stocks here, too.

It gets even better! Farther down the lake, 4 miles (7 km) past Boswell, which is 19 miles (30 km) south of the ferry terminal, is an extraordinary house made from embalming bottles. Eldon Brown, son of a funeral director, had me fascinated with stories of growing up in ◆ **The Glass House** (250-223-8372). After thirty-five years in the funeral business, his father, David Brown, retired and began building this unique house. He collected the square-shaped bottles from other funeral directors across Canada (500,000 weighing 250 tons) and built this 1,200 square-foot cloverleaf-shaped house with circular rooms. Inquisitive neighbors started showing up, and soon the Browns started charging to take a peek inside after a minister friend had advised them: "If you want to break up a congregation, either pass the plate, or ask them to sing!" Since 1952, when building began, other parts have been added—terraces, patios, a glass bridge, a saddlery, a moss-covered wishing well, and a lighthouse on the lakefront. Prices are $5.00 for adults, $4.00 for teens, $3.00 for kids six to thirteen, "and the rest are free." It's open daily from 9:00 A.M. to 5:00 P.M., May to October, and 8:00 A.M. to 8:00 P.M., June to August.

At the bottom end of Kootenay Lake, only 8 miles (13 km) from the U.S. border, lies **Creston,** population 4,743. Grain elevators and scenic fields of alfalfa give it a prairie look. As you drive through this city in the "Valley of the Swans" check out the **murals** on store walls. The surrounding valley comprises some of the province's most fertile fruit-growing land. Raspberries, cherries, and apricots are ripe in July, peaches and plums in August. In May, Highway 3A is a sea of color and the town springs to life with its **Blossom Festival.** Contact Creston InfoCentre (1711 Canyon Street, Box 268, Creston, V0B 1G0; 250-428-4342) for more information.

For a coffee stop with a view, try the **Kootenay Rose Coffee House** (250-428-7252) opposite the Post Office on Tenth Avenue. Then travel west along Highway 3 for 4 miles (7 km) to the ◆ **Creston Valley Wildlife Management Area** (P.O. Box 640, Creston, V0B 1G0; 250-428-3260), a lush 17,000-acre (7,000-ha) wetland ecosystem drained by the Kootenay River. It's a staging and nesting area to more than 240 bird species and is the only North American breeding ground of the forester's tern. During March and April, swans and geese in the thousands transform the area into a chattering, marshy amphitheater. Bald eagles, tundra swans, bank swallows, western grebe, osprey, and a rare salamander, the Coeur d'Alene, are some of the species. Viewing is made easy by boardwalks, towers, and a trail system. An interpretive center, including a gift shop, library, theater, and wildlife programs, is open April to September, 8:00 A.M. to 6:00 P.M. daily, and off-season 9:00 A.M. to 4:00 P.M. Wednesday to Sunday. The nearby **Summit Creek Campground** (250-428-7441), 7 miles (11 km) west of Creston, with fifty campsites snugly set amid 300-year-old cedars, makes visiting the area a full-on wilderness treat.

WHERE TO STAY:

1. **The Orchard Bed and Breakfast** (5615 Spencer Road, RR1, S850C C3, Grand Forks, V0H 1H0; 250-442-8583).
2. **Golden Heights Inn and Restaurant** (7342 Bluff Street, Grand Forks, V0H 1H0; 250-442-0626).
3. **Mountain Shadow Hostel,** Columbia Avenue, Rossland, V0G 1Y0; 250-362-7160).
4. **Angela's Place Bed and Breakfast** (1520 Spokane, Box 944, Rossland, V0G 1Y0; 250-362-7790).
5. **Ainsworth Hot Springs Resort** (Box 1268, Ainsworth Hot Springs, V0G 1A0; 1-800-668-1171).
6. **Wedgewood Manor** (Box 135, Crawford Bay, V0B 1E0; 250-227-9233 or for reservations 1-800-862-0022).

WHERE TO EAT:

1. **Chef's Garden Restaurant** (4415 Highway 3, Grand Forks, V0H 1H0; 250-442-0257).
2. **Grand Forks Station Pub** (7654 Donaldson Street, Grand Forks, V0H 1H0; 250-442-5855).
3. **Elmers Corner Cafe** (Second Avenue and Washington Street, Rossland, V0G 1Y0; 250-362-5266).
4. **Gold Rush Books and Espresso** (2063 Washington Street, Rossland, V0G 1Y0; 250-362-5333).
5. **Colander Restaurant** (1475 Cedar Avenue, Trail, V1R 4C5; 250-364-1816).
6. **Spinning Wheel Vegetarian Eatery** (Heritage Way, Castlegar; 250-365-7202).
7. **The Rosewood Cafe** (213 Fifth Street, Box 1435, Kaslo, V0G 1M0; 250-353-ROSE).
8. **Kootenay Rose Coffee House** (opposite the Post Office on Tenth Avenue, Creston, V0B 1G0; 250-428-7252).

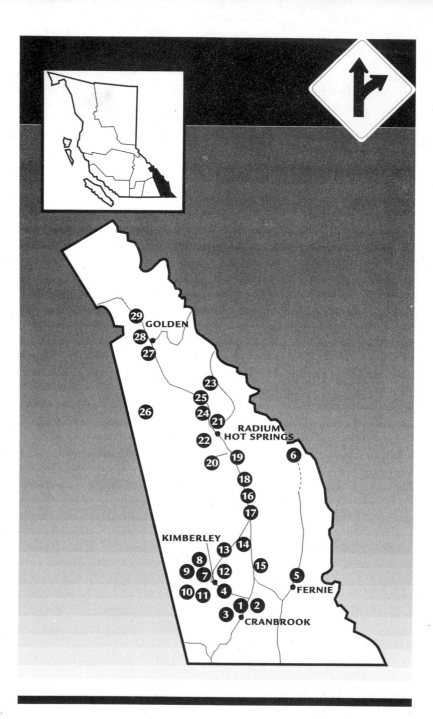

THE ROCKIES

1. Elizabeth Lake Wildlife Sanctuary
2. Mountain High River Adventures
3. Canadian Museum of Rail Travel
4. St. Eugene Mission and Church
5. Hosmer Mountain
6. Elk Lakes Provincial Park
7. Chef Bernard's Inn and Restaurant
8. Yodeling Woodcarver Arts and Crafts Shop
9. The Snowdrift Cafe
10. Cominco Gardens
11. Bavarian City Mining Railway
12. Happy Hans Campground
13. Custom Decor and Gifts
14. Wasa Lakeside Bed and Breakfast And More
15. Fort Steele Heritage Town
16. Canal Flats
17. Fairmont Hot Springs Resort
18. Crooked Tree Farm
19. Stolen Church
20. Strands Old House Restaurant
21. Radium Hot Springs
22. Village Country Inn
23. Kootenay National Park
24. Edgewater Open Market
25. Brisco General Store
26. Bugaboo Glacier Provincial Park
27. Glacier Raft Company
28. The Mad Trapper
29. Hillside Lodge Cabins Bed and Breakfast

THE ROCKIES

No matter where you stand in this rugged southeastern corner of British Columbia, there's a good chance that if you close your eyes and spin around, when you open them, you'll be facing a mountain. From rolling hills to crenelated, snow-covered peaks, the Rockies contains twenty-six provincial parks bearing names like *Top of the World Park* and *Height of the Rockies Park*. Two National parks, Yoho and Kootenay, occupy most of the northeastern section. The heart of the region is the Rocky Mountain Trench, the longest valley in North America, where the Columbia River begins its 1,245 mile (2,005 km) meandering journey to the Pacific.

On the Rockies adventure list we'll trip back to 1897 frontier life at Fort Steele Heritage Park after a sail on warm Wasa Lake. In Kimberley, where yodelers in the Platzl sing out a Bavarian theme, we'll eat German fare and ski in powder-perfect snow. In Radium Hot Springs we'll see Rocky Mountain bighorn sheep and wallow indulgently in hot springs before a trip through the fabulous Kootenay National Park. Finally, we'll kick our way out of the Rockies with some white-knuckle white-water rafting on the Kicking Horse River.

THE CROWSNEST TO CRANBROOK

As with the Okanagan and the Kootenays, we begin close to the U.S. border on the Crowsnest Highway 3, which at Yahk joins Highway 95. The highway cuts and weaves northward beside the Moyie River on its path toward Cranbrook, passing en route four provincial parks (Yahk, Ryan, Moyie Lake, and Jimsmith Lake).

Moyie Lake Provincial Park is a 222-acre (90-ha), forested playground 13 miles (21 km) south of Cranbrook, with a good swimming lake and a sandy beach. It's sure to be a winner with the kids with more than 100 well-shaded campsites, pleasant picnic shelters and showers, and lots of room on the lake for boaters, windsurfers, and fishing enthusiasts (the Dolly Varden and rainbows bite well). Reservations can be made ahead by calling the Discover Camping number 1–800–689–9025 or in Vancouver, 604–689–9025.

Just south of **Cranbrook** (population 18,500) near the Splash Zone Waterslides, the 249-acre (100-ha) ◆ **Elizabeth Lake Wildlife Sanctuary** is a must-stop for bird-lovers. Walking trails lead to blinds at different spots around the lake, allowing excellent bird-watching. You're likely to see Canada geese, mallard, teal, bufflehead, and ruddy ducks. In summer, the Cranbrook InfoCentre is located at the entrance (Box 84, Cranbrook, V1C 4H6; 250–489–5261, or 1–800–222–6174; E-mail: cbkchamber@cyberlink.bc.ca).

If bird-watching isn't exciting enough and you've always wanted to try white-water kayaking, ◆ **Mountain High River Adventures** (1424 Fifteenth Street South, Cranbrook, V1C 5N8; 250–489–2067) will have your adrenaline flowing as fast as the water. They use inflated kayaks, which makes it safe and a lot of fun. They offer trips on the St. Mary River or more difficult rivers, if you have the nerve.

Cranbrook has a lot of railway history on display at the ◆ **Canadian Museum of Rail Travel** on the highway in town (1 Van Horne Street South; 250–489–3918). The museum

BRITISH COLUMBIA FACT

Red cedar is the official tree.

features nine original cars from the luxurious CPR Trans-Canada Limited of 1929. This train, possibly the only one in the world designed as a traveling hotel, once provided service from Montreal to Vancouver. The carefully detailed dining car, the **Argyle,** is an elegant summer spot to have afternoon tea. At the museum, ask for a map to do a self-guided tour that includes many historic buildings, notably the 1888 home of Cranbrook's founder, Colonel James Baker.

North of Cranbrook on Mission Road heading toward the Cranbrook–Kimberley airport, a scenic detour leads to the ◆ **St. Eugene Mission and Church.** Restored by the St. Mary's Band and the East Kootenay Historical Association in 1983, it is viewed as the finest Gothic-style mission church in British Columbia and has beautiful, hand-painted stained glass. Phone (250) 489–2464 to arrange a tour.

THE SOUTHEASTERN CORNER

Tucked into the extreme southeastern alcove of BC are the towns of Fernie, Sparwood, and Elkford, lined up south to north in the **Elk Valley** near the Albertan border. To do a side trip to this often forgotten hunting–fishing–skiing utopia, follow the Crowsnest Highway 3 east 60 miles (96 km) from Cranbrook.

The largest of the three, **Fernie** (population 5,000), is proof that from adversity, hope occasionally springs eternal. Two fires in 1904 and 1908 destroyed the city, leaving thousands homeless. The reconstruction in brick and stone has resulted in a city full of beautiful, turn-of-the-century buildings, some of which can now be toured. Contact the Fernie

Chamber of Commerce (Highway 3 and Dicken Road, Fernie, V0B 1M0; 250-423-6868) to obtain the self-guided walking-tour map to see these architectural beauties.

The fires were just part of a series of disasters to hit the city. Floods and a horrifying coal-mining explosion in 1902, in which 128 men died, added to its woes. According to Indian legend, a curse was placed on Fernie to take revenge on the coal-mine developer, William Fernie, who spurned a young Indian woman of the Tobacco Plains band. Perhaps the proof of this curse can be seen some evenings at dusk when you look up at ◆ **Hosmer Mountain,** just north of Fernie. Some have even heard the ghostly hoofbeats filling the mountain air as a horse and rider gallop down the sheer, rocky walls. Fortunately for the town, Chief Red Eagle of the Tobacco Plains band lifted the curse shortly before he died in 1964, but the specter is still up there. Ask at the Fernie InfoCentre (250-423-6868) for the best viewing area and time.

Sparwood, 17 miles (28 km) northeast of Fernie, is a little smaller than its sister and a lot newer. The residents moved there in 1968 from nearby Michel and Natal, now bulldozed into oblivion because they were an environmental headache. Sparwood's dubious claim to fame is the **Terex Titan,** the world's largest dump truck. It weighs in at 350 tons, and its box can stuff in two buses and two pickup trucks. It stands by Canada's largest open-pit coal mine, where tours are held Monday–Friday in July and August.

Artist Don Sawatzky has spruced up Sparwood with some excellent **murals** depicting its mining history. The InfoCentre (Box 1448, Sparwood, V0B 2G0; 250-425-2423) can tell you more.

From Sparwood, Highway 43 travels north along the Elk River to **Elkford,** the jumping-off point for the ◆ **Elk Lakes Provincial Park** (250-422-3212), a walk-in-only camping park. Elkford is truly a wilderness town, with elk, bear, bighorn sheep, and deer common in the environs. Inquire at the InfoCentre (Box 220, Elkford, V0B 1H0; 250-865-4614) for details about the many hiking trails in this spectacularly scenic area.

NORTH TO KIMBERLEY

Kimberley, at 3,652 feet (1,113 m), Canada's highest city, is 20 miles (32 km) north of Cranbrook along Highway 95A. Four miles (7 km) before Kimberley, in **Marysville,** look for a sign indicating a boardwalk track to **Marysville Falls,** a thundering 100-foot (30-m) cascade quite near the highway and just before the turnoff to the scenic **Kimberley Golf Course** (250-427-4161).

If you're feeling particularly energetic, a 3.7-mile (6-km) nature and fitness trail developed by the Kimberley Rotary and Lions Clubs starts at the bridge at the north end of Main street in Marysville and leads north to Kimberley along Mark Creek. Walk quietly and you may see mule deer, Rocky Mountain elk, northern flickers, sometimes great blue heron, and lots of wildflowers. Occasionally in summer, a moose and calf can be seen in the marshes.

In Kimberley, the **Platzl** (German for *plaza*) monopolizes center stage with a brilliant red and green theme. You may enjoy (or not!) Happy Hans's yodeling as the world's largest and noisiest cuckoo clock's doors pop open at the drop of a quarter.

The clock sits in front of the amazing ◈ **Chef Bernard's Platzl Inn and Restaurant** (170 Spokane Street, Kimberley, V1A 2E4; 250-427-4820; 1-800-905-8338; http://www.cyberlink.bc.ca/chefbernards). Why amazing? First, the food is delicious. Second, the confusion of knickknacks inside will keep you gawking for the length of your dinner and then some. Model trains *toot-toot* around the ceiling, sometimes carrying birthday greetings for an unsuspecting diner. Originally the restaurant was fondue-only, until Bernard could afford a stove. His cuisine has won several awards. After many years on *Love Boat* Sunprincesses and serving the rich and famous (from Alfred Hitchcock to the King of Tonga), this Hamburg-born immigrant displays his cosmopolitan past through an eclectic menu: Cajun to curries, shrimp pots to ostrich pastas. My lobster and steak special at $18.95 went down very well as I sat below accordions and beer steins, while trophy goatheads watched clown fish swim by in colorful aquariums. No kidding!

BRITISH COLUMBIA FACT

Most easterly point: Akamina Pass in the Rocky Mountains.

Upstairs, reasonably priced accommodations, with a hot tub on the outside deck, make Chef Bernard's Platzl Inn and Restaurant a one-stop shop. His $66 "package" for bed and breakfast, plus a ski-lift ticket, is one of Kimberley's best winter deals.

The lift tickets take you to the **Kimberley Ski and Summer Resort** (1-800-667-0871), only a few minutes drive away. It has forty-seven runs, six lifts, and consistently nine feet of pure white powder each year.

Next door to Chef Bernard's at the ◈ **Yodeling Woodcarver Arts and Crafts Shop** (140 Spokane Street, Kimberley, V1A 2Y5; 250-427-7211) if you aren't quite yodeled to death, Adi Unteberger will complement your purchase with one of his famous yodels. If it sounds familiar, it's because his is the voice of Happy Hans of cuckoo-clock fame.

Still on the Platzl, ◆ **The Snowdrift Cafe** (110 Spokane Street, Kimberley, V1A 2Y5; 250-427-2001; E-mail: snowdrift@cyberlink.bc.ca) is a friendly, lively place to go for a beer or wine, play cards, or read a newspaper while you enjoy the best Manhattan clam chowder this side of the Rockies. Roy Cimolai serves "natural" foods at supernaturally low prices. His lentil soup served with homemade whole wheat bread for $2.95, and pumpkin pie for $3.95, make a great lunch between exploring Kimberley's nooks and crannies. Oversized muffins are $1.00 and his huckleberry bars—well you'd pay anything for them. Roy handpicks the huckleberries after first raking the bushes with his authentic Norwegian plastic rake. The Snowdrift Cafe is a favorite among the locals, who come not just for the great cheesecake and the best coffee in Kimberley, but also for the small-town chatty ambience.

A short, steep walk from the Platzl via Howard Street (about fifteen minutes) brings you to the ◆ **Cominco Gardens** (306 Third Avenue; 250-427-2293). In season, 48,000 blooms overwhelm your optical and olfactory senses. First planted in 1927 to advertise Cominco's Elephant Brand Fertilizer, the 2.5-acre (1-ha) site was later given to the community. It's open dawn to dusk, May through September. You can drive there also from Highway 95A. From the Platzl, head north on Wallinger Avenue, following the signs to the hospital; go one block farther and it's on the left. Entrance is free, but a donation for upkeep is welcome. **The Greenhouse Tea Garden Restaurant and Gift Shop** (306 Third Avenue; 250-427-4885) is right there and serves full meals in the original Cominco greenhouse daily from 11:00 A.M. to 7:00 P.M.

It's an adventure into the past on the ◆ **Bavarian City Mining Railway,** built as a labor of love by volunteers who salvaged the equipment from old mines. The 7.5-mile (12-km) round-trip starts at the Happy Hans Campground (on Gerry Sorensen Way) and passes through a bear-infested tunnel and by a haunted schoolhouse. It then goes through a steep-walled, tight valley, past a miner's cave, and ends up near downtown Kimberley. Alternatively pick up the train from the downtown station. It's not a luxury trip, but it's fun, and the views of the Kimberley Ski Hill and the Thousand Peaks mountain range are great. The train runs on weekends in June and daily through July to Labor Day. Find out more from the Kimberley Bavarian Society Chamber of Commerce (350 Ross Street, Kimberley, V1A 2Z9; 250-427-3666). ◆ **Happy Hans Campground** (Box 465, Kimberley, V1A 3B9;

250-427-2929 or 250-427-4877 off-season) has sites that cost from $14.50 to $18. The outdoor, heated swimming pool is a bonus.

KIMBERLEY TO CANAL FLATS

Fifteen miles (24 km) north of Kimberley, Highway 95A rolls through mysteriously named Ta Ta Creek. Here artisan Susanne Kennedy offers straight-out-of-the-garden lunch experiences in her artistically stenciled home. ◆ **Custom Decor and Gifts** (Box 123, Ta Ta Creek, V0B 2H0; 250-422-3777) is well signed behind a white house on top of the hill where you reach the 60 KPH sign. Included with lunch is a tour of her studio, where she does decorative stenciling, custom needle and lace work, stained glass, and dried flower arrangements. Many of her crafts are for sale in a small gift shop. The elegant table, with views of the mountains, seats eight. Strawberry wine, fresh iced tea, homemade soups and salads, followed by whatever vegetables are in season, fresh seafood, cheese, fruits, and berries are on the menu. Guests receive complimentary stenciled gardening gloves or other home-crafted items. Call ahead for reservations. The cost per person for the whole lovely experience is $25.

Just past Ta Ta Creek, Highway 95A joins Highway 93 heading north to Radium Hot Springs and Kootenay National Park. A mile south of the fork, **Wasa Lake Provincial Park** hugs a gem of a lake of the same name. It's a water sports utopia. A few years ago, a couple of Albertan hang gliders soared off from a road cut in nearby Mt. Estella. While

HISTORY AND HOT TUBS

It was one of those crisp, Rocky Mountain November days when I serendipitously arrived in Wasa Lake. I meandered around the lake's hypnotizing reflections and happened upon the Wasa Lakeside Bed and Breakfast. I was a stranger at the door, but that didn't concern James Swansburg, who invited me in and introduced his wife Mary and their four neat kids. I drove down to nearby Fort Steele, where a groundsman proudly unlocked every historic door. I peeked in to watch a film crew shooting a western, shot two rolls of film myself, then headed back north. My evening ended with a game of badminton in the school with James and Mary and other Wasa Lake locals, followed by a hot tub amid the silence of the dark mountains and the occasional call of a distant wolf. And only the day before, I had never heard of Wasa Lake!

ecstatically suspended over **Wasa Lake,** they decided to throw in their tidy nine-to-five Calgary life and head west for some real adventure. Now, James and Mary Swansburg operate ◆ **Wasa Lakeside Bed and Breakfast And More** (Box 122, Wasa, V0B 2K0; 250-422-3688 or 1-888-422-3636) on the northwest side of Wasa Lake. They say it's "definitely the warmest lake in Canada." The *And More* refers to Hobie Cat sailing, waterskiing, pedal boating, windsurfing, hot tubbing, hang gliding, paragliding, elegant rooms, and great breakfasts served right on the private beach. In winter, there's ice sailing, cross-country skiing, or a hike to some nearby hidden hot springs. Guests are welcome to use the beachside kitchen, barbecue, or firepit to prepare lunches and dinners. For a complete rundown on what's cooking at Wasa Lake, visit the Swansburg's home page (www.cyberlink.bc.ca/~swanys).

BRITISH COLUMBIA FACT

Special holidays: Victoria Day (May 24 weekend), Canada Day (July 1), BC Day (early August).

South of **Wasa,** almost to **Fort Steele,** history buffs can visit the site of the first gold rush—and the first town—in the East Kootenay: **Fisherville.** When a rich gold vein was discovered under Fisherville (a town of five thousand by 1885), the town site was moved farther up the hill and renamed **Wild Horse.** Stroll through the Wild Horse graveyard, following a trail past a Chinese burial ground, along Victoria Ditch to Walker's grave, and back through Fisherville. The East Kootenay Historical Association has prepared a brochure detailing the history of the area and what to look out for on your hike (allow at least an hour). You'll find brochures at the Fort Steele ticket booth or in the Kimberley and Cranbrook Chambers of Commerce. To get to Wild Horse/Fisherville, turn east off Highway 93/95 at the Fort Steele RV Resort onto Bull River Road, and left onto a logging road for about 4 miles (6 km).

There's more to discover in the Bull River Road area including a spectacular gorge on the Bull River (look for the BC Hydro Dam sign) and the **Kootenay Lake Hatchery** (250-429-3077), where millions of rainbow and cutthroat trout are raised annually. Take a free self-guided tour of the special viewing areas and displays. It's open daily from 8:00 A.M. to 4:00 P.M.

Just 12 miles (20 km) south from Wasa on Highway 93/95 (or 10 miles [16 km] northeast of Cranbrook) is the ◆ **Fort Steele Heritage Town,** named after Samuel Steele, a North-West Mounted Police superintendent blessed with conflict-resolution skills and a certain amount of

BRITISH COLUMBIA TRIVIA

According to Ktunaxa (pronounced *Tun-ah-hah*) legend, hoodoos at the north end of Columbia Lake are the remains of a giant fish that was wounded by a coyote. It tried to travel through the Rocky Mountain Trench, but finally died. Its flesh decomposed and its ribs broke up. Half of its ribs became these hoodoos, and the other half became hoodoos located farther south near St. Mary's, just north of Cranbrook.

charisma. He dealt successfully with the tension that had been rising at nearby Galbraith's Ferry between the white settlers and the Chief of the Upper Kootenay Indians. The resulting settlement was the first North-West Mounted post west of the Rockies. The restored town, set at the confluence of the St. Mary and Kootenay Rivers, with the magnificent Rockies as a backdrop, is a must-see attraction. It's open year-round 9:30 A.M. to 5:30 P.M. and operates as it would have in its heyday, with fresh bread coming from a baker's wood-fired oven, and transport provided by steam train or Clydesdale-drawn wagon. Admission (charged from June 15 to September 2) is valid for two days (you'll need two days to really experience it) and ranges from $5.50 down to free for children under six. Special events, such as an unbelievably spooky Halloween night, are held throughout the year. Phone (250) 489–3351/7352 for information.

THE WINDERMERE VALLEY

Eight miles (13 km) north of the Highway 93/95 junction, Skookumchuck does little but spew out a pulp-mill odor, but you're in for some pretty scenery around ◆ **Canal Flats,** population 680, just 17 miles (28 km) north. This legendary area, according to Ktunaxa Indian elders, is where the giant Natmuqcin molded with his knees the mile-wide portage separating the Columbia from the Kootenay River. Here, the south-flowing Kootenay is separated from the north-flowing Columbia. If you have a canoe and a couple of days to spare, a trip down the Kootenay River to Fort Steele will take you through some of the best scenery in British Columbia, with lots of wildlife viewing on the way. Two miles (3 km) north of the logging town, at **Canal Flats Provincial Park** (no campsites), the remains of the bizarrely conceived Baillie-Grohmann Canal, an 1880s endeavor to link the two rivers and reduce flooding, can be seen.

The highway caresses Columbia Lake's west bank up to the fast-growing golfing community of Fairmont Hot Springs. Two classy courses, **Mountainside Golf Course** (1–800–663–4979), in the shadow of the Rockies, and **Riverside Golf Course** (1–800–665–2112) on the banks of the Columbia, along with the famous ✦ **Fairmont Hot Springs Resort** (1–800–663–4979) make this a popular vacation center. In all, five eighteen-hole championship courses and several executive length and miniputt courses can be enjoyed in the area known as the **Windermere Valley.**

About 5 miles (8 km) north of Fairmont Hot Springs in a nook of the Rockies on Crooked Tree Road (off Kootenay No. 3 Road, a mile north of the Hot Springs Road on the east side of the highway) is the ✦ **Crooked Tree Farm** (Box 82, Fairmont, V0B 1L0; 250–345–6355). Here herbalist Donna Marie McLaughlin offers herb workshops and garden tours. You'll learn what plants can be used as medicines, how to identify wild plants, and enjoy tea and dessert in the gazebo or Crooked Tree Studio. Tours that cost $15, including tea, begin May 15 and continue until the first frost in September.

Ten miles north of Fairmont, on the eastern side of Lake Windermere, tiny **Windermere** (population 800) packs quite a punch. Glassblowers, wood-carvers, and potters are strung out funkily downtown in an artisan's village near the 1887 Whitehouse Hotel. There's even a ✦ **Stolen Church** (on the corner of Kootenay Street and Victoria Avenue). The story goes that a couple from Donald loved it so much that they purloined it, piece by piece, when they moved to Windermere back in 1897! On the highway just north of the Post Office, **Lake Windermere Adventure Golf** (250–342–7227) has eighteen, fun putting greens in a pleasant setting of ponds, waterfalls, and shrubs. It's open daily in summer from 10:00 A.M. to 11:00 P.M. In its clubhouse, **Cowpuccino on the Green Pie Company** serves homemade pies, ice cream, and coffees.

Invermere (population 2,200) is on the western side of Lake Windermere and was known by the Ktunaxa as *Kyaknuqti?it,* meaning "prairie on top of a hill." It has quite a holiday atmosphere. In 1807, David Thompson, the first European in the area, settled here calling it Kootenae House. One of its more famous establishments today is ✦ **Strands Old House Restaurant** (818 Twelfth Street, Invermere, V0A 1K0; 250–342–6344). Lovely surroundings and to-die-for food make Strands one of the best places to dine in the Rockies. Try the Rack of Lamb Anthony (named for the chef and owner, Tony Wood) or the Lamb Basil Garlic Linguini. If you eat between 5:00 and 6:15 P.M., they offer a

Radium Hot Springs

three-course early-bird special for $11.95. You'll find Strands one block west of the Invermere post office between Eighth and Tenth Avenues.

When you reach ❖ **Radium Hot Springs,** where Highways 93 and 95 diverge, you need to decide whether to head east (Highway 93) to wonderful parks and eventually Alberta, or northwest (Highway 95) along the Columbia River to Golden. My suggestion, if you have time, is to do both. To miss either **Kootenay** or **Yoho National Parks** (in one of the world's largest protected areas) would be a shame. But first, let's look at Radium Hot Springs.

Here I discovered the Victorian style ❖ **Village Country Inn** (7557 Canyon Avenue, Radium Hot Springs, V0A 1M0; 250-347-9392). Don't be surprised if a herd of Rocky Mountain bighorn sheep, refusing to let development interfere with their traditional beaten path, thunder by as you eat breakfast. The main living room–dining room area is set around a large stone fireplace, and upstairs, hosts Sasha and Gorm have decorated elegantly twelve bedrooms plus a bridal suite. Breakfasts cost $4.00–$6.00, and there's afternoon tea from 2:00–5:00 P.M. Accommodation ranges from $75 to $95.

Nearby is the "rated sixth in BC" **Springs Golf Course** (1-800-667-6444 or 250-347-6444), and just one mile from the inn, you might take a

BC Jade is the official stone.

dip in the Radium Hot Springs, where you can soak up the minerals and the stunning view from Sinclair Canyon. In winter there's skiing at **Panorama Resort** (10 miles [17 km] west of Invermere on Toby Creek Road, 1-800-663-2929), or should you be visiting in mid-September, you'll catch the **Show and Shine Columbia Valley Classic Car Show** and **Fall Fair.** To help you find these attractions and more, the Chamber of Commerce in Radium has produced a colorful, comprehensive (and artistic) map of the area. Inquire at the InfoCentre, Radium Business Association (Box 225, V0A 1M0; 250-347-9331).

KOOTENAY NATIONAL PARK TO GOLDEN

From Radium Hot Springs, you enter ⚑ **Kootenay National Park** (250-347-9615) through the dramatic Sinclair Canyon. Stop off for a dip at the Aquacourt in either the hot pool, which at an average temperature of 100°F (38°C) is great for a soak, or the cooler 84°F (29°C) pool, ideal for a swim. At the pool you can have both a coffee and a luxurious massage. Hours in summer are 9:00 A.M. to 10:30 P.M. and from October to March, noon–9:00 P.M.

Head east along Highway 93 following Sinclair Creek, then north through the Kootenay River Valley, where from the safety of your vehicle, you should see elk, white-tailed deer, and mule deer. Stop off at the **Kootenay Valley Viewpoint,** 9 miles (14 km) from Radium Hot Springs. Take a deep breath first, though, as the scenery will take it away.

At colorful **Marble Canyon,** 55 miles (89 km) from Radium Hot Springs, there's a half-mile trail through a narrow gorge to a thundering waterfall. It's a great leg-stretcher and shouldn't be missed. Four miles (7 km) farther, **Vermilion Pass,** at 5,416 feet (1,651 m) marks the Continental Divide (the rivers now flow toward the Atlantic) and the entrance to **Banff National Park** in Alberta. Canadian Heritage Parks Canada (1-800-748-7275 from anywhere in BC or Alberta) will give information on fees for all the National Parks. The Trans-Canada Highway then takes you north to Lake Louise and through Kicking Horse Pass to Golden, where you again meet up with Highway 95.

If instead you continue north from Radium Hot Springs, 7 miles (11 km) along Highway 95 is Edgewater, where every Saturday for the past twenty-five years the ◆ **Edgewater Open Market** has been the spot for farmers and artisans in the valley to show their wares.

Another 11 miles (18 km) north you'll pass through Brisco, population 140, where you may wonder, *why stop?* The ◆ **Brisco General Store** (250–346–3343), built in 1906, is why! It seems to sell everything, including liquor, videos, mousetraps, coffee, fence posts, groceries, newspapers, and rubber boots. It's also the post office and the one original general store left in the Columbia River Valley that hasn't burned down yet. Like the other small towns in this wonderful valley, Brisco has a beautiful view. And if you should be coming on horseback, the hitching post is right out front.

A 30-mile (48-km) gravel logging road just south of Brisco leads to the ◆ **Bugaboo Glacier Provincial Park,** famous for its great glaciers, church-spire mountains, and heli-skiing. Should you ever see pictures of climbers hanging off impossible, jagged, rocky cliffs, chances are they're in the Bugaboos.

From Brisco to Golden, there's not much other than rambling ranches and beautiful scenery. Some might ask, "What else do you want?" The Columbia continues its northern pursuit, and at **Golden** it's joined by the wild Kicking Horse River. Seated between the imposing Rockies and the Columbia Mountains, with five National Parks close by, Golden is indeed a crossroads. Here Highway 95 meets the Trans-Canada, from which

BRITISH COLUMBIA FACT

The legal drinking age is nineteen.

you can travel east to **Yoho National Park,** with its fabulous canyons and glaciers, or west to Rogers Pass in **Glacier National Park.**

Golden is favored by sports enthusiasts of every ilk. One gaining popularity is white-water rafting. The ◆ **Glacier Raft Company** (Box 428, Golden, V0A 1H0; 250–344–6521) offers all levels of rafting trips on the Kicking Horse River through breathtaking scenery. Half-day trips are $49, and full-day trips (including a riverside steak barbecue) are $79.

But there's lots more to do in Golden. You can paraglide in tandem with an expert on **Mount 7,** go fishing or bird-watching, rent a mountain bike, or visit the old Brisco schoolhouse at the **Golden and District Museum.** To discover these activities, contact the Chamber of

Commerce (500 Tenth Avenue, Box 677, Golden, V0A 1H0; 250-344-7125) year-round, and in summer, look for the **Discovery Centre** (250-344-6068), located in a big log cabin at the top of the hill on the Trans-Canada Highway. Here information is available at the touch of a computer screen.

The activities Golden offers are mostly energy-eaters, so it has a few good spots for refueling, such as **The Chocolate Moose Deli-Cafe** (501 Ninth Avenue North; 250-344-7978). Homemade meals and a patio view of the mountains is what brings the locals here. A good solid bowl of soup, fresh salads, and desserts are part of the menu, and local musicians add atmosphere. You'll probably run into fellow rafters or hang gliders at ◆ **The Mad Trapper** (1203 Ninth Street South; 250-344-6661), where prices are moderate and the daily specials always a bargain. Coming from the south on Highway 95, take a right on Ninth Street at the first set of lights just before the Kicking Horse River.

Leaving Golden, if you're heading toward Rogers Pass on the Trans-Canada, you'll find quiet country accommodation at ◆ **Hillside Lodge Cabins Bed and Breakfast** (1240 Seward Frontage Road, Box 2603, Golden, V0A 1H0; 250-344-7281). It's 8 miles (13 km) northwest of Golden (half-way to Donald) and just 500 yards off the highway on the Blaeberry River. The cabins are new, and the views of the river and the Rockies excellent. Rooms are $55, and cabins are $80.

From Golden the Trans-Canada follows the Columbia River north through Donald and west to Rogers Pass in Glacier National Park. Here, at 4,534 feet (1,382 m), Canadian Pacific Railway workers performed the formidable task of pushing a railway line through, while avalanches and rock slides took their toll. At Rogers Pass we head into High Country.

WHERE TO STAY:

1. **Chef Bernard's Platzl Inn** (170 Spokane Street, Kimberley, V1A 2E4; 250-427-4820 or 1-800-905-8338).
2. **Happy Hans Kampground and R.V. Park** (Box 465, Kimberley, V1A 3B9; 250-427-2929 [May-October], 250-427-4877 [November-April]).
3. **Wasa Lakeside Bed and Breakfast And More** (Box 122 Wasa, V0B 2K0; 250-422-3688 or 1-888-422-3636); E-mail: swanys@cyberlink.bc.ca). Moderately priced.
4. **Kapristo Lodge** (P.O. Box 90, 1297 Campbell Road, Golden, V0A 1H0; 250-344-6048). Moderately priced.

5. **Village Country Inn and Tea Room** (7557 Canyon Avenue, Radium Hot Springs, V0A 1M0; 250-347-9392). Moderately priced at $75-95.
6. **Hillside Lodge Cabins Bed and Breakfast** (1240 Seward Frontage Road, Box 2603, Golden, V0A 1H0; 250-344-7281). Rooms $55, cabins $80.

WHERE TO EAT:

1. **Chef Bernard's Platzl Inn and Restaurant** (170 Spokane Street, Kimberley, V1A 2E4; 250-427-4820 or 1-800-905-8338). Moderately priced. International menu.
2. **The Snowdrift Cafe** (110 Spokane Street, Kimberley, V1A 2E4; 250-427-2001). Inexpensive, healthful foods.
3. **The Greenhouse Tea Garden Restaurant and Gift Shop** (306 Third Avenue, Kimberley; 250-427-4885). Inexpensive lunches and dinners.
4. **Strands Old House Restaurant** (818 Twelfth Street, Invermere, V0A 1K0; 250-342-6344). Moderately priced. Deluxe food. Reservations.
5. **The Chocolate Moose Deli-Cafe** (501 Ninth Avenue North, Golden V0A 1H0; 250-344-7978).
6. **The Mad Trapper** (1203 Ninth Street South, Golden, V0A 1H0; 250-344-6661).

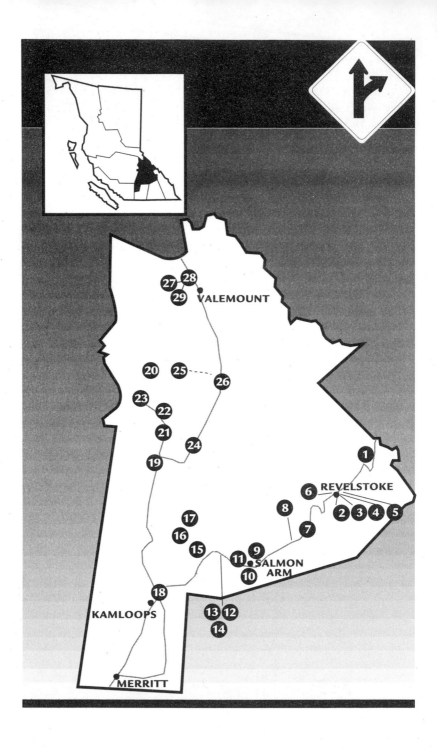

HIGH COUNTRY

1. Glacier National Park
2. Grizzly Plaza
3. Revelstoke Railway Museum
4. Revelstoke Museum
5. The Piano Keep Museum and Bed and Breakfast
6. Revelstoke Dam
7. Beardale Castle
8. Last Spike
9. Bluewater Houseboat Rentals
10. Salmon Arm Bay Nature Enhancement Centre
11. Margaret Falls
12. Pheasant Heaven
13. The Evergreens Bed and Breakfast
14. Sorrento Centre
15. Squilax General Store and Caboose Hostel
16. Squilax International Powwow
17. Adams River, sockeye salmon run
18. Kamloops Wildlife Park
19. North Thompson River Provincial Park
20. Wells Gray Provincial Park
21. Yellowhead Museum
22. Clearwater Mountain Charm Chalet
23. Helmcken Falls Lodge
24. Vavenby Trail Rides
25. Murtle Lake
26. Mike Wigele Heli-Ski Village
27. Berna's Medicine (Censored) Cabinet
28. Robert W. Starratt Wildlife Sanctuary
29. Dream Catcher Inn

HIGH COUNTRY

From the east, entry into High Country through Rogers Pass in Glacier National Park is dramatic. The Trans-Canada Highway leads west through Revelstoke, the site of Canada's largest dam, to Craigellachie, where in 1885 a plain iron spike completed the railway line linking Canada from east to west. From Canada's houseboat capital on Shuswap Lake, we follow the North Thompson River from Kamloops, British Columbia's largest city in area, past Wells Grey Provincial Park to **Mount Robson,** at 12,972 feet (3,954 m), the highest peak in the Canadian Rockies. A region of superlatives and diversity, High Country has something for all wanderers eager to find a road less traveled.

SOUTHEASTERN HIGH COUNTRY

My first trip into High Country through Rogers Pass was memorable. It was November, and the snow was falling thick and heavy. Trucks flashed like Christmas trees as they stopped to fit wheel chains, and cars littered ditches. This was Rogers Pass in its winter fury. But in warmer weather, ✦ **Glacier National Park** is a hiking and camping wonderland of more than four hundred glaciers, unique cave systems, and alpine tundra. Information is available from the Park Superintendent (Box 350, Revelstoke, V0E 2S0; 250-837-7500) or at the **Rogers Pass Information Centre** (250-837-6274), just west of the pass. Ask staff guides about joining one of their informative hikes.

From the pass, the highway blinks through snow-sheds, erected for protection from all-too-frequent avalanches. One, in 1910, buried sixty-six railway workers. To learn more about avalanches, visit the **Canadian Avalanche Centre** in Revelstoke (250-837-2435). Backcountry hikers and skiers can check snow conditions by calling 1-800-667-1105.

The Trans-Canada passes through **Mt. Revelstoke Provincial Park,** with its Giant Cedar Trail, and follows the Illecillewaet River for 40 miles (65 km) down into **Revelstoke,** which lies in the heart of the Monashees like a giant model-railroad town. Here the Illecillewaet joins the Columbia in its southerly sweep to Upper Arrow Lake.

Momma, Poppa, and baby grizzly bear sculptures guard the entrance to ✦ **Grizzly Plaza** in downtown Revelstoke, causing some locals to call it *Sesame Street*. From 7:00 to 10:00 P.M. in July and August, the plaza perks up with comedy acts, jazz combos, and Bluegrass bands.

From the plaza on Mackenzie Avenue the streets are numbered in order east or west of here, making it easy to find your way around. The city was settled in the 1800s by gold prospectors, but it was the building of the Canadian Pacific Railway that contributed to its becoming the dynamic city of 8,500 that it is today. The **InfoCentre** (Box 490, Revelstoke, V0E 2S0; 250-837-5345 or 837-3522) is open in summer at the junction of Highways 1 and 23, or year-round at 300 First Street West.

With this railway history in mind, follow the tracks (which will inevitably have a train on them, so be patient) to the new ◆ **Revelstoke Railway Museum** (719 West Track Street, P.O. Box 3018, Revelstoke, V0E 2S0; 250-837-6060; E-mail: railway@junction.net). Here you'll be able to experience the thrill of operating a diesel locomotive via a coin-operated simulated ride and learn the history of the construction of the most treacherous section of the Trans-Continental railway. The museum is open April to November from 9:00 A.M. to 5:00 P.M. and 9:00 A.M. to 8:00 P.M. in July and August. From December to March, phone for an appointment. Admission prices for adults are $5.00, seniors $3.00, youths (ages seven to sixteen) $2.00; children six and under are free. Railway memorabilia is available in the gift shop.

There's more railway history at the ◆ **Revelstoke Museum** at 315 First Street West (250-837-3067). Housed in the 1926-built original post office, the museum has interesting pieces, such as a 1911 fur press and many artifacts relating to logging.

Down the road at the end of Mackenzie Avenue, you'll find a bed and breakfast that's decidedly different. ◆ **The Piano Keep Museum and Bed and Breakfast** will appeal to anyone who has ever tickled the ivories. Impeccable Edwardian queen-size beds, a breakfast of home-made waffles, coffee, and fresh squeezed orange juice, and one of North America's best piano collections, make this bed and breakfast unique. Viennese-born artist and musician Vern Enyedy is *The Piano Man* in Revelstoke, and his wife Gwen is hostess in their restored 1905, seventeen-room residence. In the museum, there are about forty pianos, pianolas, harpsichords, and dulcimers built as early as 1783.

There are many other historical buildings in Revelstoke. A **Heritage Walking and Driving Tour** booklet (available at the museum) adds interest to a walk through the town. The most conspicuous on the list is the **Revelstoke Courthouse** at 1100 Second Street. It stands prominently about 10 blocks from the plaza, with a 30-foot (9-m) copper-covered dome. Other buildings include the **Holton House** at 1221 West First Street, another historic-home bed and breakfast.

The Piano Keep Museum and Bed and Breakfast

There's good coffee downtown at **Conversations Coffee and Gifts** on Mackenzie. But for something more substantial, the ranch-style **Frontier Family Restaurant** on Highway 23 North (where it meets the Trans-Canada) is a good bet.

♦ **Revelstoke Dam** is five minutes north of the city on Highway 23. Visitors use audio wands to learn about hydroelectricity and the dam's construction. Take the elevator to the Dam Crest Lookout to see over Lake Revelstoke reservoir and the Columbia River. The two-hour, free tour runs daily from late March till the end of October. Phone 250-837-6515 or 837-6211 for information.

Heading west past the pioneer village and resort of **Three Valley Gap** (Box 860, Revelstoke, V0E 2S0; 250-837-2109), with its ghost town and theater, you pass through the Eagle River system, known for its popular fishing spots. Twenty miles (30 km) west of Revelstoke is the **Enchanted Forest** (250-837-9477). Walking along its nature trail you'll pass an

800-year-old hollow cedar tree. Six miles (10 km) farther is ◆ **Beardale Castle** (250-836-2268), a world in miniature, which includes a medieval German village and a Canadian prairie town. It's open from May to September, 9:00 A.M. to dusk.

Just past Beardale Castle is **Craigellachie,** the site where Sir Donald Smith, a Canadian Pacific Railway financier, drove in the ◆ **Last Spike.** From mid-May to mid-October an information and souvenir shop opens, and assistants, costumed in turn-of-the-century clothing, will enlighten you with some of the stories surrounding this symbol of Canadian unity. Contact Craigellachie InfoPark (Malakwa Community Hall Association, Box 101, Malakwa, V0E 2J0; 250-836-2244).

THE SHUSWAP

The Trans-Canada moves away from the rocky peaks and follows the Eagle River past the hiking trails and ancient cedars of the **Eagle River Nature Park** to Shuswap Lake, where more than 600 miles (1,000 km) of mostly unpopulated shoreline make for a very popular vacation spot.

Sicamous, 43 miles (70 km) east of Revelstoke, is Canada's **Houseboat Capital.** You can rent houseboats from ◆ **Bluewater Houseboat Rentals** (Box 248, Sicamous, V0E 2V0; 250-836-2255; fax: 250-836-4955; or 1-800-663-4024). Some are very fancy, with hot tubs and waterslides. Contact Sicamous and District Chamber of Commerce (250-836-3313) for more information on this neat vacation idea.

Salmon Arm, farther west along the southern arm of Shuswap Lake, is the main business center for the Shuswap. Called the *Gem of the Shuswap,* it has a population of about 15,000 and boasts the largest freshwater pier in North America. **Salmon Arm Bay House Boat Vacations** (1-800-665-7782) is on the pier and rents boats that sleep up to twelve persons.

Also by the pier is the ◆ **Salmon Arm Bay Nature Enhancement Centre,** a waterfowl sanctuary. If you're there between April and June, you might catch sight of Clark's and western grebes, or any of the other 150 species familiar to the area. Fishing (Eastern brook and rainbow trout) and hiking are very popular here, too.

Over on the northwest shore of Salmon Arm, **Herald Provincial Park** (250-828-4494) is a cooling spot on a hot summer's day (quite common in the Shuswap). Located 7.5 paved miles (12 km) east of Tappen, Reinecker Creek meanders through the park. ◆ **Margaret Falls** is at the end of a trail through Reinecker Gorge. Nobody seems too sure who

Margaret was, but I've been told that if you look closely into the falls, you may see her apparition. Here the cedars are enormous, and the cool moistness of the twenty-minute round-trek is refreshing.

The Trans-Canada heads north from Salmon Arm for 20 miles (32 km) to **Sorrento,** where the air is thick with community spirit.

About 2 miles (3 km) before Sorrento, up on a hill with a great view of Copper Island and Shuswap Lake, you can roost for the night at ◆ **Pheasant Heaven** (P.O. Box 202, Sorrento, V0E 2W0; 250–675–4966; E-mail: pheasant@netshop.net). Here Mandi and Laurie Fleury run a pleasant bed and breakfast and aviaries, where they breed and raise more than forty different kinds of pheasants. Their aviaries contain many varieties including a Monal Impeyan, the national bird of Nepal. They enjoy giving personalized tours, and with plenty of parking space and the free use of their picnic tables, you can make a day of it. There's a small gift shop with displays of exotic bird eggs. Entry is by donation toward the upkeep of the pheasants and their breeding program.

BRITISH COLUMBIA FACT

Average temperatures range from 14° to 5°F (–10° to –15°C) in January, to July temperatures between 60° and 70°F (15° and 20°C).

While in Sorrento, stop at **Toby's** (250–675–4464), which is on the highway beside the hardware store, for one of Dave and Cherie's homemade pizzas and Caesar salads.

Down behind the Sorrento Elementary school on the other side of the highway, ◆ **The Evergreens Bed and Breakfast** (2853 Vimey Road, Box 117, Sorrento, V0E 2W0; 250–675–2568) is just a short walk to Shuswap Lake's western end. Berry-filled gardens provide food for delicious breakfasts and afternoon teas, served in a gazebo on Wednesdays, Fridays, and Sundays from 2:00 to 4:00 P.M. The gazebo has made the Evergreens a popular wedding spot, so hosts Linda and Verna have added a tiny chapel and an old buggy for ambience! The accommodations are pleasant, and with an aviary containing canaries, finches, and button quails, and a few wild turkeys gobbling about outside, it has a laid-back, holiday atmosphere.

Sorrento is full of surprises. The ◆ **Sorrento Centre** (Box 99, Sorrento, V0E 2W0; 250–675–2421; E-mail: sorrento@jetstream.net) is an ecumenical conference, retreat, and holiday center on Shuswap Lake just off the highway on Passchendaele Road. You can sign up for courses

BRITISH COLUMBIA TRIVIA

The Nicola Valley gets its name from a respected Okanagan Salish chief from Douglas Lake, Walking Grizzly Bear, or Hwistesme-txequen. The fur traders of the early 1800s were unable to pronounce this and referred to him as Nicholas. Ironically, the natives, too, had trouble with the anglicised word and shortened it to N'kuala or Nicola.

including such wide-ranging topics as wilderness recreation, meditation, social and environmental justice, and therapeutic touch. It can accommodate up to seventy persons in two modern lodges year-round, and there are also camping facilities. The meals are cafeteria-style with a set menu. Their Web site (http://www.sorrento-centre.bc.ca) outlines their courses.

The highway follows Shuswap Lake, and about 6 miles (10 km) farther west, the ✦ **Squilax General Store and Caboose Hostel** (RR 2, Chase, V0E 1M0; 250-675-2977) sells "funky foods and groovy groceries." Stay in renovated cabooses overlooking Shuswap Lake for $17, or if you're a Youth Hostel member, a mere $12.50.

From the store, take the bridge over the river and turn left onto Little Shuswap Lake Road to the Shuswap Band Reserve. Every July, drummers, singers, and dancers from all over North America arrive for the ✦ **Squilax International Powwow** (Box 1100, Chase, V0E 1M0; 250-679-3203). Traditional native food is served, arts and crafts are displayed, and generally a good time is had by all. There used to be a colony (or was it a congregation?) of about 3,000 female **Yuma bats** living in the attic of the old church nearby. In 1993, the church burned down, so the local Quaaout people have tried to reaccommodate them by building bat houses on poles near the administration office. Ask locally for up-to-date information.

From the bridge, the Squilax–Anglemont road leads north a short distance to **Roderick Haig-Brown Provincial Park** and the ✦ **Adams River,** famous for its October sockeye salmon run, possibly the largest on the continent. The river was called Chu Chua on early maps, but was renamed after a Shuswap Indian Chief, Selhowtken, who had been baptized Adam. Every four years (1998-2002, etc.), the river sees a boom run. A slide at Hell's Gate during railway construction in 1913 all but wiped out the run, but through the building of fishways and hatcheries, and upgrading habitats, the runs are gradually coming back to their historic numbers. To see this tide of salmon after their 305-mile (490-km) Fraser and Thompson River run, their battered crimson backs thrusting compulsively to return home to spawn and die in the gravel reaches of the Adams River, is a stirring experience. The salmon-viewing area is just past the Adams River bridge on the right. For general inquiries about provincial parks of the Shuswap, contact BC Parks, Thompson River District Office (1210 McGill Road, Kamloops, V2N 6N6; 250-851-3000).

KAMLOOPS TO MERRITT AND THE NICOLA VALLEY

Where the North and South Thompson rivers meet sits Kamloops, 130 miles (210 km) west of Revelstoke. In the Shuswap (Secwepemc) Indian tongue, it means *where the rivers meet*. It's also where three highways and two railroads meet, making it a very reachable city for the many forestry workers, miners, and ranchers for whom it exists. It's big (at 120 square miles [310 sq km], British Columbia's largest city in area), it's growing fast, and it has all the facilities you would expect to find in a city of seventy-five thousand.

One such facility is just 10 miles (16 km) east of Kamloops. The ⬧ **Kamloops Wildlife Park** (Box 698, Kamloops, V2C 5L7; 250-573-3242) is home to Zef and Czarina, two Siberian tigers, and Sheba and Shardic, two orphaned grizzly bears. As well, there are sixty-five species of local and endangered wildlife, a miniature train ride, a gift shop, a children's zoo, and trails leading to waterfalls. Prices of admission are from $3.00 to $6.00 and the park is open from 8:00 A.M. daily year-round.

Right next door in this area of Mojave-like, weirdly shaped hoodoos and rocky hills, is the **Kamloops Waterslide and R.V. Park** (250-573-3789). On a blazing hot, western summer day, these 2,000 feet of cool-water dips and curves may be the best place to hang out. It's open from May to Labor Day.

Another cooling idea is to head south toward the thriving city of **Merritt,** where the slogan *A Lake a Day, As Long As You Stay* would still hold true if you stayed almost half a year. Centrally situated where four major highways meet, Merritt is less than three hours from Vancouver via the Coquihalla (sounds like *Coca Cola*) Highway 5. But coming from **Kamloops,** you can take a more leisurely drive down Highway 5A, past forested peaks and rolling, grassy ranch lands and, nearer to Merritt, the deep, azure, and lovely **Nicola Lake.**

All the lakes in the **Nicola Valley** are popular fishing spots, and Kamloops trout, a wild strain of rainbow trout that, I hear, makes a splendid catch. Ice fishing for burbot during the winter months is popular too. Other nearby fishing spots are **Marquart** and **Lundbom Lakes,** a few miles east of Merritt off Highway 5A. They both have forestry service campsites with boat launches. The locals tell me that the best time to land rainbow, Kokanee, and brook trout is during spring and fall.

Stop off at the historic and charming **Quilchena Hotel** (Highway 5A North, Quilchena, V0E 2R0; 250-378-2611), sitting regally on the edge of Nicola Lake and at the center of one of BC's largest working cattle ranches. It's open early spring through late fall and serves excellent meals in its elegant dining room. In 1908, the hotel's builder, Joseph Guichon, believed the railway from Spences Bridge to Princeton would pass through Quilchena, and although this didn't happen, the hotel was still a success. Guichon's grandson, Guy Rose, continues to maintain the splendor and antique originality of this lovely hotel. Nearby, the **Nicola Valley Golf Course and R.V. Park** (250-378-2923) has a pleasant nine-hole course offering inexpensive golf and comfortable camping services.

Just before Quilchena on Highway 5A is the turnoff to the famous **Douglas Lake Ranch** (1-800-663-4838; E-mail: douglasl@comm-pass.awinc.com), Canada's largest cattle ranch. The ranch runs 19,000 head of cattle over almost 500,000 acres (200,000 ha). It also boasts twelve private lakes with world class fly-fishing, conducts ranch tours, and offers horseback riding. You'll find more information on Nicola Valley activities, ranging from hiking, cross-country skiing, sailing, windsurfing, and of course, fishing, at the red-roofed, log-construction **Merritt Travel InfoCentre** (Box 189, Merritt, V0K 2B0; 250-378-2281). It's at the intersection of phase one and phase three of the Coquihalla Highway. If you're needing a leg stretch, there's a nice hike along a nature trail at the back of the Infocentre.

Another major highway that meets in Kamloops is Highway 5, the Yellowhead South, named for the fair-haired Iroquois trapper Pierre Bostonais (known as Tête Jaune—*yellow head* in French), who, as a Hudson's Bay Company guide, frequently crossed through the spectacular Rocky Mountain pass that also bears his name. The Yellowhead begins in Winnipeg, Manitoba, and completes its route in Masset in the Queen Charlotte Islands. It covers 1,973 miles (3,185 km), including the 211 miles (340 km) of the Yellowhead South between Kamloops and Tête Jaune Cache, where we shall now begin.

THE NORTH THOMPSON RIVER

The first part of our Yellowhead journey hugs the eastern bank of the North Thompson River for 39 miles (63 km) to **Barriere,** a farming and forestry town, where every Labor Day weekend the **North Thompson Fall Fair and Rodeo** (Box 873, Barriere, V0E 1E0) is held.

There's excellent riverside camping 34 miles (55 km) north of Barriere at the ◆ **North Thompson River Provincial Park** (Box 70, Clearwater, V0E 1N0; 250–587–6150), 3 miles (5 km) before **Clearwater.** The park is situated where the muddy brown North Thompson River meets the green Clearwater River. There's a playground for the kids (Poggy Park) and excellent fishing. Near the river's edge in the picnic area, look for **kekuli sites,** winter pit-house depressions used by the Chu Chua or Simpcw (pronounced *simcue*) people. The **Wells Gray InfoCentre** (Box 1988, Clearwater, V0E 1N0; 250-674-2646) in Clearwater has a display describing the lives of these early native inhabitants.

Right outside the InfoCentre, which is on the corner of Clearwater Valley Road and the Yellowhead South, **Jerry the moose** stands guard. He's possibly the most photographed moose in Canada. He started life as a shiny steel creature, refusing to rust for many years. Finally, the sculptor from Victoria urged him along using saltwater-soaked cloths, and today he's a fine looking brown beast.

Don't even think of going into ◆ **Wells Gray Provincial Park** without first dropping into the InfoCentre (open daily May to September and Monday to Saturday the rest of the year). The knowledgeable staff will tell you what not to miss in British Columbia's fourth-largest park and alert you to the dangers, too. The park entrance is 25 miles (40 km) north of the InfoCentre along Clearwater Valley Road. The InfoCentre has excellent pictorials describing volcanic activity found in the park, as well as historical displays, some artifacts, and a gift and book section.

The staff will also provide directions to the ◆ **Yellowhead Museum** (250-674-3660), less than 4 miles (6 km) north along Clearwater Valley Road. It's run by a gutsy woman, Ida Dekelver, who back in 1967 at age forty-four and a mother of six, with her two donkeys, Bill and Jack, walked the Yellowhead Highway to Wadena, Saskatchewan. That's more than 890 miles (1,434 km)! She wanted to visit her aunt. Newspapers from all over the country covered her trek, giving publicity to Clearwater and Wells Gray Park. Ironically, she and her donkeys got a ride back home in a truck driven by two Saskatchewan men, Bill and Jack. She has

```
       #243  05-14-2008 12:13PM
 Item(s) checked out to Artale, Frank.

TITLE: Fodor's Montréal and Québec City.
BRCD: 32244200765721
DUE DATE: 06-11-08

TITLE: Fodor's Canada.
BRCD: 32244201075617
DUE DATE: 06-11-08

TITLE: British Columbia : off the beaten
BRCD: 32244111247421
DUE DATE: 06-11-08

TITLE: Unforgettable Canada : 100 destin
BRCD: 32244201339823
DUE DATE: 05-28-08


       Deer Park Public Library
 (631) 586-3000 www.deerparklibrary.org
```

filled two cabins with memorabilia collected during her Centennial-year trek, plus native and pioneer artifacts, and natural history displays.

If you're looking for a place to stay, 2 miles (3 km) up the Clearwater Valley Road from the InfoCentre is the ◆ **Clearwater Mountain Charm Chalet** (1048 Clearwater Valley Road, Clearwater, V0E 1N0; 250-674-2659). It's a bed and breakfast built with sunsets, guests, and spectacular views of Trophy Mountain in mind. Hosts Tom and Jean Monaghan's home makes a good base for hiking, the alpine meadows. They'll set you off on your hike with the breakfast leftovers, which could be waffles, pancakes, homemade granola, fruits, sausages, crepes, or muffins. Rates range from $40 to $55.

In those **alpine meadows** at **Trophy Mountain** you'll see subalpine daisies, cow parsnips, Indian paintbrush, Lewis's monkey flower, and arnica. To get there, take the Bear Creek Correctional Centre turnoff 6 miles (10 km) up the Clearwater Valley Road, on the right just past **Spahats Creek Provincial Park.** Ask the InfoCentre for the best time to see the flowers.

Also on Clearwater Valley Road (note that locals call it Wells Gray Road), if quilting is your passion, check out **Country Cabin Quilts** (Box 1770, RR 1, Clearwater, V0E 1N0; 250-674-3780) 15 miles (24 km) from the InfoCentre. Turn left onto Grouse Creek Road, and it's at the end. Letta Mae Colborne creates lap quilts (they fold into a pillow), and other crafts and antiques. She is open from May 1 to October 31, Tuesday to Sunday from 10:00 A.M. to 4:00 P.M., or by appointment.

In this wilderness area, you don't expect to find craft stores; it's also a bonus to find good food. At the park entrance, ◆ **Helmcken Falls Lodge** (Box 239, Clearwater, V0E 1N0; 250-674-3657) serves excellent buffet food. They'll also arrange horseback riding, guided canoeing and hiking, accommodations, and camping.

We're finally at **Wells Gray Provincial Park,** with its breathtaking scenery in all seasons. You'll see snow-covered peaks, glaciers, extinct volcanoes, old-growth cedar forests, and dozens of waterfalls, the most famous being the 450-foot (137-m) **Helmcken Falls** (more than two and a half times higher than Niagara) 6 miles (10 km) inside the park.

A few miles past Helmcken Falls is a naturally carbonated cold-water mineral spring, where you can add juice crystals to the water and presto! You have pop. At **Bailey's Chute,** a few miles farther up in the park, you can see (in season) forty-four pound (20-kg) salmon leaping up the rapids. Park your car just past the mineral springs, and it's about a fifteen-minute walk.

Back at the Yellowhead Highway in Clearwater, the road now runs slightly south and east to **Birch Island,** formed by an eddy in the North Thompson River. Either take the back road east to **Vavenby,** which runs from Birch Island via an old, one-lane wooden bridge (lots of character) and Lost Creek Road, or turn right off the highway at Vavenby, 16 miles (26 km) east of Clearwater. Here you can experience a working ranch at ✦ **Vavenby Trail Rides** (Box 250, Vavenby, V0E 3A0; 250-676-9598). The Shook family takes small groups on guided rides through open pasture, woodlands, and hay fields along the scenic North Thompson River. Help herd the cows, or just hold the reins and enjoy the scenery. They're open from April to late October, and rides are $15 per hour.

Back on the Yellowhead, heading north now, there's another entrance to the **Wells Gray Provincial Park** 67 miles (108 km) north of Clearwater. Turn onto a well-maintained, 17-mile (27-km) gravel road just past Blue River. If you can still walk after the trail ride, a 1.5-mile (2.5-km) portage from the parking lot will bring you to ✦ **Murtle Lake,** North America's largest "no-motors-allowed" freshwater lake. With more than 62 miles (100 km) of shoreline to explore, and only the call of the loon to listen to, if you have a canoe, you can really get away from it all. A dawn paddle may bring you face-to-face with black or grizzly bears, eagles, moose, beavers, deer, or wolves. And if you have a BC fishing license, the trout are very big. The camping fee is $6.00 per boat nightly, and passes are available in Blue River. Look for the large information sign just past the highway maintenance yard in Blue River.

But if roughing it on Murtle Lake is not your thing, check into the luxurious ✦ **Mike Wigele Heli-Ski Village** (Box 159, Blue River, V0E 1J0; 250-673-8381 or 1-800-661-9170) for some backcountry hiking through alpine wildflowers, fly-fishing, biking, skiing, heli-sightseeing, or picnicking (gourmet picnics at 7,000 feet!). There's a choice of accommodation from deluxe to luxury, but you get what you pay for, and they do say there are more basic accommodations available.

NORTHERN HIGH COUNTRY

Fifty-five miles (88 km) north of Blue River and far removed from the luxury of Mike Wiegele is **Valemount,** the midpoint between Edmonton and Vancouver. Here enterprising businesses sell strange gift items—real moose feet with staring glass eyes, guaranteed-to-burn wooden wood stoves, and brightly painted fungi. At ✦ **Berna's Medicine (Censored) Cabinet** (250-566-8442), pick up a *My Holiday in Valemount* traveling kit

A CENSORED STORY

It cost Berna Paquette a thousand dollars to change the name of her store—and she didn't even want to. *Berna's Medicine Cabinet* sounded simple enough for a little hometown variety store selling everything from elk's feet to aspirin, and the Valemount establishment's name was duly approved by the government Name Registration office in Victoria.

"All was well until the College of Pharmacists got wind of the fact that I'd used the word *medicine*—a word restricted to pharmacists—in my store name," Berna explained with a bit of a grin.

"I'm a little concerned now that the College of Cabinetmakers will censor the word *Cabinet*, and I'll be left with Berna's," she said, her tongue lodged firmly in her cheek!

So if you're passing through Valemount and see Berna's Medicine (with Censored obliterating the word Medicine) Cabinet, you'll understand what it's all about.

for the kids, containing coloring books, crayons, erasers, and bubble gum!

It's more than a funky little logging village with neat stores, though. Valemount sits in a valley where the Cariboo, Monashee, and Rocky Mountains meet, where the views become wondrously spectacular, and where the birds flock.

Just 2 miles (3 km) south of town, the ◆ **Robert W. Starratt Wildlife Sanctuary** (Cranberry Marsh) is the site of a Ducks Unlimited project to improve waterfowl habitat. The Canada geese love it here, as do northern harriers and red-tailed hawks. You can hike over the whole 600-acre (243-ha) marsh in an hour and a half. Contact the **Valemount InfoCentre** (Box 168, Valemount, V0E 2Z0; 250-566-4846) for information.

If you have some extra time, **Mount Robson Adventure Holidays** (Box 687, Valemount, V0E 2Z0; 250-566-4386) offers backpacking, canoeing, rafting, and fly-in/hike-out activities. Or if you'd just like to spend a night and pass on, the ◆ **Dream Catcher Inn** (Box 1012, Valemount, V0E 2Z0; 250-566-4226 or 1-800-566-9128; E-mail: dream@valemount.com) has log chalets as well as bed-and-breakfast accommodation. There's an outdoor hot tub and delicious breakfasts. My hot apple cereal, blueberry muffins, and poached eggs on toast kept me going well into the afternoon. In the bed and breakfast, you have a choice of five Indian-named rooms, each with a dream catcher (to catch your dreams before they float away) hanging above a comfortable bed. The inn is located in a ten-acre (4-ha) wooded setting just north of Valemount.

It's walking distance to the Swift Creek Chinook salmon spawning grounds (August) in **George Hicks Park,** and the nine-hole **Valemount Pines Golf Course** (250–566–4550) on the west side of the highway.

Five miles (8 km) north of Valemount is the **Mount Terry Fox Viewpoint.** In Canada, the name Terry Fox is a household name. Having lost a leg to a rare form of bone cancer, twenty-two-year-old Fox attempted to run across Canada to raise funds for cancer research. After running at a pace of almost a marathon a day, covering 3,339 miles (5,373 km), he had to retire after the cancer returned. He died ten months later, and today yearly runs are held to continue the fundraising effort and honor his memory. Look to the east at the viewpoint and you'll see the 8,694-foot (2,650-m) **Mount Terry Fox.**

Across the road there's a trail sign at Stone Road. Take this road for a little over a mile to the trailhead. It's 4.5 miles (7 km) to Mount Terry Fox—a good day-hike by the time you get back to the parking lot. It's quite steep, but the alpine views are worth the effort.

It's now time to leave the Yellowhead South Highway 5 and join the Yellowhead Highway 16 at **Tête Jaune Cache,** once a thriving town of three thousand, complete with pool halls and flophouses in the early 1900s, when the Grand Trunk Railway was under construction. Now it's all but deserted. At this point we are 63 miles (101 km) from Jasper in Alberta and 150 miles (240 km) from **Prince George.** The easterly drive is spectacular, especially when **Mount Robson** comes into view just near the **Mount Terry Fox Provincial Park.** The road to the northwest is a long and lonely drive into BC's north, which we'll explore in the chapter on the Northeast.

WHERE TO STAY:

1. **The Piano Keep Bed and Breakfast** (815 Mackenzie Street, Revelstoke, V0E 2S0; 250–837–2120). Single $65, double $75.

2. **The Evergreens Bed and Breakfast** (2853 Vimey Road, P.O. Box 117, Sorrento, V0E 2W0; 250–675–2568). Four double rooms with shared baths. Moderately priced.

3. **Sorrento Center** (Box 99, Sorrento, V0E 2W0; 250–675–2421, fax: 250–675–3032; E-mail: sorrento@jetstream.net). Inexpensive.

4. **Salmon Arm Bay House Boat Vacations** (Box 1480, Salmon Arm,

V1E 4P6; 250-832-2745 or 1-800-665-7782 in North America; fax: 250-836-4824; E-mail: kyllo@netshop.net). Rates vary with season. Inexpensive for groups of ten to fourteen.

5. **Clearwater Mountain Charm Chalet Bed and Breakfast** (1048 Clearwater Valley Road, RR 1, Box 1705, Clearwater, V0E 1N0; 250-674-2659). Single $40, double $45-55.

6. **Dream Catcher Inn** (Box 1012, Valemount, V0E 2Z0; 250-566-4226 or 1-800-566-9128; fax: 250-566-9128). Single $50, double $55-$70.

7. **Rainbow Retreat Bed and Breakfast** (11944 Essen Road, Box 138, Valemount, V0E 2Z0; 250-566-9747). Moderately priced. Near Tête Jaune Cache.

WHERE TO EAT:

1. **Frontier Family Restaurant** (Box 1239, Revelstoke, V0E 2S0; 250-837-5119 or 1-800-382-7763). Fast foods.

2. **The Chocolate Bean** (250 Alexander Street, Salmon Arm, 250-832-6681). Light lunches and good coffee.

3. **Toby's Restaurant** (Trans-Canada Highway, Sorrento, V0E 2W0; 250-675-4464). Good pizzas. Open from 7:00 A.M.

4. **Sinbads** (1502 River Street, Kamloops, V2C 1Y9; 250-372-1522). Nice riverside deck, good food.

5. **Helmcken Falls Lodge** (Box 239, Clearwater, V0E 1N0; 250-674-3657). Buffet. Moderately priced.

6. **Rainbow Retreat Bed and Breakfast** (11944 Essen Road, Box 138, Valemount, V0E 2Z0; 250-566-9747). Quality dining by reservation only; near Tête Jaune Cache.

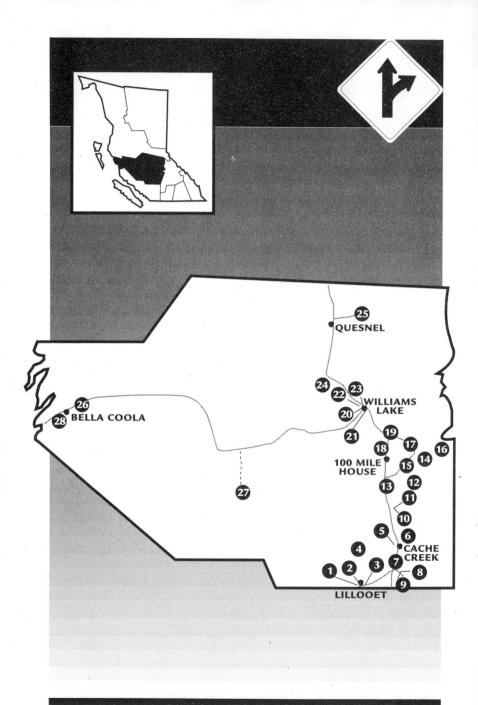

CARIBOO-CHILCOTIN

1. Lillooet Historical Museum
2. Elaine's Coffee Garden
3. Sheep Pasture Golf Course
4. Pavilion General Store
5. Hat Creek Ranch
6. Horsting's Farm Market
7. Cariboo Jade and Gift Shoppe
8. Ashcroft Museum
9. Ashcroft Manor Teahouse
10. Clinton Museum
11. Robson's Square
12. Painted Chasm
13. 59 Mile Bed and Breakfast/Arctic Artists Gallery
14. Little Horse Lodge
15. North Greenlake Gallery
16. Flying U
17. Whistle Stop Bed and Breakfast
18. Bridge Creek Falls
19. The Hills Health and Guest Ranch
20. Rowat's Waterside Bed and Breakfast
21. Scout Island Nature Centre
22. Chef's Corner
23. Williams Lake Museum
24. Xats'ull Heritage Village
25. Barkerville
26. The Hill
27. Bracewell's Alpine Wilderness Adventures
28. Barb's Pottery

CARIBOO-CHILCOTIN

Hudson's Bay fur traders could never have anticipated the gold-hungry throngs that would stampede into the area after the first of their sparkling dust and bright nuggets reached San Francisco in the late 1850s. Thousands marched north to the beckoning land in hopes of filling their pokes with the brilliant booty. And so it all began.

But in less than thirty years, towns like Barkerville, once the gold capital of the world, were empty of both the gold and its seekers. Roadhouses that had catered to exhausted travelers spread their wings to become centers for rambling ranches. Another way of life had begun.

LILLOOET: MILE ZERO

Mile Zero of the old **Cariboo Waggon Road** is at Lillooet at the junction of Highways 99 and 12, majestically perched above the muddy Fraser River. It started out as a landing point for mother-lode seekers who had come north through Harrison and Anderson lakes. Other roadhouses like 100 Mile House and 70 Mile House emerged, their names rising from their distances from Lillooet. A cairn on Main Street marks the Mile 0 spot. A busy town of sixteen thousand in the gold rush days of the 1860s, Lillooet was once the second largest settlement north of San Francisco and west of Chicago. It also holds the unenviable claim to the hottest recorded spot in British Columbia, when it reached 111.9°F (44.4°C) in 1941.

Opposite the cairn, **St. Mary's Anglican Church** houses the InfoCentre (790 Main Street, Box 441, V0K 1V0; 250-256-4308/4289) and the ◆ **Lillooet Historical Museum.** The Murray Collection in the basement is a display of newspaper and printing equipment owned by straight-talking (*and that's for damshurr*) publisher Margaret "Ma" Murray and her politician husband George. Founded in 1934, the *Bridge River-Lillooet News,* laced with her crusty commentaries, made Ma a household name in Canada. Outside the museum, there's a rusty little jail jumbled among antiquated machinery. Ask at the InfoCentre about Lillooet's Golden Mile of History from the **Bridge of 23 Camels** to the **Old Bridge,** which you can walk or bike along using a self-guided tour brochure.

Next door, ◆ **Elaine's Coffee Garden** (250-256-4633) is a lunch bar serving soups, salads, bunwiches and burgers, all deliciously homemade. It also sells a few books and souvenirs. Owner Ken Hood taught in the area for many years and is convinced that there's no place quite like Lillooet. "It's not as cold as the Cariboo, and not as wet as the Coast," he says of his and his wife Elaine's little bit of heaven.

Across at 719 Main at the **Lillooet Bakery** (250-256-4889), *bäckermeister* Axel Sterrmann and his wife Elke serve European-style breakfasts, delicious baked goods, and excellent coffee, attested to by the busloads of tourists who stop by.

If you need a place to stay, in addition to the three or four hotels there's a comfortable spot down on the river. **River-Side Bed and Breakfast** (562 Summer Street, Box 1000, V0K 1V0; 250-256-4477) has two rooms (one a family suite) starting from $45. Turn right at the Esso Station opposite the bakery (Seventh Avenue), cross the railway line, and turn left.

> ## BRITISH COLUMBIA FACT
>
> Longest river: Fraser, 851 miles (1,370 km) draining almost one-fourth of the province.

Leaving town as you head north on Highway 99 toward Cache Creek, you cross the Fraser at the **Bridge of 23 Camels,** named for the poor Bactrian beasts of burden used and abused during gold rush days. It's worth a stop to view the town and the railway line that snakes along the river at this point.

But before heading north, check out Canada's most unusual golf course. ◆ **Sheep Pasture Golf Course** (Box 217, Lillooet, V0K 1V0; 250-256-4484), 3 miles (5 km) south of Lillooet on the Texas Creek Road (turn south before the bridge), is a par thirty-five nine-holer, with quite a few moving, bleating hazards and panoramic views of the mountains and river. The green fee for eighteen holes is $13 ($12 on weekdays).

Once north of town on Highway 99, you'll twist and climb along the Fraser benchlands toward the 4,987-foot (1,520-m) Pavilion Mountain. Stop at the ◆ **Pavilion General Store,** once a one-day trip from Lillooet by horse and buggy. Here the horses were watered before continuing up over the mountain. The slope was so steep that they would have to use log "anchors" to help them down the hill, some of which can still be seen (ask at the store). Passengers would have to get out and push the wagons on the uphill sections. This is the oldest general store in BC—with an emphasis on the words *old* and *general*. Look up at the top shelf and you'll think you're in a museum. Even the Coke cooler is a collector's item. Ask to see the receipts from 1903, when twenty-five pounds of coffee cost $5.00, and try to imagine you're stocking up for the trip north, the horses hitched outside.

Farther on, after passing brilliant lakes, you'll approach Marble Canyon, about 30 miles (48 km) east of Lillooet. Watch for **Chimney Rock** on the north side of the highway and other fabulous Utah-like towering cliffs of colored limestone. Camping at **Marble Canyon Provincial Park** is available (thirty-five sites), and there's first-class swimming in Pavilion and Crown lakes.

As you leave Highway 99 and its dramatic scenery, you'll come to ❧ **Hat Creek Ranch** (Box 878, Cache Creek, V0K 1H0; 1–800–782–0922 or 250–457–9722) at the junction of Highway 97, which leads south 7 miles (11 km) to Cache Creek or north 18 miles (29 km) to Clinton. Hat Creek Ranch was originally the property of the murderous Donald McLean and his three horse-stealing sons, and was an overnight stop for early travelers on the Cariboo Waggon Road. Today it's a holiday attraction, complete with $5.00 stagecoach and $3.00 wagon rides. A blacksmith demonstrates his trade, the pigs snuffle in the troughs, and the chickens scratch in their coop. Lunch (approximately $7) is served in the restaurant. The ranch is open from mid-May to mid-October, with $10 admission costs for a family of four.

Before heading north to follow the old Cariboo Waggon Trail, take a peek at Cache Creek and Ashcroft, a few miles to the south on Highway 97. Tune into 105.9 FM to find out what's happening first, then just before Cache Creek visit ❧ **Horsting's Farm Market** (250–457–6546), with its fresh berries, vegetables, and colorful hanging baskets. Stop and try a piece of Donna Horsting's berry pies or buy a bottle of her delicious Saskatoon berry jam and a loaf of homemade bread. There's usually lots of activity year-round. The kids can play on the trampoline, go for a wagon ride, or visit the goats and rabbits after a picnic in Horsting's park.

From jam to jade. British Columbia is the Jade Capital of the World. Jade souvenirs can be bought at the ❧ **Cariboo Jade and Gift Shoppe** (1093 Todd Road, Box 280, Cache Creek, V0K 1H0; 250–457–9566) in Cache Creek. It's opposite the bus depot and is open late seven days per week in summer.

After Cache Creek, head south along the Ashcroft–Cache Creek Highway through the tumbleweed and cactus to historic Ashcroft, sitting pretty by the Thompson River. Cross the bridge into town, and at the bright red fire hall (rebuilt in 1919) go down the hill toward the riverbank to a small but lovely campground at **Legacy Park** (250–453–2642). The sites are right on the bank. Next door is the **River Inn** (Box 1359, Ashcroft, V0K 1A0; 250–453–2565 or 1–800–465–4800), where you can enjoy a meal or spend a night overlooking the river. Rates start

FROM CANNED CREAM TO CLAIM STAKING

When I arrived in Ashcroft, one of those special little towns where everybody knows everybody and conversations come easy, I headed down to the River Inn for a piece of blueberry pie and a coffee. A chat with a stranger about canned whipped cream ended with a visit to a remote cabin on a hillside. Sweet-smelling wildflowers, wandering bears, and serenity are what brings Trevor Parker, a ship's captain from Vancouver, back regularly to where he grew up. Trevor introduced me to how to stake a claim, to esoteric pictographs and hidden ice caves, and to the friendliness of Ashcroft's people. We dropped in to the Irlybird, where he bought two wooden garden chairs. When they wouldn't fit in his small Toyota, it was "no problem" for the lovely woman who served him to drop them off on the way home. That's the kind of friendly little town it is.

at $45. The restaurant is open from 7:00 A.M., and there's often live entertainment in the pub.

If you're interested in Cariboo history, the ◈ **Ashcroft Museum** on the corner of Brink and Fourth Streets (built in 1916) is (as I was told by everyone in town!) *definitely worth a visit.* Next door you'll find the *Ashcroft Journal,* started up in 1895. Originally called the *BC Mining Journal,* it was one of British Columbia's first papers and still churns out the news today.

If you head back across the bridge and turn south on Cornwall Street, you'll reach the Trans-Canada Highway and ◈ **Ashcroft Manor Teahouse** (Box 127, Cache Creek, V0K 1H0; 250-453-9983), built by the Cornwall brothers in the early 1860s and now run as a bed and breakfast. Also housed in the manor are a gift shop, restaurant (open 9:00 A.M. to 9:00 P.M.), and museum (open 9:00 A.M. to 6:00 P.M.). Accommodations (from $58) are available from March 15 to November 15. You'll be staying in one of BC's oldest roadhouses, which has served also as a post office and a court house—the "hanging judge" Matthew Begbie once presided here.

Follow the sweet smell of ponderosa pine and sagebrush for about 9 miles (14 km) south, and take a drive up the Hat Creek-Oregon Jack Road to **Cornwall Mountain.** The alpine meadows are thick with wildflowers, but this beautiful drive is really only recommended for 4 x 4 vehicles. There are no services, no campgrounds, a few bears, and

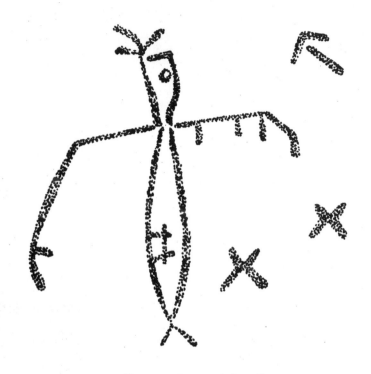

Pictograph near Ashcroft

if you're as lucky as I was to be guided by an immensely hospitable local, you'll find pictographs and a hidden ice cave containing ice stalagmites, seeming to grow like delicate ferns from the cave floor. But that's my secret!

Circle back to Cache Creek on the Trans-Canada and rejoin Highway 97 heading north to the copper-colored mountains and rolling hills surrounding laid-back Clinton, 25 miles (40 km) north of Cache Creek.

Cariboo Lodge (Box 459, Clinton, V0K 1K0; 250–459–7992) is on the highway in town. Wonderful old photos on the walls will give you a feel for the past, and with its pretty hanging baskets and warm log construction, the lodge is an inviting rest stop. The restaurant serves tasty "Lodge Burgers," and the summer room rates are from $60.

Across the road at the tiny ◆ **Clinton Museum,** built in 1892 from locally made bricks, check out the backyard, with displays including a bull-press, which was used to keep the beast from doing the blacksmith in as he bravely shoed it, a model of the now-burnt-down Clinton Hotel, and a BC Express Company sleigh. If it's Monday, then the museum won't be open, but you can still see the displays in the back.

Walk along to  **Robson's Square** and have a giggle at the Bucking Ham Palace Hotel where you can *Eat and sleep like a king for $2.00 a day.* Perhaps you'd prefer to try *Fitzwillies purifying black paste* for your *painful piles, pustules, pimples of acne, pox, bunions, tonsils, and teething grief.* If you're still a mess, at Hickory Daiquiri Doc's, you can get *mouthwash, whitewash, hogwash, distilled water, toilet water, tonic water, holy water, bones set, blood let, holes patched, and babies hatched.* It's right beside the **Grill and Chop Suey Restaurant!**

There's decidedly more refinement next door at **Crafts with Class** (1521 Cariboo Highway, V0K 1K0; 250-459-2573). Here you can buy Vallance pottery, gourmet coffee, and classy sweatshirts.

Any traveler to this part of British Columbia should not miss the spectacular **Painted Chasm,** Canada's Grand Canyon, 14 miles (22 km) north of Clinton. There's no fanfare of garish signs announcing its coming, just a small blue PROVINCIAL PARK sign on the roadside. But don't be fooled. This geological wonder, a mile wide and almost 400 feet (120 m) deep, is about 2 miles (3 km) from the highway on good road. One modern legend going the rounds is that a Scottish gold digger lost a penny, and in his effort to retrieve it, dug the mighty chasm. If you saw the movie *Grey Fox,* then you've seen scenes shot at the Chasm.

There are more colorful scenes at the **59 Mile Bed and Breakfast/Arctic Artists Gallery** (Box 518, Clinton, V0K 1K0; 250-459-7076). Fred (also known as Iyak) and Laurie Trimble offer bed and breakfast. But even if you aren't ready to bed down for the night, it's worth stopping just to see (or buy) the soapstone carvings, for which Fred (from Inuvik) is renowned. His dad, Lyle Trimble, exhibits his oil paintings of northern scenes here, too. An unusual northern find in a Cariboo setting.

BRITISH COLUMBIA FACT

BC has about 4,085 miles (6,575 km) of mainline railroad track.

Just as it happened at Arctic Artists Gallery, hitting the brakes and making a turn at 70 Mile House, 19 miles (31 km) north of Clinton, can also lead to some unexpected finds. Turn east onto Old Bonaparte Road, and less than 5 pleasant miles (8 km) later, you're at **Green Lake.** It's more than just a glorious jade-green lake. The area is inhabited by several artisans, there are three campgrounds with more than 160 sites (including several beach sites), and the plethora of guest ranches surrounding both Green and Watch Lakes means you'll probably find somewhere pleasant to stay. Many locals have their own reasons for the color of the lake (a reflection of the trees!) but the one that makes a lot of sense is that it has no outlet; hence, it has accumulated large deposits of soda, salt, and sulfur, which combine to create its glorious shade of green.

The Green Lake Park facilitators are Brenda and Bob Daub at ◆ **Little Horse Lodge** (North Green Lake Road, Comp. 1, Site E, RR 1, 70 Mile House, V0K 2K0; 250-456-7524). This lodge (a year-round resort) has everything ("Just bring a smile," says Bob) from restaurant to store to cabins to laundry, as well as a host of activities from fishing to canoeing to skiing to ice fishing (the best fishing is in winter—you can do it in your T-shirt from the comfort of a warm cabin, playing cribbage while the fishing lines bob!) and the homemade pies and bread are superb. Gymkhanas and fishing derbies are held regularly. Log cabin accommodation is $50 double, plus $7.50 for additional guests.

Bob Daub wasn't the only enthusiastic promoter of the area. Artist Judith Dodington owns ◆ **North Greenlake Gallery** (RR 1, 70 Mile House, V0K 2K0; 250-456-7326). Judith's watercolors reveal her love of the lake and the birds and animals that make it their home. Drop in and see her gallery of jewelry and dream-like paintings, and she'll fill you in on other art and craft studios in the area.

A lodge with lots of history is the ◆ **Flying U** (Box 69, 70 Mile House, V0K 2K0; 250-456-7717), an international destination with its own BC Rail whistle stop. It's Canada's oldest guest ranch (1849), with a history and spirit of the early West. Here meals are eaten ranch-style, and are announced by the clanging of a bell! There's a two-day minimum stay off-season, three-day in summer.

Tall Timbers Resort (1-888-228-8255 or 250-456-7668), **Ace High Resort** (250-456-7518), and **Watch Lake Lodge** (RR 1, 70 Mile House, V0K 2K0; 250-456-7741) are three more accommodation choices a little farther along on Watch Lake. At Watch Lake Lodge, 3 miles (5 km) on from Little Horse Lodge, you can ride on the trail, roll your own, and wear a straw hat with Shorty, Alice, Enid, and Dimps Horn, who've been doing it for more than fifty years. Just pick a pair of boots that fit from the thirty or so lined up on the verandah, and it's Happy Trails time.

If you prefer bed-and-breakfast accommodation, **Green Lake Bed and Breakfast** (S1, C5, RR 1, 70 Mile House, at 5742 North Green Lake Road; 250-456-2371) is on the water, with a dock and sandy beach.

Singles are $35 and doubles are $50. And hostess Ursula will make you feel very much at home.

Keep heading north toward Lone Butte. An easterly turn on Highway 24 will take you through the Interlakes (great fishing!) District to Little Fort, 57 miles (92 km) north of Kamloops on Yellowhead Highway 5.

A northerly turn from Lone Butte along the Lone Butte–Horse Lake Connector Road will take you past rolling, relaxing farmlands to an equally relaxing country home, the ❤ **Whistle Stop Bed and Breakfast** (Lot 2, Garrett Road, C9 McMillan Road, RR 1, Lone Butte, V0K 1X0; 250 –395–2170). Turn at the Butte (the large flat-topped volcanic crater for which the town is named) and from here, the Whistle Stop is a 2.7-mile (4.3-km) drive. When you reach McMillan Road, turn right onto the gravel section, then left onto Garrett, and it's the second house on the left. Accommodation is $50 double, including a delicious, hot breakfast.

Head into "town," which is **100 Mile House,** and you can't miss the **InfoCentre** (Box 2312, V0K 2E0; 250–395–5353) with the 36-foot-long (11-m) **World's Largest Skis** standing outside. This is a reminder that every February, 100 Mile House hosts Canada's second oldest race, the Cariboo Ski Marathon, a 30-mile (50-km) cross-country race that brings Nordic enthusiasts from all over.

Less obvious than those gigantic skis, but ever so lovely, are the ❤ **Bridge Creek Falls** near Centennial Park. They're so close to downtown, but even some locals, unfortunately, have never appreciated their beauty. Turn east on Forth Avenue (opposite the InfoCentre), take a right on Cedar, and turn immediately left by the school to the parking lot. A chip-trail leads to the falls, where a 30-foot (9-m) pipe, once used by a sawmill to harness the power of the water, still stands erect. From the pipe, trails continue upstream to the **100 Mile Village Campground.** Look out for mule deer near the falls.

There's more natural beauty right in 100 Mile House at the **100 Mile Marsh** beside the InfoCentre. This 20-acre wetland marsh, surrounded by grassy meadows and bluffs of aspen and white spruce, is a nesting ground for Canada geese and several species of ducks.

Head up the highway toward (where else?) **108 Mile House,** famous for its internationally acclaimed resorts. ❤ **The Hills Health and Guest Ranch** (Box 26, 108 Mile Ranch, V0K 2Z0; 250–791–5225; E-mail: thehills@netshop.net) is the best known. Check out the photoboard inside the main lodge to see some of the celebrities who have enjoyed cross-country skiing, horseback riding, aerobics, and other activities "The Hills" offers. You can stay overnight for $59 per person,

---

BRITISH COLUMBIA TRIVIA

You've heard of Boxing Day. They go one further in Williams Lake where, every January 2, they celebrate Wrestling Day. The civic holiday traces its roots back to the thirties, when merchants decided it wasn't worth opening their businesses to a trickle of customers. The town council made it official in 1959, and despite occasional moves to abolish it, Wrestling Day lives on.

---

including hot, ranch-style breakfast and a guided hike. Or you can sign up for a weeklong "lifestyle adjustment" vacation package of Smoking Cessation, Stress Reduction, Weight Loss, and several other wellness programs. The wilderness accommodations rival the facilities for being fabulously first class.

Highway 97, the Gold Rush Trail, continues north to Williams Lake, passing through **Lac La Hache,** the longest town in the Cariboo, and with its lakeshore setting, possibly the prettiest. There are excellent accommodations and boating activities at the north end of the lake at **Guest Log House–122 Mile Bed and Breakfast** (RR 1, Comp. 28, Kokanee Bay, V0K 1T0; 250-396-4747), where a German family has built a lovely log home and restaurant. Look for the large flags on the eastern side of the highway behind Clancy's Gas Station. Rates are $60 single and $70 double, with full breakfast. If you stop for a meal, entrees range from $9.80 to $12.80, and there's a neat walkway cut through the forest where you can walk off your dinner.

THE NORTHERN CARIBOO

Williams Lake is 40 miles (65 km) beyond Lac La Hache. Suddenly, you're back in the big city, and the signs of forestry (four major sawmills and a plywood mill), responsible for the town's incredible growth, are everywhere. It is possible to find a quiet, classy place to stay though. ◆ **Rowat's Waterside Bed and Breakfast** (1397 Borland Drive, Williams Lake, V2G 1M3; 250-392-7395) is right by the ◆ **Scout Island Nature Centre** (Box 4575, Williams Lake, V2G 3R2; 250-398-8532), a bird-watcher's paradise. From the south as you approach the city, turn left at the Husky Station onto Mackenzie Avenue, then left onto Borland Drive. Marg and Jack Rowat accept Visa and Mastercard, but it's advisable to book ahead for this quality accommodation, which starts at $55.

Scout Island (off Borland Drive) is operated by Williams Lake Field

Naturalists Volunteers, who have interactive exhibits set up in a Nature House, with an observation deck and walking trails for viewing the beaver lodge, native pit house, otters, muskrats, birds, and ducks that inhabit this conservation area. The center is open from 8:00 A.M. to 5:00 P.M. Monday to Friday, May to August, and on Sunday afternoons April through October, but the trails are open daily from 8:00 A.M. to dusk. Bring a picnic lunch and a swimsuit to make use of the tables and sandy beach.

Downtown, you can get first-class coffee at **Rockwells Cappuccino** (250-392-3633) opposite Hodgson Place Mall on Second Avenue South. Try one of Bev's Lemon Iced Apricot Squares. Kitty-corner at the new ◆ **Chef's Corner** (250-398-5622), the most popular meals are the seafood crepes ($7.95 for lunch and $13.95 for dinner). The dinner meal is served with fresh shrimp piled on top of the crepes. It's open from 11:00 A.M. to 8:00 P.M. Monday to Thursday and to 9:00 P.M. Friday and Saturday. On Sundays there's a made-to-order omelette bar. This restaurant was definitely a pleasant find in Williams Lake.

Up near the City Hall at the ◆ **Williams Lake Museum** (113 North Fourth Avenue, V2G 2C8; 250-392-7404), rodeo and ranching history is the theme. Admission is $2.00, and children are free. They're open year-round Tuesday–Saturday, 11:00 A.M. to 4:00 P.M. in winter, and Monday–Saturday, 10:00 A.M. to 4:00 P.M. in summer. To experience the real thing, visit the city in late June when the famous **Williams Lake Stampede** (1-800-71-RODEO) is held.

As you drive farther north in the Cariboo, you have a chance to experience hands-on both the native history and the more modern gold rush history. First, at ◆ **Xats'ull Heritage Village** (Site 15, Comp. 2, RR 4, Williams Lake, V2G 4M8; 250-297-6323), 23 miles (37 km) north of Williams Lake near Soda Creek Reserve, you'll share aboriginal culture in a unique way. There are one-day programs (Tuesday, Thursday, and Saturday 10:00 A.M. to 4:00 P.M. from June to the fall) at Xats'ull (pronounced *hat-sool*), where you can learn tool-making, basket-making and traditional food preparation. Stay in teepees and reconstructed pit houses (*kekulis*) near the banks of the Fraser River, and become spiritually cleansed and rejuvenated in sweat lodges. Listen to traditional storytelling and discuss the old ways with Shuswap elders for an experience very different from any other you're likely to have in the Cariboo.

BRITISH COLUMBIA FACT

BC shares twenty-two border crossings with the United States.

The hands-on gold rush experience starts where the Fraser and **Quesnel** rivers meet, 74 miles (119 km) north of Williams Lake. From here, back in the 1860s, thousands of gold seekers left the Fraser and trekked east to historic Barkerville. Today, you can try gold panning in the Quesnel River, but phone the Gold Commissioner (250-992-4301) for details first, or you could unwittingly become a claim-jumper. At low water during the fall, you're most likely to strike it rich!

From Quesnel, a turnoff 3 miles (5 km) north at the junction of Highways 97 and 26 leads 55 miles (88 km) to ◆ **Barkerville** (Box 19, Barkerville, V0K 1B0; 250-994-3332), now fully restored and surely one of British Columbia's most remote, yet biggest tourist attractions. It's a walk back into those fascinating gold rush days of yore and is open 8:00 A.M. to 8:00 P.M. year-round. In summer (when admission is charged) all activities, from live theater to guided tours, are in full swing.

Between Wells and Barkerville on Highway 26, a 14-mile (23-km) road leads northeast to **Bowron Lake Provincial Park,** one of North America's premier canoeing circuits. Six major lakes connected by several smaller lakes (and a few portages!) provide solitude and scenery unsurpassed, with plenty of wildlife as well. Reservations are necessary—call (250) 992-3111. You could take the easy way out by staying at **Becker's Lodge** (342 Kinchant Street, Quesnel, V2J 2R4; 250-992-8864 or 1-800-808-4761; E-mail: beckers@awinc.com), where overnight cabins start at $55. There are also "elite packages," where for $475 Becker's will provide meals, tents, and lightweight, easy-portage canoes for five days—all you need to bring is your sleeping bag and toothbrush. Their home page (http://advnet.com/adv/beckers) explains meals, accommodation, and canoe rentals. BC Parks (540 Borland Street, Williams Lake, V2G 1R8; 250-398-4414) has detailed information on the park.

THE FREEDOM HIGHWAY

George Dalshaug started from the west, and Alf Bracewell pushed downwards from the east. It was the summer of 1953, and the folks in the Chilcotin were tired of hearing that it couldn't be done. They would show them. And show them they did. On September 26, 1953, Dalshaug and Bracewell touched bulldozer blades, shook hands, and BC's last frontier, the vast Chilcotin, was laid open. Today, the **Freedom Highway** (Highway 20) is a tribute to those stubborn souls who said it *could* be done.

From Williams Lake to the west coast at Bella Coola, you'll cover 288 miles (463 km), of which 178 miles (287 km) are paved. Without question, the section most talked about is ◆ **The Hill,** a 5.5-mile (9-km) series of gravel switchbacks (with grades to a nail-biting 18 percent) that descend through the 5,000-foot (1,524-m) Heckman Pass in **Tweedsmuir Provincial Park** (BC's largest) into the **Bella Coola Valley.** You might ask yourself why risk this baptism of fire? There are three answers.

The first is that the views in the Chilcotin of wide open spaces, crystal clear lakes, thick forested mountains, marshes and meadows, palettes of wildflowers, and the majestic Bella Coola Valley, home of the mythical thunderbird, are second to none. You're also likely to encounter wandering bears and head-knocking California bighorn sheep.

The second reason is the people you will meet: people who are not "chicken" to try a new venture, and who love their Chilcotin. People like the Christensens of **Anahim Lake,** who for more than 100 years—three generations of the family—have provided service as **A. C. Christensen General Merchants** (Box 3449, Christensen Road, Anahim Lake, V0L 1C0; 250-742-3266). Outside, the store is decorated with a mural of rearing stallions; inside the ceiling is studded with baseball caps from the four corners of the earth. The Christensen motto is: *If we don't have it, you don't need it.* Present owner Darcy Christensen gives a double-or-nothing guarantee with purchases. Flip a coin, and if you win, it costs nothing; if you lose—well, you did agree to double or nothing!

A detour south of **Tatla Lake** will bring you to **Chilko Lake** in **Ts'ylos Park.** Chilko Lake is the largest natural high-elevation freshwater lake in North America. Fishing enters a new realm here, with rainbow and Dolly Varden trout reaching 22 pounds (10 kg). You'll find exciting rafting on the Chilko River (featured in the Alan Alda movie *The White Mile*), with thrilling rapid drops that thunder through spectacular scenery, including one section through Lava Canyon that provides an adrenaline rush for 12 miles (19 km).

Contact **Chilko River Expeditions** (Box 4723, Williams Lake, V2G 2V7; 250-398-6711) and get set for a true wilderness rafting trip that will leave you exhilarated. Ts'yl-os (sounds like *sigh-loss*) Park is situated about 100 miles (160 km) west of Williams Lake and is one of BC's newest (1994) parks. Keep a sharp eye out for bald eagles and peregrine falcons.

At **Tatlayoko Lake** (south of Tatla Lake and north of Ts'yl-os Park), you'll meet folks like the Bracewells at Circle X Ranch. The family runs ◆ **Bracewell's Alpine Wilderness Adventures** (Box 1, Tatlayoko, V0L

1W0; 250-476-1169). They'll take you riding the ranges, and in the evening they may show you their home movies of Alf Bracewell's impressive road-building feat.

Nearer the coast, halfway between **Hagensborg** and **Bella Coola,** you'll meet people like Barb of ◆ **Barb's Pottery** (Box 363, Bella Coola, V0T 1C0, 250-799-5380). Barb's studio, where she creates lovely stoneware, raku, and porcelain pottery, is in an early 1900s log heritage building of a type constructed by Norwegian settlers who arrived in Bella Coola in 1894. Look for the ARTISAN sign on the highway.

The true meaning of the title "Freedom Highway" strikes you when you emerge from the lushly forested **Bella Coola Valley,** home of the Coast Salish Nuxalk Nation. The fresh ocean smells and dockside activity of Bella Coola at the head of Bentinck Arm are in total contrast with the dramatic pinnacles, blessed with names like Stupendous Mountain and Matterhorn Peak, so recently passed. Valleys, fjords, countless islands, and thousands of miles of wilderness coastline are waiting to be explored—such as the 29-mile (47-km) drive south from Bella Coola to South Bentinck Arm. At the **Big Cedar Tree Recreational Site,** you'll see the amazing tree (15 feet [5 m] in diameter) for which the site is named.

The third tongue-in-cheek reason for driving the Freedom Highway is that you can then honestly flaunt a bumper sticker (if they don't exist, they soon will) I SURVIVED THE HILL!

The **South Cariboo Chamber of Commerce** (422 South Cariboo Highway 97, Box 2312, 100 Mile House, V0K 2E0; 250-395-5353; E-mail: sccofc@netshop.net) has prepared a two-page pamphlet on Highway 20 (*The Chilcotin–Highway 20 Guide*) outlining services and interesting spots along the road.

And finally, if you're reluctant to retrace your steps back over that awesome hill, consider booking a passage aboard **BC Ferries.** Ships leave from Bella Coola every two days from June to September (early morning) on a fourteen to twenty-four hour sail (depending on stops). You'll land in Port Hardy, from which you can drive the length of Vancouver Island to Victoria. Expect to pay approximately $110 for an adult (children half-fare) and $220 for your vehicle. Phone 1-888-BCFERRY from anywhere in British Columbia, or (604) 669-1211 for information. Their Web page at http://bcferries.bc.ca/ferries is comprehensive.

WHERE TO STAY:

1. **River-Side Bed and Breakfast** (562 Summer Street, Lillooet, Box 1000, V0K 1V0; 250-256-4477). From $45.
2. **59 Mile Bed and Breakfast/Arctic Artists Gallery** (Box 518, Clinton, V0K 1K0; 250-459-7076). From $50.
3. **Little Horse Lodge** (North Green Lake Road, Comp 1, Site E, RR 1, 70 Mile House, V0K 2K0; 250-456-7524). Cabins from $50. Campsites $9.50. Canoe rentals $30/day. Restaurant.
4. **Whistle Stop Bed and Breakfast** (Lot 2, Garrett Road, C9 McMillan Road, RR 1, Lone Butte, V0K 1X0; 250-395-2170). $50 double.
5. **The Hills Health and Guest Ranch** (Box 26, 108 Mile Ranch, V0K 2Z0; 250-791-5225; E-mail: thehills@netshop.net).
6. **Rowat's Waterside Bed and Breakfast** (1397 Borland Drive, Williams Lake, V2G 1M3; 250-392-7395).

WHERE TO EAT:

1. **Elaine's Coffee Garden** (824 Main Street, Lillooet V0K 1V0; 250-256-4633. A lunch bar serving soups, salads, bunwiches, ice creams, desserts.
2. **Hat Creek Ranch** (Box 878 Cache Creek, V0K 1H0; 1-800-782-0922 or 250-457-9722). Corner of Highways 97 and 99. Lunches $7.00.
3. **Ashcroft Manor Teahouse** (Box 127, Cache Creek, V0K 1H0; 250-453-9983). At junction of Trans-Canada Highway and turnoff to Ashcroft. Accommodations (from $58) also available seasonally.
4. **Friends** (Lakeside Inn, Highway 97, 100 Mile House, V0K 2E0; 250-395-4005). Breakfast, lunch, and dinner.
5. **Eddy's** (opposite the car dealerships at the Greyhound Bus Depot in Williams Lake). 6:00 A.M. to 9:00 P.M., seven days a week; (250) 398-8334. Great chicken burgers and homemade fries.
6. **The Bentinck Arms Pub** at **The Bay Motor Hotel** (Box 216, Bella Coola, V0T 1C0; 250-982-2212 or 1-888-982-2212 toll free). On Highway 20 in Hagensborg, 9 miles (14 km) east of Bella Coola. Patio cafe and coffee shop. Free shuttle to ferry terminal or airport. Accommodations also (from $59).

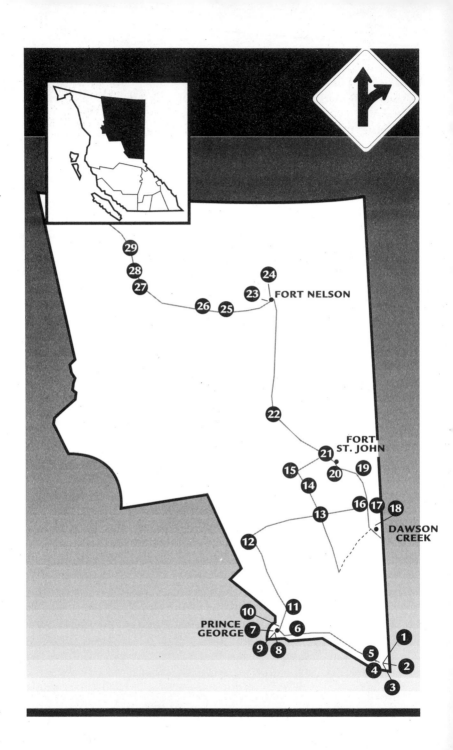

FORT NELSON

FORT
ST. JOHN

DAWSON
CREEK

PRINCE
GEORGE

THE NORTHEAST

1. Culp's farm
2. Hill's General Store
3. Terri's Attempts
4. Mountain Pottery
5. Another Roadside Attraction
6. Strider Adventures
7. The Taj
8. Prince George Native Art and Friendship Centre
9. Fraser–Fort George Regional Museum
10. Huble Homestead
11. Gitscome Portage Trail
12. Morfee Mountain
13. Chetwynd chain-saw sculptures
14. Peace Canyon Dam
15. Hudson's Hope Museum
16. Mile Zero, Alaska Highway
17. Alaska Cafe
18. Red Roof Bed and Breakfast
19. Fort St. John–North Peace Museum
20. Anna's Deli
21. Charlie Lake Provincial Park
22. Pink Mountain
23. Canadian Chopstick Manufacturing Company
24. Old Fort
25. Flower Springs Lake Trail
26. Stone Mountain Provincial Park
27. Muncho Lake
28. Northern Rockies/Highland Glen Lodge
29. Liard River Hot Springs

THE NORTHEAST

Only since the completion of the Alaska Highway in 1942 has even a scant section of this huge, beautiful region been accessible to tourists. From the Yellowhead/Trans-Canada Highway junction at Tête Jaune Cache, we'll follow the Fraser River northwest to Prince George, British Columbia's fourth largest city. From here, we'll head to the big skies of the Peace River district and Dawson Creek, where we'll tackle the legendary Alaska Highway to the Yukon border. In total we'll travel more than 930 miles (1,500 km) through some of the most spectacular scenery the province has to offer.

FOLLOWING THE FRASER TO PRINCE GEORGE

About twenty minutes northwest of Tête Jaune Cache on Highway 16 there's an easily missed sign to **Dunster.** Go down the hill and just after a one-lane Bailey bridge, take the first right to the end of the road. Another right and you're at ◆ **Bonnie and Curtis Culp's farm;** perhaps just follow the smell of the wool. Peacocks, llamas and crossbred Rocky Mountain sheep roam near antique sheep wagons built for herders 100 years ago. The Culps have redecorated the wagons to start (soon, they hope) a unique bed-and-breakfast business. The double beds are covered with Bonnie's quilts filled with wool from their sheep. Some wagons have wood stoves, and all are decorated and repainted in their original brilliant colors by the Culp's daughter Kitty. Take a tour of Bonnie's quilt-making studio above the farmhouse, where quilts can be ordered, and knitting wool is for sale. If prearranged, meals can be served. Write **Robson Valley Wools** (Station Road, Dunster, V0J 1J0; 250–968–4309) for information.

Back on the road into Dunster, drive for a mile or so to ◆ **Hill's General Store** (250–968–4488). Since 1973, Claude and Lilly Hill have sold everything and anything in this eclectic grocery-cum-post-office-cum-hardware store. It's the epicenter for a community of about 150 families who ranch, farm, log, and create in this quiet rural area. Ask Claude about the **Dunster Farmers' Market,** held in the parking lot of the Community Hall most Saturday mornings in August and September. Across the street from the store is the old **Dunster Train Station,** one of the last of the original CNR train stations built in the early 1900s.

FUR OUT FRIENDLINESS

An old black car sat abandoned in a field, a television propped on its hood. Curious, I stopped at the nearby Dunster store and met Claude Hill. He's loved this Robson Valley since he came here hunting in the sixties, and has worked at everything from logging to highway construction. But he's "never looked back" since he picked up the store in 1973.

"It's a fantastic community," he enthused, between selling eggs and stamping mail.

He told me of a board game called *Fur Out,* for "Ages 10–110" invented by trappers Rod and Deb Reimer.

"A whole bunch of us invested, thinking we had the new *Trivia,*" he joked.

When I left Hill's Store, Claude was explaining how he was happily anchored to this neat community.

"Someone will always need a rat trap, so you can't go away," he said with a laugh, insistently tucking a game of *Fur Out* under my arm.

Continue south on gravel road watching on the right for ◆ **Terri's Attempts** (Box 20, Dunster, V0J 1J0; 250-968-4468). Terri creates dream catchers and other craft items, including Nasty Drafts, bunnies that lie on window sills to keep cold drafts out—a different kind of draft dodger from those rumored to have settled in the valley in the seventies.

Seven and a half miles (12 km) from Dunster is an area called South Croydon. Here a heritage building, formerly a post office, houses the **Bear's Lair,** a studio for artists Bill and Susan Metcalf. A few hundred yards on at the foot of the Old South Croydon Ferry Road, is ◆ **Mountain Pottery** (250-968-4310), where Steficia McLean's studio bulges with aesthetic, handcrafted stoneware. It's an unlikely discovery on a sheep farm set in the fertile Robson Valley.

If you have a four-wheel-drive vehicle, you might want to drive farther south and try your luck at hooking a few rainbow trout in Shere Lake. It's about 14 miles (23 km) from Dunster. If not, head back through Dunster to the highway and drop in to Kitty Culp's ◆ **Another Roadside Attraction** (250-968-4308), possibly the cutest toy store in BC. It's at Read Road and Highway 16, a few hundred yards northwest of the Dunster turnoff. Look for Kitty's large wooden bears on the east side

Another Roadside Attraction, Dunster

of the highway. She makes children's furniture and also sells hats, quilts, and other gifts. The toys are from all over: pull-toys, ocarinas, German Ferris wheels, wind-up VWs, tin motorbikes with sidecars, puppets, and Kitty's own painted wooden Punch and Judy theaters, all waiting to tickle your memory buttons.

There are few services on the lonely Yellowhead Highway after **McBride,** about 18 miles (30 km) north of Dunster, and as Prince George is another 125 miles (202 km), make sure you're fully gassed up. The McBride Chamber of Commerce (100 Robson Center, Box 2, McBride, V0J 2E0; 250-569-3366) has information on restaurants and accommodation.

PRINCE GEORGE

Prince George (P.G. to Prince Georgians) has all the amenities of a modern city. With a population of almost seventy-seven thousand, the city enjoys first class live theater, its own symphony orchestra, a university, and modern museums and art galleries. But with 1,500 lakes in the area and 120 parks in the city alone, P.G. has managed to maintain a laid-back, northern atmosphere.

You'll see what I mean if you have a day or two to spend, and set off with ◆ **Strider Adventures** (RR 1, Site 24, Comp. 7, Prince George, V2N 2H8; 1-800-665-7752 or 250-963-9542; E-mail: strider@pgweb.com). You'll be packing out onto alpine trails with calm, inquisitive llamas on either day hikes or two-, three-, five-, and seven-day camping adventures. The llamas do all the work; you just have to walk and enjoy the scent of the wild-flowers and superb scenery. The turnoff to Strider's Adventures is at the Willow River and Upper Fraser sign on the Yellowhead Highway, 10 miles (16 km) east of the Yellowhead Bridge in Prince George. Take the first turn right for 2 miles (3 km) to an A-frame at 17075 East Perry Road. Rates are in the $100-$150 per day range, but phone, or check Dan and Dorothy's Web page (http://www.pgweb.com/strider).

In the city there are some good eating places. A curry is probably a good filler after all that fresh air, and the Indian food at ◆ **The Taj** (455 Quebec Street, 250-561-0803) is superb. It's open evenings daily, and the entree prices are very reasonable.

Along with plenty of places to eat goes plenty of places to stay. Prince George is *bed-and-breakfast city,* with many centrally located homes to choose from. Two hot-line phone numbers, (250) 561-BEDS and (250) 562-2222, will link you to most of the bed and breakfasts in P.G. I found **Adrienne's** (1467 Fraser Crescent, 250-561-2086), a pleasant base while seeing the sights of P.G. Rates are from $40 to $50. It's close to the city, but phone to get easy directions.

One of the sights I took in was the **Prince George Art Gallery** (2820 Fifteenth Avenue, V2M 1T1; 250-563-6447), which has displays of local and other British Columbia art. A new, futuristic-looking gallery will be opened in late 1998 next to the Civic Centre plaza opposite Connaught Hill Park (a good spot for a view of the city). The gallery is open Monday-Saturday from 10:00 A.M. to 5:00 P.M. and Sundays from 1:00–5:00 P.M., but it's closed Mondays in winter. If you're more interested in native arts and crafts, try the ◆ **Prince George Native Art and Friendship Centre.** Here you can also learn some native history. It's at 144 George Street, V2L 1P9; (250) 562-7385 (near First Avenue).

If you're still feeling historically inclined, visit **Fort George Park** on the banks of the Fraser River, and the ◆ **Fraser–Fort George Regional Museum** (333 Twentieth Avenue, 250-562-1612). This is where the original Hudson's Bay Trading Post was located. Displays give a good overview of the area's history, and as well there's a hands-on **Northwoods Explorations Gallery.** The Discovery Boxes here are educational and fun for the kids. In summer a small steam train gives rides. It's open daily from 10:00 A.M. to 5:00 P.M. May 15 to September 15, and noon to 5:00 P.M. Monday–Saturday off-season.

There's lots more to do in P.G., so to let you in on their secrets, **Tourism Prince George** has set up two offices—one on the corner of Victoria Street and Fifteenth Avenue (250-562-3700) and a summer site (250-563-5493) at the junction of Highways 16 and 97. Outside the Prince George area call 1-800-668-7646.

NORTH TO PEACE RIVER COUNTRY

From Prince George we leave the Fraser River and cross the Nechako River past thinning suburbs and rolling farmlands along the John Hart Highway (97 North). Twenty-five miles (40 km) north is the ◆ **Huble Homestead,** now part of a regional park. In 1900, a trapper named Albert Huble operated a trading post from here. The business became a regular stop for steamboats running the Fraser River to Tête Jaune Cache. Today, the steamboats are gone, but Huble Homestead is a historic site and a popular hiking area. To get there follow the signs from the highway for 4 miles (6 km) along Mitchell Road. Daily tours are held mid-May to October. Contact Regional District of Fraser–Fort George (987 Fourth Avenue, Prince George, V2L 3H7; 250-563-9225) for more information.

From the homestead, a pleasant hike that follows the Pacific and Arctic watershed divide, the ◆ **Gitscome Portage Trail,** runs for 5 miles (8.5 km) northwest to a pull-out on Highway 97.

Ninety-eight miles (158 km) north of Prince George on Highway 97, there's a turnoff to Mackenzie on the shores of **Williston Lake,** North America's largest man-made reservoir. A 2-mile (3-km) drive north of town takes you up ◆ **Morfee Mountain** for a spectacular view of the lake through the unpolluted crystalline air of the Rockies. Mackenzie was named for fur trader and explorer Alexander Mackenzie, who camped nearby in 1793 during his historic journey to Bella Coola on the coast. The town is a pulp, paper, and lumber manufacturing center, which doesn't sound too attractive, but it does mean there

> # BRITISH COLUMBIA FACT
>
> BC's time zones: Pacific Time in the west; Mountain Time in the east.

are countless logging roads to access the multitude of rivers and lakes. It's also home to the world's largest **tree crusher** (177 tons [160 metric tons]) sitting in state on Mackenzie Boulevard. Contact the Chamber of Commerce (Box 880, Mackenzie, V0J 2C0; 250-997-4497) year-round, or drop into the Travel InfoCentre (250-997-5459), open from May to September at the junction of Highways 97 and 39.

The next town traveling northeast along Highway 97 is Chetwynd, 190 miles (306 km) north of Prince George. It's here that you decide whether to go north to Fort St. John via the **Bennett Dam,** or east via Dawson Creek. The former is very scenic, following the Peace River to join the Alaska Highway 8 miles (13 km) past Fort St. John. The latter is slightly longer but will take you to Mile Zero of the Alaska Highway.

While in Chetwynd try out the wave pool or take a walk around to search out the ◆ **Chetwynd chain-saw sculptures.** After being greeted by three huge bears at the entrance, you may want to see more of the two dozen or so carvings that decorate the town. Ask at the **Chamber of Commerce** (North Access Road, Box 1000, Chetwynd, V0C 1J0; 250-788-3345), for a brochure showing their locations.

The drive northwest from Chetwynd along Highway 29 passes Moberly Lake and the ◆ **Peace Canyon Dam** (250-783-9943). Drop in at the dam's visitors center (open mid-May to October daily from 8:00 A.M. to 4:00 P.M., but only on weekdays in winter) to learn of dinosaur evidence discovered when the Peace River was dammed. You'll see two life-size dinosaurs and some photographic displays of the building of the dam.

If you're still interested in dams, 14 miles (23 km) upstream from the Peace Canyon Dam is the **W.A.C. Bennett Dam** (250-783-5211), an enormous structure (1.2 miles [2 km] wide) constructed from glacial moraine left over from the last Ice Age. This damming formed the 225-mile-long (362-km) Williston Lake, which took a whole five years to fill. Take the Dam Access Road just west of Hudson's Hope and drive along good road for 15 miles (24 km). Tours of the dam are held daily in summer from 9:30 A.M. to 4:30 P.M. and weekdays in winter.

If you enjoy looking at fossils, the ◆ **Hudson's Hope Museum** (10506 105th Avenue, 250-783-5735), housed in a turn-of-the-century Hudson's Bay Company store in Heritage Park opposite the InfoCentre (250-783-9154) has a great collection. It's beside the highway near the dam access road. **St. Peter's Church,** built in 1938, is next door. It's of log construction, very small, and quite beautiful.

Stop off on this pretty 55-mile (88-km) drive between Hudson's Hope and Fort St. John along the banks of the **Peace River** and cast a line for rainbow trout, arctic grayling, Dolly Varden, or northern pike. And keep the camera handy, as the views of the island-stippled Peace River are lovely. The road twists and bends steeply as it approaches Fort St. John.

Should you choose the southern route from Chetwynd, 62 miles (100 km) to Dawson Creek, you'll cross the Pine River at the entrance to the **East Pine Provincial Park,** a nice picnic spot, where you can cast for a fish or launch your boat.

But there's yet another side trip to consider before starting the journey north along the Alaska Highway.

A mile or so east of Chetwynd, Highway 29 South leads to **Tumbler Ridge,** home of the world's largest open pit coal mine. Incorporated as recently as 1981, the town prides itself on having the lowest crime rate in BC and the province's highest average family income. Its two large coal mines produce annual exports of $500 million. In BC's history, Tumbler Ridge is its largest single industrial undertaking. But it's not all industry—far from it.

En route to Tumbler Ridge, you'll pass two parks, **Sukunka Falls Provincial Park** and **Gwillim Lake Provincial Park** (250-787-3407), the latter with first-rate camping facilities and miles of wilderness blue-lake shoreline to explore. Twelve miles (20 km) south of the park (42 miles [68 km] south of Chetwynd), is the **Bullmoose Mine** (250-242-4702), where from mid-June to late August, ninety-minute mine tours are held every Tuesday and Thursday at 10:00 A.M. The town of Tumbler Ridge is 23 miles (37 km) south of the mine. But the jewel of the area is even farther south.

BRITISH COLUMBIA TRIVIA

Down near Dawson Creek is a village called Pouce Coupe. This means *cut thumb* in French, but the origins of the village's name are vague, ranging from a story of a French *voyageur* who cut his thumb skinning a buffalo, to that of a Sekanni trapper who lost a digit in a gun accident, to meaning *an abandoned chief's lodge by a deserted beaver dam* in the Beaver language. Whatever the origin, the area is rich with rustic views and colorful grainfields.

Monkman Provincial Park is a 79,000-acre (32,000-ha) wilderness park, where the 210-feet-high (64-m) **Kinuseo Falls** provides fantastic photographic opportunities, especially in winter when the falls freeze over—offering an unforgettable snowmobile adventure. In summer, jet boats take tourists up the Murray River to visit this unspoiled wonder, which is higher than Niagara Falls. If you don't mind a little gravel under your tires (about 30 miles [45 km] of it, in fact), an industrial road leads from Tumbler Ridge to **Kinuseo Falls Campground** (250-787-3407) from which you can hike a trail to the falls viewing platform. The thunderous sounds and spray are incredible. Contact the **Tumbler Ridge InfoCentre and Chamber of Commerce** on Southgate Road (Box 606, Tumbler Ridge, V0C 2W0; 250-242-4702) for information.

A mostly unpaved road (Highway 52 North) heads 60 miles (98 km) northeast from Tumbler Ridge to Arras, where you rejoin Highway 97, 10 miles (17 km) west of Dawson Creek.

THE ALASKA HIGHWAY: DAWSON CREEK TO FORT NELSON

The **Alaska Highway** has its official beginning in **Dawson Creek;** hence, the popular thing to do there is to have your photo taken at the ◆ **Mile Zero Alaska Highway** post. The InfoCentre (250-782-9595) is right next door in the **Railway Station Museum** at 900 Alaska Avenue. Check on Alaska Highway driving conditions and information there.

In March 1942, Dawson Creek's population went from about 500 to 10,000 in a few short days when the United States military started arriving in droves. Eight months and three weeks later, the highway was officially opened, an amazing feat, considering that the distance covered was 1,421 miles (2,288 km), and it traversed impossible terrain to its end in Fairbanks, Alaska. Today, the Canadian and Yukon governments spend about $40 million annually on its maintenance and reconstruction. Although a thousand times better than when first opened to the public in 1948, patience and a good spares kit are still key ingredients to enjoying the **Alaska Highway.**

Before hitting the highway, you'll find a decent meal at the ◆ **Alaska Cafe** (250-782-7040), housed in the quaint **Dew Drop Inn** at 10209 Tenth Avenue. The menu is varied, not too expensive, and very tasty.

And for a down-on-the-farm place to stay, the ◆ **Red Roof Bed and Breakfast** (Box 524, Pouce Coupe, 250-786-5581), is a perfect choice. It's about twenty minutes toward the Alberta border from Dawson Creek in a picturesque valley surrounded by lush green fields. Contact the **Pouce Coupe InfoCentre** (Box 190, Pouce Coupe, V0C 2C0; 250-786-5555 or 786-5794 off-season) for more information on this pioneer community.

The city of **Fort St. John** is 45 miles (73 km) north of Dawson Creek and is the site of the first nonnative settlement on the British Columbia mainland. (It started with twelve men, four women, and five children!) In 1793, Alexander Mackenzie marked it as an excellent fur-trading center during his journey to the coast. There's a monument to him in Centennial Park on Mackenzie Street. But it was the **Alaska Highway** (then the Alcan Military Road) that in the early forties caused Fort St. John's great growth spurt. Discovery of oil and gas south of the city in 1951 was the icing on the cake for this *Energy Capital of BC*. The ◆ **Fort St. John–North Peace Museum InfoCentre** complex (Ninety-third Avenue and 100th Street, 250-787-0430) behind the 150-foot-high (46-m) oil derrick has all the information and history on this thriving city that you'll need to know. Nearby, there's healthful light food at ◆ **Anna's Deli** in the Totem Mall (9600 Ninety-third Avenue, 250-785-9741).

BRITISH COLUMBIA FACT

BC has 26,409 miles (42,500 km) of public highways.

About 4 miles (7 km) north of Fort St. John is the ◆ **Charlie Lake Provincial Park.** Archaeological findings from caves here show evidence of huge bison having occupied the area. A 10,500-year-old bead was found here, thought to be the oldest evidence of human adornment in North America. You can see a replica on display in the museum complex.

Between Fort St. John and Fort Nelson, you have only the scenery and the occasional moose or caribou to entertain you for 240 miles

(387 km). It's these long, desolate stretches that give the Alaska Highway its mystery and magic, and occasionally its boredom. After **Wonowon** (at Mile 101 of the Alaska Highway!) the road follows the Blueberry River through densely forested areas as it slowly climbs to 3,600 feet (1,100 m) at **Pink Mountain,** the halfway point between Dawson Creek and Fort Nelson. Services here include **Mae's Kitchen/Ed's Garage** (at Mile 143, 250-772-3215), a restaurant, garage, motel combo, and **Pink Mountain Campsite** (at Mile 147, 250-774-1033). You'll often see wildlife, mainly moose, on the roadside around here.

A little-known side trip at Mile 147, west on Road 192 for 10 miles (16 km) brings you to a summer road that ascends to a communications tower and lookout at ◆ **Pink Mountain.** The lowlands to the north and west sides of the mountain are the only areas in the province where you are likely to see wild Plains bison.

The Alaska Highway descends steeply down **Suicide Hill** into the Beatton River Valley and drops to 1,383 feet (411 m) near **Fort Nelson,** the lowest point on the Alaska Highway. Here long, hot summers and excellent soil provide good growing conditions. It's not unusual to hear of forty-pound cabbages.

But gigantic vegetables aren't the only "biggests" that Fort Nelson has to boast. Its most unusual is probably the world's largest chopstick plant. Nine million pairs of chopsticks are produced daily at the Japanese-owned ◆ **Canadian Chopstick Manufacturing Company.** It's also home to North America's largest gas processing plant (complete with ugly storage tanks) and a big plywood/sawmill operation. Despite all the industry, there are still a few hundred fur trappers in the area, working mostly as their ancestors have done for centuries.

After so many miles on the road, you might want to wash up at the **Coachouse Inn** (4711 Fiftieth Avenue South, Box 27, Fort Nelson, V0C 1R0; 250-774-3911). Rates are from $60, and it's open year-round. The restaurant at the inn serves fair-sized tasty meals at moderate prices. Comfortable bed-and-breakfast accommodation is available at **Home on the Hill Bed and Breakfast** (5612 Fifty-first Street, Box 1689, Fort Nelson, V0C 1R0; 250-774-3000), with rooms year-round at $40 and $50.

Locals assured me that the best meal in town could be had at the **Fort Nelson Flight Centre,** located by the airport. It originally catered only to airline personnel, but word of the scrumptious food hit the airwaves, and the rest is history. Homemade soups, breads, sandwiches, and desserts are eaten in a small room just like at home, with the kitchen right there. Coffee is always "on," and drinks are located in the refrigerator, from which you can help yourself. Talk to the locals, read a book from the shelf, or play one of the games provided in this laid-back atmosphere.

For those wanting to find out more about these offbeat spots and the many hiking areas near Fort Nelson, or do tours of the chopsticks factory and the gas processing plant, information is available at the **Fort Nelson Travel InfoCentre,** located in the Recreation Centre on the highway at the west end of town. Write Bag Service 399, Fort Nelson, V0C 1R0; (250) 774-6400 (summer) or 774-2541 in winter.

They may or may not tell you about the ◆ **Old Fort,** an exciting place not only to visit, but also getting to this site of the original Fort Nelson is an adventure in itself. You'll need a four-wheel-drive vehicle, though. The trip takes about an hour, and the road is either extremely muddy when wet or very bumpy when dry. It isn't plowed in winter and is often merely a track. So you are warned!

To get there, take the road to the Helmut Oil Field, just south of the Husky station in Muskwa Heights on the southern outskirts of town. Cross a rickety rail bridge (controlled by a traffic light) and drive until the road forks at a gas-line pumping station (about twenty minutes). Follow a rough road straight to the Old Fort. In winter, access is by an ice bridge across the river. Once there, explore the settlers' first church, now abandoned, and the rectory and graveyard behind it. I've heard that the only ghost in the Fort Nelson area is the one haunting the basement of this church. A couple of families still live in the vicinity, so respect their homes while you explore.

FORT NELSON TO THE YUKON BORDER

As you travel west from Fort Nelson, you'll start to get the feeling of the true North, of its strength, its freedom, and its beauty. There are 326 miles (525 km) of diverse and spectacular scenery ahead of you between Fort Nelson and Watson Lake in the Yukon, so get ready for a little visual ecstasy.

To appreciate the North is to enjoy the outdoors. The ◆ **Flower Springs Lake Trail** takes you up almost 1,000 feet (300 meters) for 3 miles (5 km), hiking through breathtaking scenery along the North Tetsa River, past waterfalls to Flower Springs Lake, looking brilliantly blue in an alpine setting. To get there take the Alaska Highway about 100 miles (160 km) west from Fort Nelson to **Summit Lake Lodge.** About 100 yards past the lodge there's a left turn, which is an access road to a microwave tower. Keep an eye out for moose, mountain caribou, stone sheep, and grizzly bears. Stone Mountain is visible across the valley. A drive up to the tower (about thirty minutes) will give you a spectacular view of the park.

Either before or after your hike, you may want to stop at the cafe at the highway turnoff where they make wonderful homemade chili and bread, and huge "bear" burgers. These are highly recommended by Fort Nelsonites, who aren't too sure if it really is bear meat but love them just the same. If you have more time and really want to explore ◆ **Stone Mountain Provincial Park,** there's a list of outfitters available at the Fort Nelson InfoCentre willing to share their knowledge of the park and hoodoo-filled **Wokkpash Recreation Area** adjoining the southwestern limit of Stone Mountain Park. These hoodoos (pillars caused by erosion) reach heights of 100 feet (30 meters) and give the area

> # BRITISH COLUMBIA FACT
>
> BC's population of black bears is estimated at 120,000 to 160,000.

an otherworldly aura. There are a couple of close-by hoodoos along a short trail just west of the Summit Lake Campground. Ask at the lodge or campground for directions.

Your first vision (the word "view" is too tame) of ◆ **Muncho Lake** will leave you (as it left me in 1980) speechless. I now have to take a deep breath before turning that special corner when I know a lake so blue-green and clear, surrounded by snow-covered Rocky Mountains at their awe-inspiring best, will be revealed. The jade color comes from reflection and refraction of light on the suspended sediments brought into the lake by glacial melt water, but if you prefer, simply enjoy the beauty unhindered by explanations. Keep your eye out for stone sheep (a southern subspecies of Dall sheep) and woodland caribou, attracted to the salt left on roadsides after winter maintenance.

At Mile 462 of the Alaska Highway, the new ◆ **Northern Rockies Lodge** is the largest log building in British Columbia. Sitting right by Muncho Lake, it has a 45-foot (13-m) stone fireplace that dominates a European-style restaurant. Together with the older ◆ **Highland Glen Lodge,** there are a total of forty units. A campground, R.V. Park, boat rentals, and other facilities are available. Owners Marianne and Urs Schildknecht will organize complete package holidays whether you're into fishing, photography, or mere sight-seeing. Urs has bush-piloted in the area for almost twenty years; with their own float-planes (Liard Air) the Schildknechts can help you explore a large part of this magnificent area. Write Box 8, Muncho Lake, V0C

1Z0; (250) 776-3481, fax (250) 776-3482, or 1-800-663-5269 for reservations. Lodge prices start at $60.

After leaving Muncho Lake, 16 miles (27 km) on is ◆ **Liard River Hot Springs,** another spot worthy of waxing poetic. Not only are the waters intensely hot and soothing, but there are some interesting organisms living here that can be found nowhere else in BC, including the tiny Plains forktail damselfly. There's also a small snail called the hotwater physa, which is unique to these waters. The two pools, Alpha and Beta, are a pleasant stroll along a 760-yard boardwalk (originally built by U.S. servicemen) from the parking lot near the campground. On your walk check the steamy bogs for little lake chub darting about, and several species of orchids, lobelias, cow parsnips, and ostrich ferns. It's almost tropical! In fact it's hard to believe that not far from here at Smith River, the province's coldest temperature was recorded in 1947, a chilling −74°F (−58.9°C).

Cold or not, there is nothing quite like a winter stop at Liard River Hot Springs. Not only are there fewer people, but it's also comical watching hair turn into spaghetti, as the steam combines with bitter cold air, aging each thread into hoarfrost. The first pool you come to is tiered, with each tier a slightly different temperature water that then runs off in a stream. Take care though, as the waters are so hot (from 100-120°F [38-49°C]) that you can easily become hyperthermic before realizing it. The recommended times for immersion are fifteen to twenty minutes. The second, deeper, cooler pool is another ten- to fifteen-minute walk through the lush vegetation, but it is well worth it. Occasionally moose and black bears come to the pools to graze on the aquatic vegetation, so take particular care. A resident park naturalist is a great source of knowledge about the flora and fauna in the area and offers summer hikes. Don't miss the **hanging gardens,** which can be viewed from the boardwalk, just past Alpha pool.

A couple of lodges nearby provide rustic accommodation. **Trapper Ray's Liard Hotsprings Lodge** (Mile 497, Liard River, V1G 4J8; 250-776-7349), is a log building with campground, R.V. Park, and attached cafe. It's open year-round. **Lower Liard River Lodge** (Mile 496, Alaska Highway, Box 9, Muncho Lake, V0C 1Z0; 250-776-7341) also provides very friendly service. The **Liard River Hot Springs Provincial Park Campground** is just east of the 500-mile signpost. Phone 1-800-689-9025 for reservations.

The Alaska Highway straddles the BC-Yukon border passing through Watson Lake and Upper Liard before it meets the Stewart-Cassiar Highway, which we will explore in the next chapter.

WHERE TO STAY:

1. **Adrienne's Bed and Breakfast** (1467 Fraser Crescent, Prince George, V2M 3Y4; 250-561-2086).
2. **Red Roof Bed and Breakfast** (Box 524, Pouce Coupe, V0C 2C0; 250-786-5581).
3. **Pink Mountain Campsite** (Mile 143-TG96, Alaska Highway, Pink Mountain, V0C 2B0; 250-774-1033). Gas, diesel, and propane available. Liquor store. Cabins. Year-round.
4. **Home on the Hill Bed and Breakfast** (5612 Fifty-first Street, Box 1689, Fort Nelson, V0C 1R0; 250-774-3000).
5. **Northern Rockies/Highland Glen Lodge and Restaurant** (Box 8, Muncho Lake, V0C 1Z0; 250-776-3481, fax 250-776-3482 or 1-800 -663-5269 for reservations). Lodge prices start at $60.
6. **Lower Liard River Lodge** (Mile 496, Alaska Highway, Box 9, Muncho Lake, V0C 1Z0; 250-776-7341).

WHERE TO EAT:

1. **The Taj** (1310 Fifth Avenue, Prince George, V2L 3L4; 250-561-0803). Moderate prices. Curries.
2. **Rosels** (1624 Seventh Avenue, Prince George, V2L 3P6; 250-562-4972). Corner of Vancouver Street. Fine dining; lunch 11:00 A.M. to 3:00 P.M.; dinner from 5:00 P.M.
3. **Anna's Deli** (9600 Ninety-third Avenue, Fort St. John, V1J 5Z2; 250-785-9741). In the Totem Mall near the InfoCentre. Serves appetizing sandwiches. Inexpensive.
4. **Alaska Hotel, Cafe and Pub** (10209 Tenth Avenue, Dawson Creek, V1G 4G7; 250-782-7040 [cafe], 782-7998 [hotel]). At the Dew Drop Inn. Moderately priced.
5. **Mae's Kitchen** (Box 35 TG, Pink Mountain, Mile 147, Alaska Highway, V0C 2B0; 250-772-3215). Roadside homemade bread, pies; nonsmoking.
6. **Trapper Ray's Liard Hotsprings Lodge and Cafe** (Mile 497-TG96, Alaska Highway, V1G 4J8; 250-776-7349). Year-round.

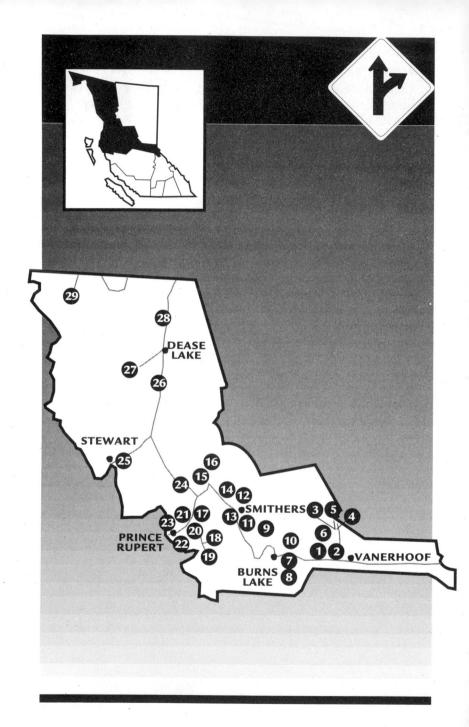

THE NORTHWEST

1. Vanderhoof Bird Sanctuary
2. OK Café
3. Big Bay Bed and Breakfast
4. Mt. Pope
5. Fort St. James National Historic Site
6. Tannis Gold
7. Darter's Misty Willow Bed and Breakfast
8. Likkel's Lakeside Store and Resort
9. Fulton River Salmon Project
10. Eveneshen Nature Trail
11. Telkwa
12. Stork Nest Inn
13. Berg's Valley Tours Bed and Breakfast
14. Moricetown Canyon
15. 'Ksan Model Village
16. Bent Box Native Arts Gallery
17. Kleanza Creek Provincial Park
18. Kitimat Centennial Museum
19. Violet Patch Bed and Breakfast
20. Mount Layton Hotsprings Resort
21. Northern Light Studio and Gardens
22. North Pacific Cannery Village Museum
23. Cowpuccino's Coffee House
24. Kitwanga Fort National Historic Site
25. Bear Glacier
26. Red Goat Lodge
27. Telegraph Creek
28. Mighty Moe's
29. MV *Tarahne*

THE NORTHWEST

This region, approximately one-third of British Columbia, ranges from the rolling plains of the interior plateau west of Prince George, follows the Yellowhead Highway past myriad fishing lakes and the haunting totems of First Nations' villages to the smell of the sea at Prince Rupert. It then heads north along the Stewart–Cassiar Highway, past the stirring Bear Glacier and the Grand Canyon of the Stikine, to the Yukon border.

VANDERHOOF–BULKLEY VALLEY

The big-city feel of Prince George is replaced by open country and ranches along the banks of the Nechako River, as Yellowhead Highway 16 heads to **Vanderhoof,** 60 miles (98 km) west. Vanderhoof began as a railway town for the Grand Trunk Pacific Railway, but today it's more a gathering-hole for loggers and ranchers—it's the kind of town where trucks sport bumper stickers such as the one I saw declaring BEATEN PATHS ARE FOR BEATEN MEN.

Most travelers rush through Vanderhoof, unaware that on the northern edge of town, the ◆ **Vanderhoof Bird Sanctuary,** bordering 3 miles (5 km) of the Nechako River, swarms with migrating birds, notably Canada geese. To find out more, contact the Nechako Valley Sporting Association (Box 1077, Vanderhoof, V0J 3A0) or the **InfoCentre** (Box 126, Vanderhoof, V0J 3A0; 250–567–2124) on Burrard Street, one block north of the highway.

Learn Vanderhoof's history at the reconstructed **Heritage Village Museum** (250–567–2991) where costumed waiters in the ◆ **OK Café** (250–567–2594) serve reasonably priced food. It's on the highway as you head west out of town.

FORT ST. JAMES

As you leave Vanderhoof, look for the **buffaloes** grazing at the Fort St. James turnoff. Historic **Fort St. James** is 34 miles (54 km) north along Highway 27; it's a "don't miss" area.

Just before entering Fort St. James, visit **Paarens Beach Provincial Park** and, a little farther on, **Sowchea Bay Park.** Take Sowchea Bay Road just before the bridge over the Stuart River. The campsites on the beach all have excellent views across 62-mile-long (100-km) Stuart Lake. Just before the Sowchea Bay Park entrance, on the corner of Heavenor and Sowchea Bay Roads, the ◆ **Big Bay Bed and Breakfast** (Box 1849,

Fort St. James, V0J 1P0; 250–996–8857) is a new Victorian-style home, with a wheelchair-accessible elevator. Jo Anne and Martial Desrochers run five, large guest rooms. Accommodation ranges from $35 to $75, and the hot breakfasts are delicious. Jo Anne also runs **Step Back in Thyme,** a gift shop selling Victorian-style gifts and ice cream.

The beach across the road is sandy, and there are plenty of hiking or snow-mobiling/ski trails. The nearby **Antimony Mine hiking trail** leads to an old mining site. And for divers, there's a **freshwater coral reef** on Battleship Island.

To get an eagle-eye view of Fort St. James, do the hike up ◆ **Mt. Pope** to T-shaped caves. Inside, they're full of bat poop, but the view is spectacular. The trailhead begins along Stones Bay Road, 3 miles (5 km) from town. Allow about five hours. For the fish-eye view, **Patty Lou Charters** (4319 Otway Road, Prince George, V2M 6X6; 250–562–9105) takes guests to see native pictographs, where you can look up to see the T-caves high above. A hiking map is available at the **Fort St. James Chamber of Commerce and Travel InfoCentre** (115 Douglas Avenue, Fort St. James, V0J 1P0; 250–996–7023).

> **BRITISH COLUMBIA FACT**
>
> Highest temperature ever recorded in BC was 111.9°F (44.4°C) at Lillooet and Lytton in 1941.

For skiers, **Murray Ridge Ski Area** (250–996–8513), twenty minutes from Fort St. James, has some excellent trails, both cross-country and downhill. **Whisky Jack Restaurant** (250–996–8828), just past the mill, serves great burgers. To get there, take North Road out of town toward Germansen Landing.

The big attraction in Fort St. James is the ◆ **Fort St. James National Historic Site** (P.O. Box 1148, Fort St. James, V0J 1P0; 250–996–7191). You'll learn here about the Carriers (the Indians named for their widows who carried the cremated remains of their deceased husbands on their backs until a potlatch could be held). In summer, actors become early Hudson's Bay Company officers and Carrier Indians. Chickens and geese run around, and you feel as if you have walked in on a scene from the fur-trading past. "The Fort" is open from 9:00 A.M. to 5:00 P.M. mid-May to September. Admission ranges from $2.00 to $4.00, to a maximum of $12.00 for a family.

Across the road from the fort is the **Nak'azdli Handicraft Shop** (250–996–7400/7368, open seasonally from 9:00 A.M. to 5:00 P.M.). Here an elder's society makes traditional moose-skin crafts and beaded jewelry.

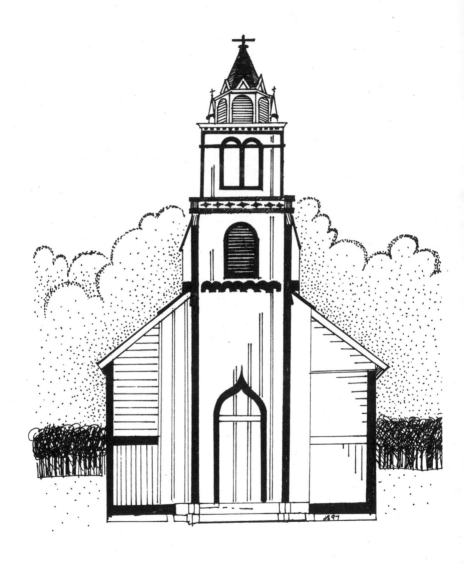

Our Lady of Good Hope Church

From the fort, follow Lakeshore Drive past Cottonwood Park to one of the oldest Catholic churches in BC. **Our Lady of Good Hope Church** was in regular use until 1951. It was completed in 1836 by Fr. Blanchet, O.M.I. A graveyard nearby has headstones written in the Carrier syllabics that were developed by another Oblate, Fr. Morice. Behind the church is an old log hut in which Fr. Morice printed the Carrier books and newspapers, which can be seen in the "Old Fort" museum.

Gold mining is part of Fort St. John's history. Pick up some Manson Creek nuggets at ✦ **Tannis Gold** (3-264 Douglas Avenue, 250-996-2189). Then head to the **Gourmet Deli** for a healthful, loaded sub.

THE LAKES DISTRICT

The area known as the **Lakes District,** with its center at Burns Lake, is an excellent recreation area. Fort Fraser, Fraser Lake, and Endako dot the highway leading to Burns Lake. They exist today mainly because of a nearby molybdenum mine, but ranching and recreational fishing are also important. **Fraser Lake** is famous for the hundreds of trumpeter swans that nest close by.

In downtown Burns Lake, take a drive up **Boer Mountain Road** to a lookout that will give you a great overview of the district. To the south in **François Lake,** large rainbow trout and char are common. To get to these big fish, take a left just before Burns Lake (Highway 35), passing pretty Tchesinkut Lake (pronounced *te-sink-it*), and drive 15 miles (24 km) south to the ferry landing.

Close to the ferry landing, ✦ **Darter's Misty Willow Bed and Breakfast** (P.O. Box 455, Burns Lake, V0J 1E0; 250-695-6573) has more than 300 acres of aspen groves, rolling meadows, and waterfowl ponds, and a lovely view of François Lake. In this 1906-built home, I enjoyed swapping stories beside a grand old wood stove in the big country kitchen with Marie Darter and her neighbors. Bed-and-breakfast rates start at $45.

Darters is also the site of the **Burns Lake Bluegrass Country Music Festival,** held the first weekend in July. Each year the place swings with more than 1,000 dancing, fiddling, and singing Bluegrass enthusiasts from all over the globe. For information on the festival write Box 113, Fraser Lake, V0J 1S0; (250) 699-8697.

Free ferries leave the north side of the lake on the half-hour, and the south side, on the hour. Fifteen paved miles (24 km) south is **Takysie Lake,** where you'll have no trouble filling your creel with rainbow trout.

BLUEGRASS GHOSTS

Goats, turkeys, a curious cat, and a dog or two greeted me as I drove into Darter's Misty Willow farm. Before you could sing "Hot Corn, Cold Corn," I was wearing Marie Darter's gumboots and dragging bales of hay to sheep troughs. Later, over roast dinner and excellent wine, Marie reminisced about when she and her late husband Charlie added music to their yearly picnics—and the Burns Lake Bluegrass Country Music Festival was born. Marie told of the history of her home, built by Jacob Henkel in 1906. Before the ferry service, settlers across François Lake would signal with fires, and Henkel would row a canoe over to fetch them. That evening, I listened as the ferry crunched through the ice and imagined I could hear the stomp and twang of a Bluegrass banjo beat. Across the lake, a brightly glowing fire sent tingles up my spine.

◆ **Likkel's Lakeside Store and Resort** (Box 11, Takysie Lake, V0J 2V0; 250-694-3403) has campsites, cabins, a restaurant (popular with the locals after Sunday church), a post office, and a Laundromat.

Back in Burns Lake (originally *Burnt Lake* because of an enormous bush fire), **Process 4 Gallery** (Box 200, Burns Lake, V0J 1E0; 250-692-3434) sells local art. Owner Wayne Brown has fished and explored most of the area and reveals readily his good fishing spots. He tells of the **Fulton River spawning grounds,** where the fish are so thick "you can walk across their backs." The best time to see this run is early September. The BC Fisheries ◆ **Fulton River Salmon Project** (Box 9, Granisle, V0J 1W0; 250-697-2314) is one of the largest in the world and welcomes visitors. Take the road north from Topley (32 miles [51 km] west of Burns Lake) for 25 miles (40 km), watching out for moose, black bears, and bald eagles.

Before going fishing, though, fill up at the **China Moon** (250-692-7411) in the Lakeview Mall (on the highway opposite Mulvaneys). They serve Subgum Wonton Soup loaded with jumbo shrimp, chicken, pork, and vegetables. After eating you can take a walk along the ◆ **Eveneshen Nature Trail.** It starts behind the **InfoCentre** (Box 339, Burns Lake, V0J 1E0; 250-692-3773), which is on the highway in town. While at the InfoCentre, check out the **Bucket of Blood** beside the **museum;** once a gambling den, a shooting over a game of poker gave the little building its gruesome name.

HOUSTON TO THE HAZELTONS

Houston is 50 miles (81 km) past Burns Lake, and home of the 60-foot-long (18 m) **world's largest fly rod.** It's located at the **InfoCentre** (3289 Yellowhead Highway 16, P.O. Box 396, Houston, V0J 1Z0; 250–845-7640) and is perhaps a hint at how to catch the steelhead in the Bulkley and Morice Rivers running through town.

Thirty miles (49 km) past Houston is picturesque ◆ **Telkwa,** where the Bulkley River meets the Telkwa. Maps at the museum in the old schoolhouse describe a village walking tour. Accommodation is available at the **Douglas Motel** (Box 291, Telkwa, V0J 2X0; 250–846-5679) overlooking the green Bulkley River rapids. Telkwa is halfway between Prince George (226 miles [364 km] to the east) and Prince Rupert on the Pacific coast.

Smithers, fifteen minutes past Telkwa, is at the center of the Bulkley Valley, sitting snugly below the towering (8,600 feet [2,621 m]) Hudson Bay Mountain and glacier. In winter Smithers becomes a skiing paradise, with eighteen runs to choose from. Lodgings range from the popular-with-skiers **Hudson's Bay Lodge** (3251 East Highway 16, Smithers, V0J 2N0; 250-847-4878) on the eastern edge of town, to the newer, cheaper ◆ **Stork Nest Inn,** closer to the western end (1485 Main Street, 250-847-3831). Here they serve endless free breakfasts in a friendly talk-to-the-chef atmosphere. **Tumbleberries,** at 3774 Third Avenue (250-847-8849), makes delicious sandwiches and great ice cream.

If you can find a few days to enjoy the scenic Bulkley Valley, ◆ **Berg's Valley Tours Bed and Breakfast** (3924 Thirteenth Avenue, Box 3235, Smithers, V0J 2N0; 250-847-5925) runs valley and mountain safari tours, where you can visit historic ◆ **Moricetown Canyon,** 20 miles (32 km) west. In fall, fishers armed with gaffs or spears challenge the rushing waters of the Wa Dzun Kwuh (Bulkley River) as it roars through a 50-foot (15-m) chasm. The village has some interesting, original totem poles.

BRITISH COLUMBIA FACT

Biggest snowfall in BC in one day: 46.5 inches (118.1 cm) at Lakelse Lake near Terrace.

An attractive log building houses the **New Hazelton Travel InfoCentre** (Box 340, New Hazelton, V0J 2J0; 250-842-6571), 22 miles

(35 km) northwest of Smithers. It's on the highway and worth a stop to find out what's *off* the highway in 'Ksan Village and Kispiox.

Head down the Hazelton High Road (Highway 62) and cross the one-lane **Hagwilget Bridge,** suspended like a tightrope high over the Bulkley River. Built in 1931, it replaced a rickety footbridge of poles lashed together with cedar bark rope, that was once used as a trading route by the Gitxsan Wet'suwet'ens (*the people of the lower drainage*).

Cross over the bridge, and about 3 miles (5 km) north, where the Skeena and Bulkley rivers meet, seven communal houses and some fabulous totems comprise the ◆ **'Ksan Model Village** (Box 326, Hazelton, V0J 1Y0; 250-843-5544). Guides will take you through the houses and relate the area's history. The museum, video presentations, art shows, carving school sessions, and dramatic events are open seven days per week mid-April through September, as is the Gift Shop, but you can walk through the village any time of year.

In the **'Ksan Museum** (Box 333, Hazelton, V0J 1Y0; 250-842-5723) "blankets" (robes worn by high-ranking chiefs), cedar-bark boxes, and "coppers" (the chief's most valuable item) are displayed. On Friday nights, the 'Ksan Performing Artists Group entertains.

Continue on to Hazelton, sitting like a western movie set on the banks of the Skeena River. Eight paved miles (13 km) north, the Kispiox River joins the Skeena, and here you'll find some of the best totems in all of BC. Kispiox's fifteen poles have been moved from their original sites in the village to a spot by the water's edge. Nearby the ◆ **Bent Box Native Arts Gallery** (250-842-6179) sells beautiful silk-screen prints that tell stories of the Gitxsan people's rich history. The **Kispiox Travel InfoCentre** is at Box 25, Kispiox, V0J 1Y0; (250) 842-5248.

TERRACE TO KITIMAT

Ten miles (16 km) east of Terrace is one of British Columbia's loveliest parks. ◆ **Kleanza Creek Provincial Park** (250-847-7320) features cascading waterfalls and a hiking trail to a beautiful view spot at the top of a canyon. "Kleanza" in Gitxsan means *gold,* so some people like to try a little panning here. Don't laugh—back in 1934 some lucky panner took out a 6.3-ounce (180-gram) nugget.

At the eastern edge of Terrace, Highway 37 leads to **Kitimat,** 36 miles (58 km) south, at the head of Douglas Channel. In 1995 the combined value of Kitimat's industrial products was more than $1 billion, and its industry accounted for 7 percent of the province's total merchandise exports. Tours of what keeps Kitimat booming—**Alcan Smelter**

BRITISH COLUMBIA TRIVIA

At Mount Layton Hotsprings Resort by Lakelse Lake Provincial Park, south of Terrace, you'll hear tales about the big-tipping, luggage-lacking "Catholic priests," who were guests there for two weeks in October 1928. They turned out to be none other than Al Capone and three of his henchmen, escaping the heat of their rum-running in Prohibition-wracked Chicago.

(250-639-8400), **Eurocan Pulp and Paper** (250-639-3597), and **Methanex/Pacific Ammonia** (250-639-9292), can all be done (for free) in a day. Or if you prefer, the kids can feed salmon hatchlings at the **Kitimat River Fish Hatchery** (250-639-9616). For information write or phone **Kitimat Chamber of Commerce and InfoCentre** (4511 Keith Street, Box 214, Kitimat, V8C 2G7; 250-632-6294).

In town at the ◆ **Kitimat Centennial Museum** (293 City Center, 250-632-7022; E-mail: kitmuse@sno.net), learn about oolichan trading and the grease trails, then head over to the Kitimat River to see BC's largest Sitka spruce tree. It's more than 500 years old, measures 36.7 feet (11.2 m) around, and is 165 feet (50.32 m) tall. There's apparently enough wood in it to frame nine houses. The **Chalet Restaurant,** 852 Tsimshian Boulevard (250-632-2662), serves good fish meals, and the **Ol' Keg Pub,** 874 Tsimshian Boulevard (250-632-6920), often has entertainment. For accommodation try the ◆ **Violet Patch Bed and Breakfast** (250-639-9643) at 30 Kokanee Street, where the fishing is just a cast away from the door. Accommodation ranges from $55 for a single to $65 for a double.

Kitamaat *(people of the snow)* **Village** is 7 miles (11 km) across Douglas Channel. Watch for killer whales, eagles, and sea lions. Here you can learn about the untouched **Kitlope Valley,** an area 60 miles (100 km) south-east of Kitimat. In 1994 this 780,000-acre (317,000-ha) valley was set aside as a protected area to preserve the world's largest intact coastal rain-forest. Contact the **Nanakila Institute** at 260 Kitlope Street (Box 1101, Kitamaat Village, V0T 2B0; 250-632-3308) for information on ecotours.

On the way back to Terrace, the ◆ **Mount Layton Hotsprings Resort** (Box 550, Terrace, V8G 4B5; 250-798-2214 or 1-800-663-3862) is near **Lakelse Lake Provincial Park** (250-847-7320), with its old-growth giant cedars, hemlock, and Sitka spruce. The public is invited to use the resort's odorless, open-air hot pools and waterslides.

Accommodation is $60–$80, and the sunset views of the snow-capped mountains are wonderful. Cross-country ski trails at **Onion Lake** are just five minutes away.

We're almost back to Terrace. Keep your eyes peeled, as you may catch a glimpse of the rare Kermode, the elusive "white" black bear, found in the Skeena Valley. The **Terrace InfoCentre** (Box 107, Terrace, V8G 4A2; 250–656–2063), on the highway, has information on this protected animal. In town, the ◆ **Northern Light Studio and Gardens** (4820 Halliwell Avenue, 250–638–1403) is a restful spot with a Japanese-style garden, where you can purchase local artwork and jewelry. It's not far from the **Terrace Heritage Park** (4011 Sparks Street), with its panoramic views of the Skeena River winding through the city and surrounds.

PRINCE RUPERT AND THE COAST

From Terrace there are 90 miles (144 km) of lovely twisting Yellowhead Highway to cover as it follows the Skeena River to Prince Rupert. Drive it by day or you'll miss towering snow-covered peaks, waterfalls, and possibly a bear or two.

Don't miss the ◆ **North Pacific Cannery Village Museum** (1889 Skeena Drive, Port Edward, V0V 1G0; 250–628–3538. The turnoff to this National Historic Site is about 8 miles (12 km) before Prince Rupert. Students act as guides and storekeepers in this restored cannery. Admission is $3.00–$5.00 (under six free).

Prince Rupert is Canada's deepest, ice-free harbor and a major shipping port. It's the terminus for ferry traffic to Alaska, the Queen Charlotte Islands, and Vancouver Island, and for more than ten thousand years has been home to Tsimshian First Nations people. Their culture is depicted in the many totem poles seen throughout the city.

Back in the eighties I had sailed into Cow Bay, so when I arrived in 1997 by car I headed straight to the waterfront, keen to see if it had changed. The town was originally called Vickersville, but after a herd of cows was unloaded in 1909, the name Cow Bay stuck. Today, instead of a dairy, you'll find fresh seafood for sale on the docks, cute shops and eateries, and cow-patch black-and-white hydrants and fuel drums looking like a herd of Friesians. It has certainly changed from what I had remembered, but it still has that familiar salty allure. To get to Cow Bay from the highway, turn right on Third Avenue East, cross the railway line onto Manson Way, and turn right onto Cow Bay Road.

"See You Latte" says the reverse of the business card at ◆ **Cowpuccino's Coffee House** (25 Cow Bay Road, Prince Rupert, V8J 1A4;

Canoe and Totem, Prince Rupert

250-627-1395). For breakfast here, try a large, fresh-fruit salad and granola loaded up with yogurt and a choice of Latte, Moocha, or Cowpuccino coffee. It's open 7:30 A.M. to 10:00 P.M. (Sundays 9:00 A.M. to 9:00 P.M.) and often plays foot-tapping Bob Marley music.

Other interesting restaurants in the area include **Smiles Seafood Café** (250-624-3072), famous for its halibut, and **Cow Bay Café** (250-627-1212), serving a colorful menu of fresh halibut with sun-dried tomato pesto, red Thai chicken curry, and vegetarian moussaka. And you can lose yourself in a library of books as you wait for your meal or watch the fleet come in.

There are accommodations at **Eagle Bluff Bed and Breakfast** (201 Cow Bay Road, 250-627-4955 or 1-800-833-1550), right on the docks overlooking the Yacht Club, perfect for the landlubber with a secret desire to wake up to the sounds and smell of the sea. It was originally a cannery house. Accommodation with a cozy nautical theme ranges from $45 to $75. Next door is **Eagle Wind on the Waterfront Native Arts** (250-624-9772), selling Northwest Coast jewelry, masks, talking sticks, and other native arts and crafts.

Across from Cowpuccino's on Cow Bay Road, **The Rain Store** is full of wet-weather stuff—gumboots with bells attached, umbrellas, rain sticks, and colorful raincoats, which may give you a hint at what to expect with the weather! But if it should be raining, visit the **Museum of Northern British Columbia** (Box 669, Prince Rupert, V8J 3S1; 250-624-3207) in its new quarters at the cedar-beamed **Chatham Village Longhouse** on First Avenue. Exhibits include Tsimshian settlement history and smooth, black argillite carvings. In summer, two-hour **archaeological harbor tours** are held. On these, you'll see native middens, the **Digby Island Finnish fishing village,** and **Metlakatla Village,** considered by many to be one of the richest archaeological sites in the world.

Across the road, the **Prince Rupert InfoCentre** (100 First Avenue East, Box 669, Prince Rupert, V8J 3S1; 250-624-5637 or 1-800-667-1994) has maps for a tour of the city's totem poles, information on the **Fire Museum** (200 First Avenue West, 250-624-2211), and **Kwinitsa Station Museum** (250-627-1915), down on the waterfront.

There's a great photo view of Prince Rupert from the top of Fifth Avenue West, or you could take a flight-seeing tour of **Khutzeymateen,** the valley of the grizzly bear, from the seaplane base at **Seal Cove. Harbour Air** (250-627-1341) and **Inland Air Charters** (250-624-2577) are two of the companies offering this flight close to the Alaskan border. To get there take Sixth Avenue East (off McBride Street) and follow the seaplane signs.

THE STEWART–CASSIAR

We return east to Kitwanga, 138 miles (223 km) from Prince Rupert, and join the **Stewart–Cassiar,** which after 450 miles (725 km) joins the Alaska Highway at the Yukon border.

At Kitwanga, cross the Skeena River Bridge and turn right, driving slowly along a very narrow loop road to Gitwangak, *place of the rabbits.* Here you'll see twelve totems telling the story of Kitwanga Fort and its defender, the fierce Nekt, who wore a suit of armor made from grizzly skins lined with pitch and slate. **St. Paul's Anglican Church** (1893), across the road from the totems, is one of BC's lovelier old wooden churches.

The ❖ **Kitwanga Fort National Historic Site** is 3 miles (5 km) north on Highway 37. The Gitwangak people devised a defense system whereby logs were rolled on enemies who tried to attack the fort. Interpretive panels along a trail up to Battle Hill (*Ta'awdzep*) tell its history. For more information write Fort St. James National Historic Park (Box 1148, Fort St. James, V0J 1P0; 250-996-7191).

> **BRITISH COLUMBIA FACT**
>
> Canada's first covered stadium: BC Place, Vancouver (1983), the world's largest air-supported, domed stadium, home to the BC Lions football team.

Nine miles north of the fort, and still appearing on some maps as Kitwancool, is **Gitanyow.** Carvers working in the shed near eighteen or so impressive totem poles will show you *Hole in the Ice,* believed to be the oldest totem in the world.

SIDE TRIP TO STEWART

Highway 37 forks at Meziadin Junction, and Highway 37A (the Glacier Highway) travels 40 miles (65 km) to **Stewart,** at the head of Portland Canal. It passes the magnificent ❖ **Bear Glacier,** 21 miles (34 km) from the Junction, at Stohn Lake, where even on hot days you can feel the cool air flowing off the glacier. It's a fantastic sight, with the glacier so opalescent and blue that it glows at night. Along the 40 miles (65 km) to Stewart you'll see over twenty glaciers poking through spectacular craggy mountains.

Stewart (and its American sister Hyder) is a frontier town with a history of hard-rock gold, silver, and copper mining, but with its natural beauty, tourism is fast becoming a mainstay. The area is also valued as a movie backdrop (*Bear Island, The Thing,* and *Iceman*). By 1910 the population was booming at ten thousand; today it's just over a thousand. Around morning teatime you'll see a good percentage of that thousand around **Brothers Bakery,** when the steaming aroma of delicious doughnuts and pastries waft from within.

Seaport Limousine (Box 217, Stewart, V0T 1W0; 250-636-2622) provides bus service to Terrace and Kitimat, and will also take you into the glacier country for a breathtaking trip through the steep Salmon River Valley. Colorful commentary of the valley's interesting history and characters adds to the tour as you travel past alpine meadows, bears, eagles, spawning salmon, and the spectacular **Salmon Glacier.** It's a restful alternative to wrecking your vehicle on a rutted road.

Drop into the **Historical Society Museum and InfoCentre** (250-636-2111, off-season 2251). The friendly staff will reveal the good hiking and fishing spots. If you're camping, the **Stewart Lions Campground** (Box 431, Stewart, V0T 1W0; 250-636-2537) on Eighth Avenue borders a trout stream. It's just a few minutes walk to the shops and a mile or so from Hyder, Alaska, where you can get into the *spirit* of things at the **Glacier Inn** bar, and earn an I'VE BEEN HYDERIZED certificate. While there, you may as well continue to follow tradition and sign a dollar bill, which you then add to the multitude already on the wall of the inn. Nothing's too serious in this friendly little ghost town.

THE GRAND CANYON OF THE STIKINE

From **Meziadin Junction,** the Stewart-Cassiar follows the Bell Irving River to **Bell II,** 57 miles (92 km) north. From Bell II, you cross several creeks, then skirt Kinaskan, Tatogga, and Eddontenajon Lakes on the way to **Iskut** and the **Grand Canyon of the Stikine.** There are about 75 miles (120 km) of dusty, unpaved road to cover, and lots of logging trucks, so drive cautiously.

BRITISH COLUMBIA FACT

Lowest temperature ever recorded in BC was -74°F (-58.9°C) in Smith River in 1947.

On Eddontenajon Lake, about 2 miles (3 km) before Iskut, ◆ **Red Goat Lodge** (P.O. Box 101, Iskut, V0J 1K0; 250-234-3261) is open from June to September, and the $85 double includes mulled wine with truffles in the evening and sourdough crepes for breakfast. There's also a campground with hot showers and a laundry, and for members of Hosteling International, bunk rooms for $12. It's perfectly positioned for hiking, canoeing, and fishing, with **Spatsizi Plateau Wilderness Park** to the east, and **Mt. Edziza Park** to the west. Another highly recommended place to stay is **Bear Paw Ranch** (Box 69, Iskut, V0J 1K0; Radio phone 2M3 858 Whitehorse operator, Meehaus channel), 5 miles (8 km) north of Iskut in beautiful surroundings.

> # BRITISH COLUMBIA FACT
>
> Highest annual sunshine in BC: Victoria, 2,426 hours in 1970.

Dease Lake should be renamed Halfway. It's halfway between Seattle and Anchorage, and halfway between Whitehorse and Smithers. It's also 52 miles (83 km) north of Iskut, and at the junction of the 74-mile (119 km) rough and winding but spectacularly scenic road to ◆ **Telegraph Creek.** Leave your trailer in Dease, and check locally for road conditions. At about 50 miles (80 km) it starts to twist and roller-coast along narrow canyons, with rock walls almost 1,000 feet (300 m) high, past fish camps and lava beds along the Stikine River, till it reaches Telegraph Creek, where the Tahltan community has the high view, and the nonnative community is a terrace below.

Accommodation in Telegraph Creek is limited. The original Hudson's Bay Company store is now the **Stikine River Song Lodge** (250-235-3196). You'll be able to meet the locals and arrange fishing charters here.

NORTH TO THE YUKON BORDER

Back on Highway 37, about 50 miles (85 km) north of Dease Lake, look for ◆ **Mighty Moe's** sign on the east side of the highway. The camping here by Cotton Lake is scenic, and the hot showers (heated by a potbellied wood stove) are great. Take time to chat with Moe in his memorabilia-filled cabin. He's one of the originals!

At the Cassiar Junction you can pick up souvenirs at **Jade City;** then, as Cassiar is now abandoned, continue north through the Kaska village of Good Hope Lake for 20 miles (33 km) to one of the prettiest campsites I've ever stayed in, **Boya Lake Provincial Park.** The sites are set beside a turquoise lake and are a boater's and photographer's joy.

At Boya Lake, the **60th Parallel** (the Yukon border) is 50 miles (80 km) north, and the Alaska Highway, 2 miles (3 km) farther on. Since we left the Yellowhead, we've covered many a dusty mile, but there's still one littlegem hidden way up in the far northwestern corner.

Atlin is 290 miles (460 km) from the junction of the Alaska and Stewart–Cassiar highways. The turnoff is at Jakes Corner, 52 miles (84 km) southeast of Whitehorse. Although Highway 7 is mostly gravel, the 60-mile (98-km) scenic trip along Little Atlin Lake and Atlin Lake, with the stunning, snow-clad Coast Mountains towering splendidly over them, is nothing short of magnificent. Once a thriving gold rush town, now its streets are paved with creativity and a certain spirituality. Recently the community has experienced tension and division, with pressure from a mining company that wants to build a 100-mile (160-km) road south to tidewater near Juneau. Many of its mixed-culture residents want to preserve its unique isolation and fragility at any cost.

Politics aside, there's lots to see and do in Atlin. A good starting point is the **Atlin Historical Museum** (250-651-7522) on the corner of Third and Trainor Streets in a little 1902 schoolhouse. In summer museum staff members conduct walking tours of the town and the historic, elegantly restored ◈ **MV** *Tarahne.* In 1928 it took wealthy tourists on round-the-island cruises, but since 1936 it has lain idle on the shores of Atlin Lake. It's now the site of an annual **Tea Party,** held the first weekend of July, when period-costumed hostesses serve delicious refreshments.

A delightfully rustic place to stay in Atlin is **Kirkwood Cottages** (Box 39, Atlin, V0W 1A0; 1-800-688-ATLIN) on Lake Street. The cozy cottages occupy a spot on the lakeshore, where, until the depression, the three-storey White Pass Hotel sat so majestically. If you prefer bed-and-breakfast accommodations, try the **Fireweed Inn** (250-651-7729) or **The Noland House** (250-651-7585).

One of the neatest things to do in Atlin is to pan for gold—legally and with hope! East of town, on Spruce Creek, there's a "Keep all you find" panning claim, to which the friendly staff at the Visitors Centre (Box 365, V0W 1A0) will direct you; they'll also direct you to the artists and outfitters who make this wild but exquisite part of British Columbia their home.

WHERE TO STAY:
1. **Big Bay Bed and Breakfast** (Box 1849, Fort St. James, V0J 1P0; 250-996-8857).
2. **Darter's Misty Willow Bed and Breakfast** (P.O. Box 455, Burns Lake, V0J 1E0; 250-695-6573).

3. **Berg's Valley Tours Bed and Breakfast** (3924 Thirteenth Avenue, Box 3235, Smithers, V0J 2N0; 250-847-5925).

4. **Mount Layton Hotsprings Resort** (Box 550, Terrace, V8G 4B5; 250-798-2214 or 1-800-663-3862 in Canada).

5. **Eagle Bluff Bed and Breakfast** (201 Cow Bay Road, Prince Rupert, V8J 1A2; 250-627-4955 or 1-800-833-1550).

6. **Red Goat Lodge** (P.O. Box 101, Iskut, V0J 1K0; 250-234-3261).

7. **Kirkwood Cottages** (Box 39, Atlin, V0W 1A0; 1-800-688-ATLIN) on Lake Street.

WHERE TO EAT:

1. **OK Café** (250-567-2594), located in Vanderhoof's Heritage Village Museum.

2. **China Moon** (250-692-7411), in the Lakeview Mall, Burns Lake.

3. **Tumbleberries** (3774 Third Avenue, Smithers V0J 2N0; 250-847-8849), makes delicious homemade bread sandwiches and great ice cream.

4. **Chalet Restaurant** (852 Tsimshian Boulevard, Kitimat, V8C 1T5; 250-632-2662). Moderately priced meals.

5. **Cowpuccino's Coffee House** (25 Cow Bay Road, Prince Rupert, V8J 1A4; 250-627-1395).

6. **Cow Bay Café** (205 Cow Bay Road, Prince Rupert, V8J 1A2; 250-627-1212) offers fresh halibut on the waterfront.

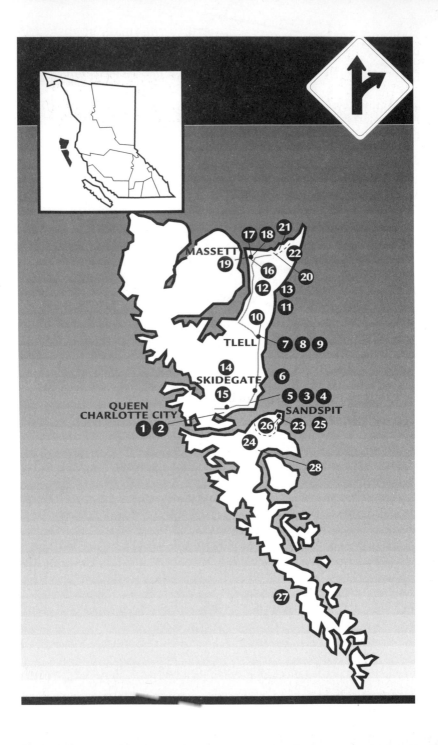

QUEEN CHARLOTTE ISLANDS

1. Tufted Puffin
2. Rainbows Gallery
3. *Loo Taas*
4. The Haida Gwaii Museum
5. Dogfish Pole
6. Balance Rock
7. Bottle and Jug Works
8. Crystal Cabin Rock and Gem Gift Shop
9. Sitka Studio
10. Sitka Lodging
11. H'ltunwa Kaitza (Cacilia's Bed and Breakfast)
12. Naikoon Provincial Park
13. *Pesuta* shipwreck
14. Marie Lake Fish Hatchery
15. Rennell Sound Wilderness Campsites
16. Café Gallery
17. Ed Jones Haida Museum
18. Haida Arts and Jewelry
19. Delkatla Wildlife Sanctuary
20. Dixon Entrance Golf and Country Club
21. Alaska View Lodge Bed and Breakfast
22. Tow Hill
23. Seaport Bed and Breakfast
24. Pallant Creek Fish Hatchery
25. TimberWest Forest Tours
26. Logger Sports Day
27. Gwaii Haanas
28. Moresby Explorers

QUEEN CHARLOTTE ISLANDS

Tell any Canadian that you're trekking around British Columbia, and the first question is inevitably: *Have you been to the Charlottes?* Canadians think of them much as a new mother does her baby. They're precious. Recently, when a drifter took a chain saw to a beloved golden spruce tree near Port Clements, not only were residents and scientists horrified, the whole country was in an uproar.

I'd dreamed for years of visiting these misty, myterious islands, known for 10,000 years to their outspoken native inhabitants as Haida Gwaii (*Islands of the People*). Their appeal lies in the mythology and artistry surrounding the Haida culture, combined with their isolation and stormy, rugged loveliness.

BRITISH COLUMBIA FACT

The longest frost-free period in BC (685 days in 1925–26) occurred in Victoria.

Consisting of two main islands, the more populated Graham in the north, and Moresby in the south, four smaller islands, and about 150 teeny specks of islands, Haida Gwaii stretches like an elongated, curved triangle for 166 miles (251 km) from Langara Island in the northwest to Kunghit in the southeast. The remote southern part of Moresby is entirely Gwaii Haanas National Park Reserve, an area cherished by wilderness adventurers, and the Haida people who make up about one-sixth of the population of 6,000.

We begin our journey with an eight-hour sailing across a sometimes boisterous Hecate Strait on a BC ferry trip from Prince Rupert to Skidegate, a few minutes from Queen Charlotte City on Graham Island. Vehicle reservations (1–800–663–7600) are required, as there are only five to six sailings per week from each port in summer, and three in winter. BC Ferries has a handy Web site (http://bcferries.bc.ca/ferries) that lists fares and schedules and allows on-line reservations. (As a general guide, expect to pay about $23 one-way per person, and $87 per vehicle, with an extra $40 if you want an overnight cabin.) From Sandspit, which is just 3 miles (5 km) from Queen Charlotte City, a paved road (Highway 16 and still the Yellowhead) leads to Masset and clam-filled northern beaches, or a twenty-five-minute ferry ride will take you south to Alliford Bay, 8 miles (13 km) from the village of Sandspit on Moresby Island, gateway to the Gwaii Haanas National Park Reserve and UNESCO World Heritage Site, Ninstints.

QUEEN CHARLOTTE CITY

Queen Charlotte City is the administrative center for the islands. Don't be fooled by the word *city*, though. It's about as laid-back as a city can be. You'll see what I mean if you start with a 6:30 A.M. coffee at **Margaret's Café** on Wharf Street (250-559-4204). Margaret's has been around for about forty-five years and has that homey help-yourself-to-the-coffee friendly feel about it. Don't come after 2:45 P.M., though, as the owners, Deb and Larry Demers, close up early. I tried the hamburger and seafood chowder lunch special for $6.50, and it was excellent.

Across the road, **Joy's Island Jewellers** (Box 337, Queen Charlotte, V0T 1S0; 250-559-4742) sells local crafts. Carved driftwood by Ernie Burnett from Tlell is unique and humorous. Farther along the main drag at 3205 Third Avenue, you can't miss a smug-looking wooden puffin standing outside the ❖ **Tufted Puffin** (Box 1048, Queen Charlotte, V0T 1S0; 250-559-8689). Inside there's a selection of hand-crafted works (ever seen tatted earrings?) made almost exclusively by local artists.

Nearby, at ❖ **Rainbows Gallery** (Box 489, Queen Charlotte, V0T 1S0; 250-559-8420; E-mail: rainbows@qcc.island.net), there's a large selection of Haida art, including antique Native heritage crafts and collectibles, books, carved gold, and the famous black argillite, a soft slate found only on Slatechuck Mountain, west of Queen Charlotte City, and reserved exclusively for the Haida.

A quick look in at **Hanging by a Fibre,** a clothing store/cappuccino bar with unusual Queen Charlotte–theme T-shirts, then on to **Meegans Store** (*The Best Little Lure House in the Charlottes,* 250-559-4428), where they hand out *lurist* information if you're here for the wild steelhead or trophy halibut, and I was ready to explore this Canadian Galapagos.

BRITISH COLUMBIA FACT

The Queen Charlotte Islands have the highest density of Peale's peregrine falcons in the world.

Less than a mile north of the ferry landing, at the blue "M" sign on Highway 16 at Second Beach, is the Haida Gwaii Watchmen office (250-559-8225), where you register to visit the ancient villages in South

Moresby. Next door lie totems and ⚜ *Loo Taas* (*Wave Eater*), a 50-foot (15-m) cedar dugout canoe, whose carving was overseen by the famous Haida artist Bill Reid. Traditional techniques were used in this Expo 1984 commission, which was paddled home from Vancouver when the fair ended. In true Haida style, a great potlatch celebration greeted its arrival.

Right next door, ⚜ **The Haida Gwaii Museum** at Qay'llnagaay (Box 1373, Skidegate, V0T 1S1; 250-559-4643) has a collection as eclectic as the people of the Charlottes. Magnificently displayed totem poles, two from Tanu (the ancestral home of many of Skidegate's residents), and two from Skedans, are the museum's most distinctive features. Other displays range from an old washing mangle, to fossils, to the world's largest argillite collection. There are photos of Mexico Tom (the area's first rancher) and a seismometer, a reminder that the strongest earthquake (8.1) ever recorded in Canada occurred on Aug 22, 1949, off the west coast of Graham Island. The museum is open daily in summer. Off-season it varies, so phone for information. Admission is $2.50.

Before heading north, make sure to stop at the Skidegate Band office on the highway to see the tall ⚜ **Dogfish Pole,** also created by Bill Reid. Just north of Skidegate look for ⚜ **Balance Rock,** a strange phenomenon left on the beach thousands of years ago by moving glaciers. From late April to June, a plume of rainbowed mist rising out of the water may enhance the scene, as a gray whale pauses to feed on its Mexico to Alaska migration.

GRAHAM ISLAND CENTRAL

Tlell is becoming noted for its community of artists. The first studio you pass driving north on Highway 16 (peacefully hidden on the beach, but there's a sign) is ⚜ **Bottle and Jug Works** (250-559-4756). John and Jennifer Davis, teachers who arrived on these isolated islands in 1965, named the studio for their two previous dogs. They create bowls and other interesting, functional pottery.

North of the post office on Highway 16 in Tlell, follow the "A" signs left onto Wiggins Road, and right onto Richardson. Tucked away, just a minute from the highway, are a few little treasures. At one, the ⚜ **Crystal Cabin Rock and Gem Gift Shop** (Box 88, Tlell, V0T 1Y0; 250-557-4383), French-born Dutes Dutheil creates fabulous gold and silver gemstone jewelry. His wife, Laura (Tlegaa Gaathlandaay to the Haida), makes spirit dolls, ceremonial pipes, intricately beaded purses, and other unique fiber-art sculptures. Her embroidered and beaded dolls have spellbinding stories associated with them. From Copper

THE DAWN WATCH

I had just driven off the ferry from Prince Rupert and was now between Skidegate and Tlell. A delicate first blush of sunrise added sheen to views across Hecate Strait. I quietly unlocked my Pentax, eager to capture the magic. I looked up. A lone bald eagle eyed me inquisitively from a stark conifer. Exhilarated, I clicked, hoping I wouldn't destroy the dawn's serenity. As I drove off, huge wings spread out above me. A few hundred yards on, another rose-tinted seascape had me reaching for my camera. As if reading my mind, the brown-black body and radiant white head swooped, sharp talons finding a tall gray snag above me. Again, the golden-brown eyes pierced me intensely. I felt like an intruder, but furtively stole another image. Unbelievably, the eagle followed my journey, continuing to sear my soul with its glare, as together, we kept this lonely vigil.

Woman to Medicine Woman to Jade Woman they're all unique, all beautiful. Hidden inside there may be a stick of sage, a crystal, something special to the doll. The gift shop also sells fossils, crystals, and Island Scenic Stone, a local stone surreally embedded with natural scenes.

Across the gravel road is ♦ **Sitka Studio** (Box 460, Queen Charlotte City, V0T 1S0; 250–557–4241). Barbara Small and artist Noel Wotton sell quality artwork, batiks, birds-eye yellow cedar boxes, black-and-white photographic prints and, upstairs, a large range of BC books.

They also have a two-story cottage, ♦ **Sitka Lodging** (250–557–4386/4241), fully equipped, and with verandahs overlooking geese, ducks, and wild swans by the Tlell River. Don't leave without asking Noel to show you his unique cottage. It's the butt of an enormous burled spruce tree, roofed with cedar shakes and a droopy copper peak looking a little like a giant guard-cockatoo. Some might say it's the butt of an enormous joke. It's furnished with chain-saw–hewn chairs, and the story goes that the famous Canadian author/artist/filmmaker James Houston, who can often be seen around Tlell in the summer, had a hand in it. If you're lucky, as I was, you'll find some of Houston's original work in Sitka Studio.

Tlell has been the site of fish camps, farms, artists' hideouts, and more recently, Naikoon Provincial Park headquarters. The spread-out community, 22 miles (36 km) north of Skidegate, also has some intriguing places to stay.

Austrian Cacilia Honisch runs ♦ **H'ltunwa Kaitza** (*feathered headress*

Sitka Lodging burled tree house

star), better known as simply **Cacilia's Bed and Breakfast** (Box 3, Tlell, V0T 1Y0; 250-557-4664). There's loads of space for backpackers ($15 including breakfast—what a deal!) and more elegant double bedrooms from $30 single. *Rustic* (the toilet-roll holders are driftwood and the shower-stall floor is pebbled) and *beachy* (the dunes are right outside) are key words. You never know who you might meet sitting in the drift-wood/macrame barstools. You may even get to join in the weekly tai chi exercises. It's easy to find—heading north on Highway 16, turn right after the 2 KM TO NAIKOON PARK sign 25 miles (40 km) north of the Skidegate ferry dock.

Just north of Tlell, near the **Misty Meadows Campsite** at the southern tip of ❦ **Naikoon Provincial Park** (250-557-4390), a 3-mile (5-km) trail beginning at the Tlell River Bridge leads along the river to Hecate Strait and the 1928 ❦ *Pesuta* shipwreck. Do the hike on an outgoing tide, as the water comes up to the dune cliffs on high tides.

If you keep walking, it's another 52 miles (84 km) to **Rose Point,** the most northerly spot in the Charlottes. As one local commented: *Why would anyone want to do that?* It's total wilderness hiking, with no drinking water, nothing but rugged beach scenery, Sitka blacktail deer, tufted puffins, possibly even a few wild cows (although it's a while since they've been seen), and a few streams to ford. Tide tables and a lot of common sense are necessary items, especially considering how the surf can pound against the 400-foot (120-m) cliffs just north of **Cape Ball.** There's a little respite, though, with three rustic wilderness shelters en route, off the beach, but open at one end for the wind to whistle through! Ask for information at park headquarters on this unspoiled 179,490-acre (72,640-ha), boggy, wild tract.

From Tlell, the highway crosses the island for 13 miles (21 km) northwest to **Port Clements,** home to loggers and purse seiner fishers on Masset Inlet. The famous **Golden Spruce,** a feature of Haida mythology that was sadly destroyed in an act of madness in 1997, was its claim to fame. There's still a piece of history left in the area though, the beginnings of an ancient 50-foot (15-m) **Haida dugout canoe.** Follow the signs into Port Clements, staying on Bayview Drive heading toward **Juskatla.** The road quickly deteriorates and becomes a MacMillan-Bloedel logging road, so if you value your life, get permission first, drive with headlights on, expect a logging truck at every corner, pull over and stop when you do see one, and obey all road signs. The canoe is on its original site on the east side of the road. Look for the trail sign 8 miles (13 km) south of Port Clements.

This road from Port Clements is called the Charlotte Main and makes for an exciting circle tour. Before starting, especially if you plan to do the trip in logging operating hours (Monday to Friday, 6:30 A.M. to 5:30 P.M.), phone MacMillan-Bloedel (250–557–4212) or stop at their Queen Charlotte Division headquarters in Juskatla, or their shop at the west end of Queen Charlotte City, to obtain permission to use the road.

The gravel road follows the Mamin River south across a couple of bridges to the ◆ **Marie Lake Fish Hatchery,** 15 miles (24 km) from Port Clements. The program is run by the Massett Band Council and is designed to enhance chinook stocks in the Yakoun River. A short walk from the 40Q bridge on the Yakoun River, renowned for its steelhead fishing, there's a campsite called **Papa John's,** popular with fishing fanatics.

When you see sign 23S, you're at the turnoff to **Rennell Sound.** Other than by boat, this logging road is the only way to get to the rugged west coast. It passes Yakoun Lake, and near the end there's a very steep hill, with an appropriate STEEP HILL sign. This is followed by an equally appropriate NO SHIT sign. BC Forest Service operates campsites here. ❖ **Rennell Sound Wilderness Campsites** has seven beach sites, picnic tables, and pit toilets. You're free to use the sites to enjoy the pounding surf and miles of empty beaches.

Back at the junction, the main logging road continues south from the Yakoun River Bridge for 14 miles (22 km) to Queen Charlotte City, coming out at MacMillan-Bloedel's shop, and dustless (Yes!) paved roads. You may wish to do the circle clockwise, starting in Queen Charlotte City at **Hooterville,** a squatter community of weather-beaten float homes at the west end of town.

GRAHAM ISLAND NORTH

Masset, 25 miles (40 km) due north of Port Clements on Highway 16, has until recently been a Canadian Forces Base. I discovered a superb restaurant there. ❖ **Café Gallery** at 2062 Collison Avenue (250-626-3672), run by Thi Hai and Fritz Engelhard, is one of those unexpected treats you sometimes stumble on in the most out-of-the-way places. It's right beside the Royal Canadian Mounted Police station and has Haida prints gracing the walls to add local flavor. I enjoyed an evening special, a delicate chicken vegetable soup followed by Potatoes William, Fillo Purse (stuffed with peppers and onion) and Steak and Prawns Marsellaise, and completed by sinfully rich chocolate mousse cake for $17.95, the equal of any big-city haute cuisine. It's open every day except Sundays.

Old Massett (different spelling, and sometimes called *Haida*) is the largest Haida village in the Charlottes and stands on the site of three ancient Haida townsites; you can learn about them at the ❖ **Ed Jones Haida Museum** at the north end of the village. To get there from Masset, travel west on Collison Avenue and turn right at the beach. The village is about a mile along. It's spread out parallel to the beach on two main streets, Raven and Eagle.

The first thing you'll notice is the number of totems in the village. There are some erected outside homes, one outside St. John's Anglican Church (carved in 1969 by famous Haida artist Robert Davidson), and in the ball field there are replicas of two that stood in the old village of Yan. Two Reg Davidson poles stand in front of the **Adams Family House of Silver** longhouse (250-626-3215) and ❖ **Haida Arts and Jewelry** (250-626-5560). Behind a frontal house painting of Raven and Eagle, Sarah Davidson sells Haida art and souvenirs, including large

Haida Arts and Jewelry, Old Massett

argillite carvings, painted cedar bark woven hats and baskets, and painted drums and paddles. Ask Sarah to show you the halibut-skin wall hanging, complete with buttons!

Before leaving the Masset area, visit the ◆ **Delkatla Wildlife Sanctuary,** where trails and viewing platforms make it easy to spot some of the rust-colored sandhill cranes and white trumpeter swans that stop over during the spring and fall migration in this diverse marsh ecosystem. More than 100 species of waterfowl have been identified including great blue herons, pied-billed grebes, peregrine falcons, hairy woodpeckers, and sandpipers. Trails start from points along Trumpeter Drive on the west side of the bridge, where the streets are named delightfully, Brant, Widgeon, Pintail, Swan, and Teal.

Recently on a cool fall day, I drove northeast from the Delkatla Wildlife Sanctuary past *The Elephant Pen,* as some locals refer to the Canadian Forces Base signal station, and past one of the world's most remote golf courses. The ◆ **Dixon Entrance Golf and Country Club** works on an honor system. It's set in the dunes, has grass greens, great views, and lots of deer. I was soon at Graham Island's northern coastline looking across 37 miles (60 km) of Dixon Entrance waters at soft pinkish-grey shapes. I was looking at Alaska.

It seemed fitting then that I should stay at the ◆ **Alaska View Lodge Bed and Breakfast** (Box 227, Masset, QCI, V0T 1M0; 250-626-3333 or 1-800-661-0019). It's directly on South Beach on Tow Hill Road, 8 miles (12 km) from the Masset Causeway. Eliane and Charly Feller's hospitality is unparalleled. Fabulous Swiss antique furniture, views of Prince of Wales Island, and scrumptious breakfasts make this a memorable retreat. Some of Eliane's unique, esoteric collages are displayed on the walls. There's great beachcombing—you may pick up agates or those elusive, delicious razor clams. Whales, eagles, and occasionally northern lights add to this special experience. Rates range from $50 for the bed and breakfast, and there's also a separate guest house.

From Alaska View Lodge, it's just a short drive on a gravel road east to ◆ **Tow Hill.** Park just before the Heillen River bridge and follow the map directions (on a bulletin board) to the boardwalks leading to the top of this 358-foot (109-m) basalt cliff. From here enjoy the great view of the Coast Mountains (on a clear day), and North Beach, which seems to run forever. Nearby is a trail to a **blowhole,** all that remains of a whale turned to stone in a famous Haida legend.

MORESBY ISLAND

There are only 62 miles (100 km) of paved roads separating Masset from Skidegate in the south, where the MV *Kwuna,* a small car and passenger ferry, will take you to Moresby Island and the magic of Gwaii Haanas. The crossing time to **Alliford Bay** is about 20 minutes, and the round-trip fare is paid on the Skidegate side. From Alliford Bay, the road hugs the ocean for 8 miles (13 km) to the little village of **Sandspit** and the islands' main airport.

On the seafront in Sandspit there are a couple of cozy bed and breakfasts. The ◆ **Seaport Bed and Breakfast** (Box 206, Sandspit, V0T 1T0; 250-637-5698) is different, in that it has separate accommodations from its hosts, with a self-serve hot breakfast. A complete kitchen and laundry, and plenty of lawn to clean out your kayak, makes it an ideal base for Gwaii Haanas explorers. Rates range from $30 for a single.

As on Graham Island, the only in-depth way to really see anything is via logging roads (requiring permission) or by water. All too many tourists come to the islands expecting to see ancient totems and wilderness, only to be disappointed that so much of it is inaccessible. Gwaii Haanas is a World Heritage Site, but for environmental concerns, only 2,500 tourists may experience its beauty each year.

Perhaps the quickest way to titillate the taste buds is to do a **circle tour** (approximately two hours) from Alliford Bay. After leaving the ferry, turn right, sticking to the coast road for 6 miles (10 km) to South Bay. You're onto active logging roads now, so abide by the rules stressed before. Turn left at South Bay, and 4.5 miles (7 km) south, the Moresby Road turnoff leads to the ◆ **Pallant Creek Fish Hatchery** (250–559–8695) and Moresby Camp. This is the gateway for small boats to the national park.

> **BRITISH COLUMBIA FACT**
>
> Endangered species list includes the sea otter, burrowing owl, American white pelican, and Vancouver Island marmot.

Go back to the South Bay Main, which then passes through forty-year-old western hemlock and Sitka spruce to Skidegate Lake. The road follows the Copper River to Copper Bay, Sandspit, and Alliford Bay. A variety of **seashells,** ranging from large moon snails to slender *Bittium eschrichtii,* are waiting to be picked up on the gravel beach between Copper Bay and the airport. If you have the time, take another side-trip (14 miles [23 km] from South Bay) to the rugged **Gray Bay** campsite on the ocean. Phone TimberWest in Sandspit (250–637–5436) or stop at their information center on the road into Sandspit from the ferry (just before the baseball field and the Lions Community Hall) to find out about their ◆ **TimberWest Forest Tours** held every Wednesday and Friday from noon to 4:30 P.M. They'll give you a map/brochure *Forests for Our Future,* which will simplify your appetite-whetting drive.

If there's one fair not to miss, it's the annual ◆ **Logger Sports Day** held at the Sandspit baseball field, usually in late June. You'll see record-setting pole climbs, ax throws, speed sawing, and birling at its best when hulking loggers dance like cats on fire trying to spin a log and dump their opponent into the freezing water. King and Queen Logger Trophies go to the male and female loggers with the highest aggregate scores.

If you're passing the new airport terminal, take a peek inside at the 14-foot (4-m) dugout canoe *BiJaBoJi* used by Sandspit's Betty Carey in a gutsy west coast trip with her son Gene in 1962. Since the mid-fifties, Betty and Neil Carey have had a love affair with the Charlottes, which can be shared in Neil's famous *Guide to the Queen Charlotte Islands*. For thirty years they lived and explored from Puffin Cove on Moresby's remote west coast; today, home is on the sea front in Sandspit. They're avid collectors of anything nautical, or recyclable.

But if it's the ghosts of Ninstints, Skedans, and Tanu, and the magic of ✦ **Gwaii Haanas** that you've been patiently waiting for, you must first get permission at the Watchmen building in Skidegate (250-559-8225). Tour operators authorized to take you there can also help.

✦ **Moresby Explorers** (Box 109, Sandspit, V0T 1T0; 250-637-2215 or 1-800-806-7633) is a Sandspit-based business owned and operated by a lifetime local. Doug Gould will take you on day-trips to nearby Louise and Hot Springs Islands, or four-day excursions to the hallowed, abandoned village of Ninstints in Anthony Island Provincial Park, a World Heritage Site on the remote and rugged southern part of the island. If you're experienced, try a kayak rental, ranging from $200 single per week, which includes transportation to the Moresby Float Camp. Doug's Web page (http://www.cybersurf.net/~Moresby) has complete information. South Moresby National Park Reserve (P.O. Box 37, Queen Charlotte, V0T 1S0; 250-559-8818) has general park information.

WHERE TO STAY:

1. **H'ltunwa Kaitza—Cacilia's Bed and Breakfast** (Box 3, Tlell, V0T 1Y0; 250-557-4664). Rustic, beachy, different! $25-50.
2. **Sitka Lodging** (Box 460, Queen Charlotte, V0T 1S0, 250-557-4386/4241). Very private cottage on Tlell River. $75.
3. **Alaska View Lodge Bed and Breakfast** (Box 227, Masset, QCI, V0T 1M0; 250-626-3333 or 1-800-661-0019). $50-$80.
4. **Seaport Bed and Breakfast** (Box 206, Sandspit, V0T 1T0; 250-637-5698). $30-$40. Home baking to put in the fridge!
5. **Rose Harbour Guest House** (Box 578-P, Rose Harbour, Gwaii Haanas, Haida Gwaii, V0T 1S0; 250-624-8707 [April-October], 250-559-8638 [October-March]). $95 per day includes three meals. Wilderness accommodation on the north shore of Kunghit Island. Kayak rentals. Accessible only by boat or float plane.
6. **Jo's Bed and Breakfast** (Site 1, C5, Skidegate Landing, V0T 1S0; 250-559-8865). Across from Ferry Terminal, $30 single, $40 double.
7. **Copper Beech House Bed and Breakfast** (1590 Delkatla, Masset, V0T 1M0; 250-626-5441). Beachfront. $50-$75.

WHERE TO EAT:

1. **Café Gallery** (2062 Collison Avenue, Masset, V0T 1M0; 250-626-3672).

2. **Oceana Chinese and Continental Restaurant** (3119 Third Avenue, Queen Charlotte City, V0T 1S0; 250-559-8683).

3. **Daddy Cool's Pub and Grill** (Collison Avenue, Masset, V0T 1M0; 250-626-3210).

4. **Sandspit Inn Restaurant** (at the airport, 250-637-5334).

5. **Tlell River House** (Beitush Road, Tlell, 250-557-4211).

6. **The Yakoun River Inn** (overlooking government wharf in Port Clements, 250-557-4440).

7. **Margaret's Café** (Wharf Street, Queen Charlotte City, V0T 1S0; 250-559-4204), opens 6:30 A.M.

USEFUL INFORMATION

For general information and bookings: **Super, Natural BC** 1-800-663-6000 (from anywhere in North America). From overseas: (250) 387-1642. Greater Vancouver: 663-6000. Web site: http://www.travel.bc.ca.

REGIONS

1. **Tourism Association of Vancouver Island** (302-45 Bastion Square, Victoria, V8W 1J1; 250-382-3551; fax: 250-382-3523; E-mail: tavi@islands.bc.ca; Web site: http://www.islands.bc.ca).

2. **Vancouver, Coast and Mountains Tourism Region** (Suite 204, 1755 West Broadway, Vancouver, V6J 4S5; 604-739-9011; 1-800-667-3306; fax: 604-739-0153; E-mail: VCM_Tourism@mindlink.bc.ca).

3. **Okanagan Similkameen Tourism Association** (1332 Water Street, Kelowna, V1Y 9P4; 250-860-5999; fax: 250-861-7493; E-mail: osta@awinc.com).

4. **Kootenay Country Tourist Association** (610 Railway Street, Nelson, V1L 1H4; 1-800-661-6603, 250-352-6033; fax: 250-352-1656).

5. **Rocky Mountain Visitors Association** (P.O. Box 10, Kimberley, V1A 2Y5; 250-427-4838; fax: 250-427-3344; E-mail: bcrockies@cyberlink.bc.ca). Location: 1905 Warren Avenue, Kimberley.

6. **Cariboo Tourism Association** (P.O. Box 4900, Williams Lake, V2G 2V8; 250-392-2226; 1-800-663-5885; fax: 250-392-2838). Location: 190 Yorston Street, Williams Lake.

7. **High Country Tourism Association** (2-1490 Pearson Place, Kamloops, V1S 1J9; 250-372-7770, 1-800-567-2275; fax: 250-828-4656).

8. **North by Northwest Tourism Association** (P.O. Box 1030, Smithers, V0J 2N0; 250-847-5227, 1-800-663-8843; fax: 250-847-7585; E-mail: nxnw@mail.netshop.net). Location: Unit 11, 3167 Tatlow Road, Smithers.

9. **Peace River Alaska Highway Tourist Association** (Box 6850, Fort St. John, V1J 4J3; 250-785-2544; fax: 250-785-4424; E-mail: prahta@awinc.com). Location: 9908 106th Avenue, Fort St. John.

OTHER USEFUL INFORMATION

BC Ferries (1112 Fort Street, Victoria, V8V 4V2; 1-888-223-3779. In Victoria: 250-386-3431; in Vancouver: 604-669-1211; fax: 250-381-5452; Web page: http://www.bcferries.bc.ca/ferries).

BC Museums Association (514 Government Street, Victoria; 250-387-3315; Web site: http://www.museumsassn.bc.ca/~bcma/).

BC Parks (Second Floor, 800 Johnson Street, Victoria, V8V 1X4; 250-387-5002; Web site: http://www.bcparks.gov.bc.ca).

Fishing regulations and licenses: At most local fishing outlets or Ministry of Environment, 250-387-9589.

Forest recreation: Ministry of Forests, Forest Practices Branch (Box 9513, Station PROV GOVT, Victoria, V8W 9C2; 250-387-6656; fax: 387-6751; Web site: http://www.for.gov.bc.ca/hfp/hfp.htm).

Hunting and fishing regulations: Ministry of Environment, Lands and Parks, Wildlife Branch (780 Blanshard Street, Victoria, V8V 1X5; 250-387-9739).

Alaska Highway Park information: BC Parks District Manager (10003 110th Avenue, Fort St. John, V1J 6M2; 250-787-3407; fax: 250-787-3490).

Cranbrook Chamber of Commerce (P.O. Box 84, Cranbrook, V1C 4H6; 250-426-5914, 1-800-222-6174; E-mail: cbkchamber@cyberlink.bc.ca).

Kamloops Visitor InfoCentre (1290 West Trans-Canada Highway, Kamloops, V2C 6R3; 1-800-662-1994; Web page: http://www.city.kamloops.bc.ca).

Kimberley InfoCentre (350 Ross Street, Kimberley, V1A 2Z9; 250-427-3666; E-mail: kimbchamber@cyberlink.bc.ca).

Osoyoos Chamber of Commerce (Box 227, Osoyoos, V0H 1V0; 250-427-4838; fax: 250-427-3344).

Queen Charlotte Islands Chamber of Commerce (Box 38, Masset, V0T 1M0; 250-626-5211).

Revelstoke Chamber of Commerce (P.O. Box 490, 206 Campbell Avenue, Revelstoke, V0E 2S0; 250-837-5345).

Summerland Travel InfoCentre (15600 Highway 97, Box 1075, Summerland, V0H 1Z0; 250-494-2686; fax: 250-494-4039).

Tourism Shuswap (Box 1670, Salmon Arm, V1E 4P7; 250-832-5200, 1-800-661-4800; E-mail: shuswap@mail.netshop.net; Web page: http://www.shuswap.bc.ca/sunny).

Tourism Vancouver (Plaza Level, Waterfront Centre, 200 Burrard Street, Vancouver, V6C 3L6; 604-683-2000; fax: 604-682-6839; Web site: http://www.tourism-vancouver.org).

Tourism Victoria (812 Wharf Street, Victoria, V8W 1T3; 250-953-2033, fax: 250-382-6539).

INDEX

ABOUT THE AUTHOR

As an experienced traveler to many of the world's little-known places, and with a sailing circumnavigation to her credit, Tricia Timmermans is well qualified to uncover British Columbia's unique destinations. Australian by birth, she has a background in teaching and is a recent graduate in photojournalism. She has lived in some of Canada's more remote areas, from Baffin Island to the Yukon, and presently resides in Victoria, BC, where she is a keen photographer and travel writer.